Everyday Diversity

Developing Cultural Competency and Information Awareness

first edition

Edited by Angela Cartwright and Emily Reeves
Midwestern State University

Bassim Hamadeh, CEO and Publisher
John Remington, Senior Field Acquisitions Editor
Michelle Piehl, Project Editor
Alia Bales, Associate Production Editor
Don Kesner, Interior Designer
Miguel Macias, Senior Graphic Designer
Trey Soto, Licensing Coordinator
Natalie Piccotti, Senior Marketing Manager
Kassie Graves, Vice President of Editorial
Jamie Giganti, Director of Acquistions

Everyday Diversity

Developing Cultural Competency and Information Awareness

first edition

Table of Contents

Chapter Four: Introduction

Appendices

Introduction: Positionality

The purpose of this course reader is to help you, as citizens and future professionals, to increase your cultural competency and information awareness. Our advances in technology and communication have made it possible to get information from an infinite number of sources, and that can make it difficult to know what sources can be trusted and how the information they provide has been created. Because we don't know which sources to trust, it can be easy to trust sources and opinions that match our own. This is particularly true about controversial issues or those that have a lot of emotional involvement. While this may be easy and comfortable, it doesn't always provide us with the best information, information that we will need as we act as both citizens and professionals.

Some of the more "touchy" issues that we face today revolve around culture, diversity, multiculturalism, and social justice. The words have become pretty politicized, but we don't always have the same meaning when we use them. The meaning we attach to the words is largely based on our own positionality (which we'll discuss momentarily), which we'll call the word's connotation. The word's connotation and our feelings about it are not necessarily the same thing as the word's true meaning, which we'll call the word's denotation. In order to be responsible citizens and professionals, we need to learn how to assess information, especially information about which we have some feelings regarding the connotation, in order to be able to see the issues with as little bias as possible.

For the purposes of this reader, we'll use the following definitions, which build upon each other, for these important words. Culture is our shared way of life; it is fluid, as all cultures are constantly evolving due to technological advances in the areas of economic production, transportation, and communication. Diversity, quite simply, is the ways in which we are different. This is much more nuanced than we normally make it, because we tend to focus on intergroup (between cultural groups) differences and ignore intragroup (within cultural groups) differences. Multiculturalism is a perspective that values cultural diversity and pluralism (it's okay to be different), as opposed to assimilation (we should all be the same). Social justice is a perspective that actively works toward equity (as opposed to equality—Google "equity" versus "equality" if you're not sure what the difference is) by challenging systems that promote and sustain inequity.

The initial reactions we have to these ideas are largely based on our positionality. Positionality is kind of like our point of view, but on a systems-level scale. It includes things that we can't control or change, things that are the luck of the draw, so to speak. These things are so much a part of us that we probably don't even realize how much they influence the ways in which we see the world. Just like our literal point of view is limited by where we are standing, so our positionality is limited by our standing in a variety of social contexts. None of us can see everything from our positionality; we each have our own little slice of reality, and we need everyone's little piece of the puzzle to make a full picture of the reality of any given situation. When we can only see our own piece, we can get a skewed version of reality. For example, what do you see in this image?

Figure 0.1 Dorothy Counts (cropped)

What do you think is happening in this situation? What context clues (which will be based in your own personal experiences, your positionality) did you use to interpret the image? What feelings did the image cause you to experience? Take a minute to consider this image and unpack your feelings about it and why you think it makes you feel that way. Ok, now that you've gotten your initial thoughts on paper, let's look at some additional pieces of the puzzle.

Figure 0.2 Dorothy Counts

How did your initial interpretations and feelings about the situation hold up when you were able to see more of it? This is kind of how our positionality impacts the ways in which we see the world, and it can be a similarly surprising (and not necessarily in a good way) experience when we get additional pieces of the puzzle by learning from someone with a different positionality and experience. It can come as a shock that our perception has been so limited, but it isn't really unusual. We all struggle to see things that don't impact us or someone about whom we care. A few largely subconscious processes increase this likelihood: filtering, confirmation bias, and identity reification.

Filtering is the process through which our brains decide what information or stimuli to give attention. Our brains are trained by confirmation bias, in which we tend to unconsciously seek out and give priority to those things that confirm our existing beliefs. Confirmation bias is encouraged by our desire for identity reification, which is the process of solidifying our positive self-perception by interpreting information in ways that make us feel good about ourselves.

As you can see, our epistemology (the way we create knowledge) is a largely subconscious process that has a lot to do with our positionality. Bucher (2014) describes it as an ongoing and nonlinear process.

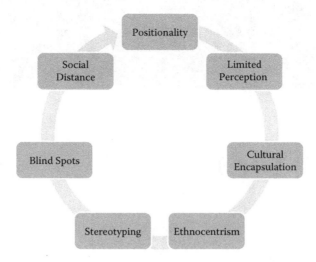

Figure 0.3 Positionality Loop

As the diagram above illustrates, our positionality contributes to our limited perception, both of which lead to cultural encapsulation. Cultural encapsulation is when, through homogenous social-ization (lack of exposure to other cultures and ideas), we begin to think that our culture represents the totality of reality, not just a piece of it. Cultural encapsulation leads to a skewed view of the world because it becomes very difficult to see beyond our own culture; this leads us to judge other cultures and individuals by our own cultural standards, which are not always applicable.

Our lack of exposure leads to a caricaturized view of those who are different from us; our ideas of them are oversimplified and exaggerated. The tricky thing about them is that we may not know they are stereotypes, as they might really be all we have been exposed to (usually through the media) about people with whom we may differ. The stereotypes we have lead us to have blind spots in which we make judgements without real evidence, but it's hard for us to see that this is what's happening. Those blind spots create social distance where, for a variety of reasons, we don't interact with the very people with whom we need to interact to get a more complete picture of the world around us, which perpetuates the cycle.

This reader and the core assessments that go with it are designed to help us disrupt this cycle so we can be informed and effective citizens and professionals. We start by looking at what science really has to say about our differences and diversity, and we address the issues of opinion discourse (where we disregard evidence that contradicts our predispositions by saying "everyone is entitled to their own opinion," as if all opinions were equally rooted in facts). We then proceed into self-examination, followed by data collection and literature analysis. The core assessments, and their relationship with each other, will be discussed in the next chapter.

FIGURE CREDITS

chapter one

Core Assessments

Four core assessments that build on each other are the primary ways that this course is assessed: 1) Cultural Autobiography, 2) Academic Analysis, 3) Field Notes and Report, and 4) Final Synthesis. It is critical that each of these assignments be completed in order, as they literally inform each next assignment. For example, the cultural autobiography is designed to help determine positionality of the researcher, or student. This assignment will also help inform the topic selection for the remainder of the course. "Remainder of the course" is a key phrase here, and it is essential that this concept be emphasized as each researcher/student moves through the core assessment. Think about these assessments as one large, cohesive research project. For the project to be cohesive, all assessments for the course must align with each other. Below is a big picture of the four assessments, followed by a breakdown of each assessment and its requirements. Examples, rubrics, and templates may be found in the appendix. It is strongly encouraged that you use the examples, rubrics, and template.

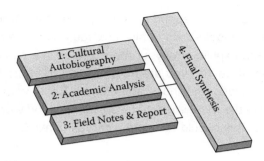

Figure 1.1 Cultural Autobiography

1: Cultural Autobiography

As a constant reminder of the necessary cohesion between assignments, the culminating project, the final synthesis, will remain in each graphic.

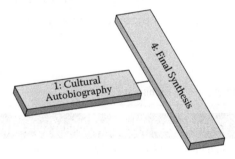

Figure 1.2 Creating a Cultural Autobiography

Creating a Cultural Autobiography to Explore and Interrogate Researcher Positioning

To better understand researcher positioning, you will create a cultural autobiography that explores the sociocultural factors that inform your own positioning. There are many factors that contribute to our identity. All of us belong to many cultural groups and sub-groups, and our "identity is based on 1) the relation between us and the dominant group/subgroup and 2) on the interaction among groups/subgroups.

In your cultural autobiography, you must address many aspects of your identity. It is not enough merely to state, for example, that you are a White, Irish American,

English-speaking male, etc. or a second-generation Chinese American, multilingual female who was raised in a middle-class family, etc. You must take each cultural group/subgroup one at a time and explain how your membership in a particular subgroup has helped to create the kind of person you are and how it is likely to influence the ways in which you perceive the world and those around you. Begin with the cultural group/subgroup that currently has the most impact on your identity and work down to the least influential group/subgroup. This should take some careful thinking.

> If you are part of any dominant subgroups, you must address the concept of privilege, particularly White, (upper) middle-class, and language privilege. The cultural autobiography should be an honest expression of who you perceive yourself to be along a cultural continuum. Think carefully about each category and provide enough details to create a vivid portrait of your unique cultural identity."[1]

The cultural groups/subgroups below should be used to help you work through your cultural positioning. Below is a chart of cultural groups/subgroups as well as immutable and dominant subcultures. It is expected that the cultural autobiography help you think about the specific topic you want to explore through research. This topic will be what you focus on throughout the rest of the course. For a great example and a not-so-great example, see the appendix.

Table 1.1 Cultural Group/Subgroup—The Dominant Subcultures

Cultural Group/Subgroup	* = immutable ** = the dominant subcultures
A. Class (socioeconomic status)	Underclass—below poverty level, homeless
	Working class—lower middle class, blue collar
	Middle class—white collar and low-level managerial/administrative **
	Upper middle class—professionals, high-level managerial/administrative
	Upper class—professionals, top-level managerial/administrative, inherited wealth and social status
B. Race *	Caucasian (Whites) **
	African American (Blacks)
	American Indian
	Eskimo
	Asian/Pacific Islander
	Hispanic
	Other

---

1   Peebles, Marybeth. *Cultural Autobiography Guidelines.* http://w3.marietta.edu/~peeblesm/452%20 Cultural%20Autobiography%20guidelines.htm

Cultural Group/Subgroup	* = immutable ** = the dominant subcultures
C. Ethnicity *	Western European **
	Central/Eastern European
	Asian
	African
	Latino
	Other
D. Gender/sexual orientation *	Male **
	Female
	Heterosexual **
	Homosexual
	Bisexual
	Transgender
E. Language	Monolingual (English only) **
	Bilingual (English as primary language)
	ESL (English as a second language)
	Multilingual (fluent in more than two languages)
F. Religion	Christianity—Protestantism **
	Christianity—Catholicism
	Christianity—Other (e.g., Mormon, Jehovah's Witness, Christian Scientist, Eastern Orthodox)
	Judaism
	Islam
	Buddhism
	Hindu
	Other
G. Exceptionality *	Nondisabled **
	Physically disabled
	Mentally challenged
	Learning disabled
	Gifted/talented
H. Age *	Infancy
	Youth
	Adolescence
	Young adulthood **
	Middle age
	Aged (elderly)
Geography	Regional (e.g., Midwest, New England, Southwest, etc.)
	Location (e.g., urban, suburban, rural)
	Environmental (e.g., mountains, desert, coastal)

(adapted from materials by Marybeth Peebles, Marietta College)

The links in Table 1.2 provide additional information on the topics covered in the cultural autobiography.

Table 1.2 Topic—Links

Topic	Links
Identity and access to power	https://www.youtube.com/watch?v=t2XFh_tD2RA
Meritocracy and social mobility	https://www.youtube.com/watch?v=khRX1Oo93AY
Healthcare disparity	https://www.youtube.com/watch?v=7qAld9bGwlA
Intersectionality	https://www.youtube.com/watch?v=n2kUpKP18z8
Segregation	https://www.youtube.com/watch?v=eejmYzOO3YE
Geography	https://www.youtube.com/watch?v=0L2xCwD5RNI https://www.youtube.com/watch?v=PYZhVX6rr08 https://www.youtube.com/watch?v=KBsOwZRKzcE http://www.bravenewfilms.org/deaavoidsthesub https://www.youtube.com/watch?v=SyWWgn5YEZo https://www.youtube.com/watch?v=XTdvyM2PT_4
Race and ethnicity	http://www.pbs.org/race/000_General/000_00-Home.htm http://newsreel.org/transcripts/race.htm https://www.youtube.com/watch?v=4WliConeatM http://www.bravenewfilms.org/racismisreal http://www.bravenewfilms.org/whiteriots http://www.bravenewfilms.org/prisonsystembynumbers
Class	https://www.youtube.com/watch?v=JYxspCbwZVs https://www.youtube.com/watch?v=amv4Ed15YMY https://www.youtube.com/watch?v=ShJqEBcyiBg https://www.youtube.com/watch?v=IjbJZ5jspzE https://www.youtube.com/watch?v=fAUUHCZMJH8
Sex versus gender	https://www.youtube.com/watch?v=Hkmsu9TI7NE
Perception and positionality	https://www.youtube.com/watch?v=slLo6xYbsc0 https://www.youtube.com/watch?v=tfk3b6BAaYc https://www.youtube.com/watch?v=QQsBM1dZLO4 https://www.youtube.com/watch?v=4qoE3OVy4Vo https://www.youtube.com/watch?v=PF7m1fFr2eQ https://www.youtube.com/watch?v=hx8bYUF30Gg https://www.youtube.com/watch?v=_RrZggEhSJA https://www.youtube.com/watch?v=uK3M7RGqJFQ https://www.youtube.com/watch?v=nuAVtkCVOsw https://www.youtube.com/watch?v=XYWFGJ2aYRU

2: Academic Analysis

As demonstrated in the graphic, the academic analysis is the second assessment that links directly to the final synthesis paper and builds on what you discovered about yourself and interests in the cultural autobiography.

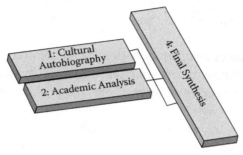

Figure 1.3 Academic Analysis

To better understand research methods, you will obtain and analyze two conflicting articles on the diversity issue of your choice. You will explore the ways in which they are and are not examples of credible scholarship by answering the guiding questions below for each piece of literature. While there are questions provided below to help guide you through your paper, remember that this should be a formal APA-style paper and should not be numbered or bullet point answers but a cohesive, formal APA paper complete with citations, an abstract, and a running head. The website Purdue Owl (https://owl.english.purdue.edu/owl/section/2/10/) is an excellent resource for formatting your paper.

1. Identify the author's/authors' research question.

2. Identify the hypothesis/es being tested.

3. Document at least three instances where statistical information was displayed. Where did these numbers come from? Were they believable or trustworthy?

4. If you sought to answer the same research question, what two things would you do to improve the credibility of the study and your findings?

5. Should findings from the study (or your own) be used to modify law? Explain your opinion.

6. What is your personal response to the author's/authors' argument?

In what ways does your positioning influence the way you perceive the author's/authors' argument?

(adapted from materials by Amy Cass, CA State Univ.)

3: Field Notes and Report

Your field notes and report will be based on the ethnography that you conduct after you complete your academic analysis. Again, your field notes and report should be directly related to your academic analysis and will then be used in your final synthesis paper. In fact, the cultural autobiography, academic analysis, and field notes and report will all come together to complete your final synthesis paper. This must be one cohesive research project.

The researchers/students will partner with existing community organizations specifically selected for their potential to increase students' multicultural competency. The setting in which you choose to do your ethnographic field notes should be one that takes you out of your comfort zone, one in which you do not normally spend time. The purpose is for you to immerse yourself (thirty minutes a week for eight weeks in a normal semester or one hour a day on four different days in a mini/shortened term) in a situation in which you can begin to see the world through another's eyes in order to see more of the picture than you can see through just your own. While working with these community organizations to achieve their organizational goals, you will record ethnographic field notes that focus on the community's perception of and approach to your chosen diversity issue as well as your personal reactions and experiences during the partnership. You will propose a community partnership, record ethnographic field notes, and produce a field write-up in accordance with the syllabus schedule. Use the template and example in the appendix as a guide.

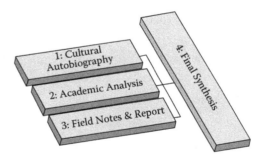

Figure 1.4 Field Notes and Report

4: Synthesis Paper

You are to take the data that you gathered from your community partnership experience, along with your cultural autobiography and scholarship analyses, and synthesize your findings in a 4–5-page APA-style paper. Remember to use Purdue Owl as a resource for formatting a formal paper. In the synthesis paper, you will take a position on the diversity issue of your choice, acknowledging the impact of your own positioning on your perception, and defend your position with the ethnographic data you collected during your community partnership experience. This is a culminating paper that directly links the cultural autobiography, academic analysis, and field notes and report. See the appendix for an outline and rubric for the synthesis paper to know exactly what is expected and how you will be graded.

chapter *two*

Introduction

*Anthropologists are those who write
things down at the end of the day.*

—Jean Jackson in Emerson, Fretz, & Shaw (2011)

This chapter contains two readings (two chapters from a larger book) on how to take ethnographic field notes. The purpose of taking ethnographic field notes is twofold: 1) It will provide you with data for your research paper, and 2) it will encourage you to actively observe as you try to increase your cultural competency, to see the world through another's eyes.

After you complete the readings, please answer the following questions to help you prepare for taking your own ethnographic field notes.

When, where, and how will you write your jottings (pages 22–28)?

How should we judge the actions of those we observe (page 14)? Why is this important? Why is this difficult?

How do we respond to those things in the field to which we have a strong reaction (page 14)?

What should you begin looking for in the course of your field observations (page 13)?

How do we avoid writing evaluative summaries and instead produce detailed descriptions without our opinions (pages 44–53)?

When should you write up your field notes (page 36)? Why?

What is the purpose of the initial write-up (page 37)?

In the Field: Participating, Observing, and Jotting Notes

◆

From *Writing Ethnographic Fieldnotes* By Robert M. Emerson, Rachel I. Fretz, and Linda L. Shaw

Ethnographers ultimately produce a written account of what they have seen, heard, and experienced in the field. But different ethnographers, and the same ethnographer at different times, turn experience and observation into written texts in different ways. Some maximize their immersion in local activities and their experience of others' lives, deliberately suspending concern with the task of producing written records of these events. Here, the field researcher decides where to go, what to look at, what to ask and say so as to experience fully another way of life and its concerns. She attends to events with little or no orientation to "writing it down" or even to "observing" in a detached fashion. Indeed, an ethnographer living in, rather than simply regularly visiting, a field setting, particularly in non-Western cultures where language and daily routines are unfamiliar, may have no choice but to participate fully and to suspend immediate concerns with writing. A female ethnographer studying local women in Africa, for example, may find herself helping to prepare greens and care for children, leaving no time to produce many written notes. Yet in the process of that involvement, she may most clearly learn how women simultaneously work together, socialize, and care for children. Only in subsequent reflection, might she fully notice the subtle changes in herself as she learned to do and see these activities as the women do.

Field researchers using this ethnographic approach want to relate naturally to those encountered in the field; they focus their efforts on figuring out—holistically and intuitively—what these people are up to. Any anticipation of writing fieldnotes is postponed (and in extreme cases, minimized or avoided altogether) as diluting the experiential insights and intuitions that immersion in another social world can provide.[1] Only at some later point does the ethnographer turn to the task of recalling and examining her experiences in order to write them down.

But the ethnographer may also participate in ongoing events in ways that directly and immediately involve inscription. Here, the fieldworker is concerned with "getting into place" to observe interesting, significant events in order to produce a detailed written record of them. As a result, participation in naturally occurring events may come to be explicitly oriented toward writing fieldnotes. At an extreme, the fieldworker may self-consciously look for events that should be written down for research purposes; he may position himself in these unfolding events to be able to observe and write; and he may explicitly orient to events in terms of "what is important to remember so that I can write it down later."

Each mode of field involvement has strengths and drawbacks. The former allows an intense immersion in daily rhythms and ordinary concerns that increases openness to others' ways of life. The latter can produce a more detailed, closer-to-the-moment record of that life. In practice, most field researchers employ both approaches at different times, sometimes participating without thought about writing up what is happening and, at other times, focusing closely on events in order to write about them. Indeed, the fieldworker may experience a shift from one mode to another as events unfold in the field. Caught in some social moment, for example, the field researcher may come to see deep theoretical relevance in a mundane experience or practice. Conversely, a researcher in the midst of observing in a more detached, writing-oriented mode may suddenly be drawn directly into the center of activity.[2]

In both approaches, the ethnographer writes fieldnotes more or less contemporaneously with the experience and observation of events of interest in the spirit of the ethnographer who commented, "Anthropologists are those who write things down at the end of the day" (Jackson 1990b:15). In the experiential style, writing may be put off for hours or even days until the field researcher withdraws from the field and, relying solely on memory, sits down at pad or computer to reconstruct important events.[3] In the participating-to-write approach, writing—or an orientation to writing—begins earlier when the researcher is still in the field, perhaps in the immediate presence of talk and action that will be inscribed. The ethnographer may not only make mental notes or "headnotes"[4] to include certain events in full fieldnotes, but he may also write down, in the form of jottings or scratch notes, abbreviated words and phrases to use later to construct full fieldnotes.

Furthermore, in both styles, field researchers are deeply concerned about the quality of the relationships they develop with the people they seek to know and understand. In valuing more natural, open experience of others' worlds and activities, field researchers seek to keep writing from intruding into and affecting these relationships. They do so not only to avoid distancing themselves from the ongoing experience of another world but also because writing, and research commitments more generally, may engender feelings of betraying those with whom one has lived and shared intimacies. Ethnographers who participate in order to write, in contrast, pursue and proclaim research interests more openly as an element in their relationships with those studied. But these field researchers often become very sensitive to the ways in which the stance and act of writing are very visible to, and can influence the quality of their relationships with, those studied. And they also may experience moments of anguish or uncertainty about whether to include intimate or humiliating incidents in their fieldnotes.

In the remainder of this reading, we focus on a participating-in-order-to-write fieldwork approach that confronts writing issues directly and immediately in the field. This approach brings to the fore the interconnections between writing, participating, and observing as a means of understanding another way of life; it focuses on learning how to look in order to write, while it also recognizes that looking is itself shaped and constrained by a sense of what and how to write. We will begin by examining the processes of participating in order to write in detail, considering a number of practices that ethnographers have found useful in guiding and orienting observations made under these conditions. We then take up issues of actually writing in the presence of those studied by making jottings about what we see and hear, even as these interactions are occurring. Here, we first present illustrations of actual jottings made in different field settings and discuss a number of considerations that might guide the process of making jottings. We then consider choices confronting field researchers in deciding how, where, and when to make jottings in field settings.

Participating in Order to Write

In attending to ongoing scenes, events, and interactions, field researchers take mental note of certain details and impressions. For the most part, these impressions remain "headnotes" until the researcher sits down at some later point to write full fieldnotes about these scenes and events. In the flux of their field settings, beginning students are often hesitant and uncertain about what details and impressions they should pay attention to as potential issues for writing. We have found a number of procedures to be helpful in advising students how initially to look in order to write.

First, ethnographers should take note of their *initial impressions*. These impressions may include those things available to the senses—the tastes, smells, and sounds of the physical environment, and the look and feel of the locale and the people in it. Such impressions may include details about the physical setting, including size, space, noise, colors, equipment, and movement, or about people in the setting, such as their number, gender, race, appearance, dress, movement, comportment, and feeling tone. Writing down these impressions provides a way to get started in a setting that may seem overwhelming. Entering another culture where both language and customs are incomprehensible may present particular challenges in this regard. Still, the ethnographer can begin to assimilate strange sights and sounds by attending to and then writing about them.[5]

Furthermore, this record preserves these initial and often insightful impressions, for observers tend to lose sensitivity for unique qualities of a setting as these become commonplace. Researchers who are familiar with the setting they study, perhaps already having a place in the setting as workers or residents, have lost direct access to their first impressions. However, such fieldworkers can indirectly seek to recall their own first impressions by watching any newcomers to the setting, paying special attention to how they learn, adapt, and react.

Second, field researchers can focus on their personal sense of *what is significant or unexpected* in order to document key events or incidents in a particular social world or setting. Particularly at first, fieldworkers may want to rely on their own experience and intuition to select noteworthy incidents out of the flow of ongoing activity. Here, for example, the fieldworker may look closely at something that surprises or runs counter to her expectations, again paying attention to incidents, feeling tones, impressions, and interactions, both verbal and nonverbal.

Similarly, field researchers may use their own personal experience of events that please, shock, or even anger them to identify matters worth writing about. A fieldworker's strong reaction to a particular event may well signal that others in the setting react similarly. Or a fieldworker may experience deeply contradictory emotions, for example, simultaneously feeling deep sympathy and repulsion for what he observes in the field. These feelings may also reflect contradictory pressures experienced by those in the setting.

To use personal reactions effectively, however, requires care and reflection. One must first pay close attention to how others in the setting are reacting to these events; it is important to become aware of when and how one's own reactions and sensitivities differ from those of some or most members. But in addition, in taking note of others' experiences, many beginning ethnographers tend to judge the actions of people in the setting, for better or worse, by their own, rather than the others', standards and values. Prejudging incidents in outsiders' terms makes it difficult to cultivate empathetic understanding and to discover what import local people give to them. The field researcher should be alive to the possibility that local people, especially those with very different cultures, may respond to events in sharply contrasting ways. For example, an ethnographer in a Chokwe village may react with alarm to an unconscious man drugged by an herbal drink in a trial-for-sorcery court, only to realize that others are laughing at the spectacle because they know he will soon regain consciousness.

Yet, fieldworkers should not go to the other extreme and attempt to manage strong personal reactions by denial or simply by omitting them from fieldnotes. Rather, we recommend that the ethnographer first register her feelings, then step back and use this experience to ask how others in the setting see and experience these matters. Are they similarly surprised, shocked, pleased, or angered by an event? If so, under what conditions do these reactions occur, and how did those affected cope with the incidents and persons involved? Whether an ethnographer is working in a foreign or in a familiar culture, she needs to avoid assuming that others respond as she does.

Third, in order to document key events and incidents, field researchers should move beyond their personal reactions to attend explicitly to *what those in the setting experience and react to as "significant" or "important."* The field researcher watches for the sorts of things that are meaningful to those studied. The actions, interactions, and events that catch the attention of people habitually in the setting may provide clues to these concerns. Specifically: What do they stop and watch? What do they talk and gossip about? What produces strong emotional responses for them? "Troubles" or "problems" often generate deep concern and feelings. What kinds occur in the setting? How do people in the setting understand, interpret, and deal with these troubles or problems? Such "incidents" and "troubles" should move the field researcher to jot down "who did what" and "how others reacted."

Often, however, a researcher who is unfamiliar with a setting may not initially be able to understand or even to identify local meanings and their significance. Hence, the researcher may have to write down what members say and do without fully understanding their implications and import. Consider, for example, the following fieldnote written by a student ethnographer making her first visit to a small residential program for ex-prostitutes:

> We walk inside and down the hallway, stopping in front of the kitchen. One of the girls is in there, and Ellen [the program director] stops to introduce me. She says, Catherine this is our new volunteer. She says, "Oh, nice to meet you," and thanks me for volunteering. We shake hands, and I tell her it's nice to meet her as well. Ellen adds, "Well most people call her Cathy, but I like the way Catherine sounds so that's what I call her." Catherine is wearing baggy, navy blue athletic shorts and a loose black tank top. Her thick, curly hair is pulled into a bun resting on the side of her head. She is barefoot. She turns to Ellen, and the smile leaves her face as she says, "Julie cut her hair." Ellen responds that Julie's hair is already short, and asks, "Is it buzzed?" Catherine responds no, that it's cut in a "page boy style and looks really cute." Ellen's eyebrows scrunch together, and she asks, well, is she happy with it? Catherine smiles and says, "Yeah, she loves it." To which Ellen responds, "Well, if she's happy, I'm happy," and that she's going to finish taking me around the house. I tell Catherine, "See you later."

Here, the program director's response to Catherine's report treats Julie's haircut as simply a decision about personal style and appearance—"is she happy with it?" On its face, it does not seem to be an important or significant statement and could easily have been left out in the write-up of this encounter.[6]

But events immediately following this encounter made it clear that Julie's haircut had important implications for the institution and its program. Leaving Catherine, the program director continued to show the ethnographer around the home:

[In an upstairs bedroom] Ellen tells me to take a seat while she "makes a quick phone call." She begins the conversation, "Hey, so I just got home, and Catherine told me that Julie cut her hair." She listens for awhile, and her voice becomes more serious as she says, "Yeah, I know. I'm just thinking she's headed toward the same bull-shit as last time." [Later in her office] Ellen explains to me that Julie used to be a resident of the house but left and went back into pros-titution. When Julie wanted to come back "we took her back on one condition, that she doesn't focus on her physical appearances but works on what's inside instead." That is why she was so concerned about the haircut: "It seems like she's going back to the same things as before," because this is how it starts.

The program director's phone call, immediately reporting Julie's haircut to someone else connected with the program, displays the local importance of this event. Later, the program director explains to the observer that, given Julie's history in the program, her haircut is a likely indicator of a troubled psychological state and weakening commitment to the program.

As this incident illustrates, the field researcher discerns local meanings, not so much by directly asking actors about what matters to them, but more indirectly and inferen-tially by looking for the perspectives and concerns embedded and expressed in naturally occurring interaction. And in gleaning indigenous meanings implicit in interaction, the ethnographer is well placed to apprehend these meanings, not simply as static cate-gories, but, rather, as matters involving action and process. This requires not just that the ethnographer describes interactions but that she consistently attends to "when, where, and according to whom" in shaping all fieldnote descriptions. Those in different institutional positions (e.g., staff and clients) may evaluate different clients as doing well or poorly in "working the program" and may do so by invoking different evaluative criteria. Indigenous meanings, then, rarely hold across the board but, rather, reflect particular positions and practical concerns that need to be captured in fieldnote descriptions.

Fourth, ethnographers can begin to capture new settings by focusing and writing notes as systematically as possible, focusing on *how routine actions in the setting are organized and take place.* Attending closely to "how" something occurs encourages and produces "*luminous descriptions*" (Katz 2001c) that specify the actual, lived conditions and contingencies of social life. Consistent with our interactionist perspective, asking *how* also focuses the ethnographer's attention on the social and interactional processes through which members construct, maintain, and alter their social worlds. This means that field researchers should resist the temptation to focus descriptions on *why* events or actions occur; initially focusing on "why" stymies and prematurely deflects full descrip-tion of specific impressions, events, and interactions because determining "why" is a complex and uncertain process requiring explanation and, hence, comparison with other instances or cases. Consider the difference in understanding that Katz develops between asking *why* one decides to get gas for one's car and *how* one does so:

> I can describe how I did that on a given occasion, but why I did it is never really as simple as top-of-the-head explanations suggest, for example, "because I was low on gas" or "because I needed gas." I needed gas before I entered the station; I did not rush to the station the first moment I noticed the gas gauge registering low; and usually I get there without having to push the car in because it ran completely dry. In any case, my "need" for gas would not explain the extent to which I fill the tank, nor why I pay with a credit card instead of cash, nor which of the pumps I choose, nor whether I accept the automatic cut-off as ending the operation or top up with a final squeeze. As the description of how the act is conducted improves, the less convincing becomes the initially obvious answer to "why?" (Katz 2001c:446)

Finally, ethnographers' orientations to writable events change with time in the field. When first venturing into a setting, field researchers should "cast their nets" broadly; they should observe with an eye to writing about a range of incidents and interactions. Yet, forays into a setting must not be viewed as discrete, isolated occasions that have little or no bearing on what will be noted the next time. Rather, observing and writing about certain kinds of events foreshadow what will be noticed and described next. Identifying one incident as noteworthy should lead to considering what other incidents are similar and, hence, worth noting. As fieldwork progresses and becomes more focused on a set of issues, fieldworkers often self-consciously document a series of incidents and interactions of the "same type" and look for regularities or patterns within them.

Even when looking for additional examples of a similar event, the field researcher is open to and, indeed, searches for, *different forms* of that event, and for *variations from, or exceptions to, an emerging pattern*. Beginning field researchers are often discouraged by such discoveries, fearing that exceptions to a pattern they have noted will cast doubt upon their understanding of the setting. This need not be the case, although noting differences and variations should prod the field researcher to change, elaborate, or deepen her earlier understanding of the setting. The field researcher, for example, might want to consider and explore possible factors or circumstances that would account for differences or variations: Are the different actions the result of the preferences and temperaments of those involved or of their different understandings of the situation because they have different positions in the local context? Or the ethnographer may begin to question how she decided similarity and difference in the first place, perhaps coming to see how an event that initially appeared to be different is actually similar on a deeper level. In these ways, exploring what at least initially seem to be differences and variations will lead to richer, more textured descriptions and encourage more subtle, grounded analyses in a final ethnography.

In summary, ethnographic attention involves balancing two different orientations. Especially on first entering the field, the researcher identifies significant characteristics gleaned from her first impressions and personal reactions. With greater participation in that local social world, however, the ethnographer becomes more sensitive to the concerns and perspectives of those in the setting. She increasingly appreciates how people have already predescribed their world in their own terms for their own purposes and projects. A sensitive ethnographer draws upon her own reactions to identify issues of possible importance to people in the setting but privileges their "insider" descriptions and categories over her own "outsider" views.

What are Jottings?

While participating in the field and attending to ongoing scenes, events, and interactions, field researchers may, at moments, decide that certain events and impressions should be written down as they are occurring in order to preserve accuracy and detail. In these circumstances, the field researcher moves beyond mere "headnotes" to record jottings—a brief written record of events and impressions captured in key words and phrases. Jottings translate to-be-remembered observations into writing on paper as quickly rendered scribbles about actions and dialogue. A word or two written at the moment or soon afterward will jog the memory later in the day when she attempts to recall the details of significant actions and to construct evocative descriptions of the scene. Or, more extensive jottings may record an ongoing dialogue or a set of responses to questions.

In order to convey how field researchers actually write and use jottings, we provide two illustrations. Each identifies specific scenes, observed actions, and dialogue rather than making evaluations or psychological interpretations. But each researcher approaches interaction in their settings in different ways, noting different sensory and interpretive details.

"Too Many Sexual References"

A student ethnographer jotted the following notes while sitting in on an after-school staff meeting attended by a continuation school principal, four teachers, and the school counselor:

Sexual Harassment
Andy—too many sexual references
    PE frisbee game "This team has too many sausages"

Reynaldo—(*Carlos—in jail for stealing bicycle, 18 yrs old*) [circled]

Laura → Wants to propose sexual harassment forms

    Thinking about detention for these students but already too much work for keeping track of tardies/truancies/tendencies

Here, the observer begins by marking off one of the topics that came up during this meeting—"sexual harassment." His jottings then identify a student—Andy—who has been accused of making "too many sexual references." The next line records a specific incident: When placed on a team composed mostly of boys during an Ultimate Frisbee game on the physical education field, Andy had commented that "this team has too many sausages." There follows the name of another student—Reynaldo—but no indication of what he said or did. Adjacent to this name was a circled phrase, including another name "Carlos" and a comment "in jail for stealing bicycle, 18 yrs old." The rest of the jotting names a teacher—Laura—and sketches her proposal to create "sexual harassment forms" to be filled out in response to such "inappropriate" sexual talk by students. Detention is mentioned as one possible punishment for such offenders, but this idea is countered by the observation that staff already has too much paperwork in dealing with students in detention.

"You Can Call His Doctor"

In contrast to the focus on named individuals and a variety of events linked to them, the following jottings focus strictly on dialogue, recording bits of talk in a formal court proceeding. The case involved a woman seeking a temporary restraining order against her two landlords, one of whom is not present in the courtroom. The landlord who is present disputes the woman's testimony that the missing landlord is "well enough to walk" and, hence, could have come to court:

> you can call his doctor at UCLA and
>
> he can verify all this
>
> I just don't call people on the
>
> telephone—courts don't operate that way—
>
> it has to be on paper or
>
> (in person)[7]

Here, only spoken words are recorded; specific speakers are not indicated but can be identified by content—the landlord defendant in the first two lines and the judge in the last four lines. The words represent direct quotes, written down as accurately as possible when spoken; an exception occurs in the last line where the observer missed the judge's exact words ending this sentence (because of jotting down the preceding dialogue) and inserted a paraphrase "in person" (indicated by parentheses). As in the prior illustration, there is no indication of what the ethnographer had in mind in noting these pieces of the flow of social life; they "speak for themselves," making no reference as to why they were recorded or about their possible implications.

Each of the jottings in these illustrations is "a mnemonic word or phrase [written] to fix an observation or to recall what someone has just said" (Clifford 1990:51). As preludes to full written notes, jottings capture bits of talk and action from which the fieldworker can begin to sketch social scenes, recurring incidents, local expressions and terms, members' distinctions and accounts, dialogue among those present, and his own conversations.

Making jottings, however, is not only a writing activity; it is also a mindset. Learning to jot down details that remain sharp and that easily transform into vivid descriptions on the page results, in part, from envisioning scenes as written. Writing jottings that evoke memories requires learning what can be written about and how. We have found the following recommendations helpful for making jottings useful for producing vivid, evocatively descriptive fieldnotes.[8]

First, jot down details of what you sense are key components of observed scenes, events, or interactions. Field researchers record immediate fragments of action and talk to serve as focal points for later writing accounts of these events in as much detail as can be remembered. The field researcher studying the continuation school staff meeting, for example, relied on the jotted names of two youth, supplemented by one direct quote, to recall two accounts provided by the complaining teacher about students' "inappropriate" sexual comments. In this way, jottings serve to remind the ethnographer of what was happening at a particular time, providing a marker around which to collect other remembered incidents. But the fieldworker does not have to have a specific reason or insight in mind to make a jotting about what she has seen and heard. For example, one field researcher teaching in a Headstart Program described a series of incidents that occurred while supervising children playing in a sandbox. Included in her jottings, but not in her full fieldnotes, was the phrase, "Three new bags of sand were delivered to the sandbox." In discussing this scratch note later, she commented: "I don't think it is so important as I would want to include it in my notes because I think it is just—I wrote it down to remind me more what the day was like, what was happening."[9]

Second, jot down concrete sensory details about observed scenes and interactions. Sensory details will later help to reconstruct the feel of what happened. Pay particular attention to details you could easily forget. Since jottings must later jog the memory, each field researcher must learn which kinds of details that they best remember and make jottings about those features and qualities that they might easily forget. Thus, fieldworkers come to develop their own jotting styles reflecting their distinctive recall propensities, whether visual, kinetic, or auditory. Some focus on trying to capture evocative pieces of broader scenes, while some jot down almost exclusively dialogue; others record nonverbal expression of voice, gesture, and movement; still others note visual details of color and shape. Through trial and error, field researchers learn what most helps them to recall field experiences once they sit down to write up full notes.

Third, avoid characterizing scenes or what people do through generalizations or summaries. Many novice field researchers initially tend to jot down impressionistic, opinionated words that lend themselves better to writing evaluative summaries than to composing detailed, textured descriptions. For example, it is problematic for a field researcher to characterize the way someone works as "inefficient." Such cryptic, evaluative jottings are likely to evoke only a vague memory when the fieldworker later on attempts to write a full description of the social scene. Such jottings also convey nothing of how people in the setting experience and evaluate worker performance. Similarly, jottings that a probation officer "lectures about school" and that a youth is "very compliant—always agrees" during a probation interview are overly general; such summary statements are not helpful for writing close descriptions of how the probation officer and the youth actually talked and acted during a particular encounter.

Fourth, fieldworkers use jottings to capture detailed aspects of scenes, talk, and interaction; short or more extended direct quotes are particularly useful for capturing such detail, as reflected in the previous two illustrations of jottings. In general, field researchers note concrete details of everyday life that *show*, rather than tell, about people's behavior. By incorporating such details, jottings may provide records of actual words, phrases, or dialogue that the field researcher wants to preserve in as accurate a form as possible. It is not enough, for example, to characterize an emotional outburst simply as "angry words." Rather, the ethnographer should jot the actually spoken words, along with sensual details such as gestures and facial expressions, suggesting that the speaker's emotional experience involved "anger." Jotting these words should evoke recall, not only of the details about what happened, but also of the specific circumstances or context involved: who was present, what they said or did, what occurred immediately before and after, and so on. In this way, jottings may be used to reconstruct the actual order or sequence of talk, topics, or actions on some particular occasion.

Fifth, use jottings to record the details of emotional expressions and experiences; note feelings such as anger, sadness, joy, pleasure, disgust, or loneliness as expressed and attended to by those in the setting. Beginning ethnographers sometimes attempt to identify motives or internal states when recording observed actions. Having witnessed an angry exchange, for example, one is often tempted to focus on the source or "reason" for this emotional outburst, typically by imputing motive (e.g., some underlying feeling such as "insecurity") to one or both of the parties involved. But such psychologized explanations highlight only one of a number of possible internal states that may accompany or contribute to the observed actions. Anger could, for example, result from frustration, fatigue, the playing out of some local power struggle, or other hidden factors; the ethnographer who simply witnesses a scene has no way of knowing which factors are involved.[10] When witnessing social scenes, then, the ethnographer's task is to use his own sensibilities and reactions to learn how others understand and evaluate what happened, how they assess internal states, and how they determine psychological motivation. Useful jottings should correspondingly reflect and further this process of writing textured, detailed descriptions of interactions rather than attributing individual motivation.

Sixth, use jottings to signal your general impressions and feelings, even if you are unsure of their significance at the moment. In some cases, the ethnographer may have only a vague, intuitive sense about how or why something may be important. Such feelings might signal a key element that in the future could enable the field researcher to see how incidents "fit together" in meaningful patterns. For example, at another point the ethnographer in the Headstart Program made a jotting about a student, "Nicole showing trust in me," which she decided not to write up in her full notes: "It was just an overall feeling I had throughout the day; … at that point when I wrote the jottings I couldn't remember an exact incident." But this jotting served as a mental note, subsequently stimulating her to appreciate (and record) the following incident as a revealing example of "children trusting teachers":

> At one point, Nicole got on the swings without her shoes on and asked me for a push. I told her that I would push her after she went and put her shoes on. Nicole paused and looked at me. I repeated my statement, telling her that I would save her swing for her while she was gone. Nicole then got off of the swing and put her shoes on. When she came back to the swing, I praised her listening skills and gave her a hug. I then gave her a push. I found this incident to be a significant accomplishment for Nicole, as usually she doesn't listen to the teachers.[11]

Through thinking about whether or not to write this jotting up as full notes, this student developed sensitivity to the issue of "trust." The jotting later acted as a stimulus to observe and write up a "concrete event" involving such "trust."

In summary, by participating in a setting with an eye to making jottings, an ethnographer experiences events as potential subjects for writing. Like any other writer, an ethnographer learns to recognize potential writing material and to see and hear it in terms of written descriptions. Learning to observe in order to make jottings thus is keyed to both the scene and to the page. Ethnographers learn to experience through the senses in anticipation of writing: to recall observed scenes and interactions like a reporter; to remember dialogue and movement like an actor; to see colors, shapes, textures, and spatial relations as a painter or photographer; and to sense moods, rhythms, and tone of voice like a poet. Details experienced through the senses turn into jottings with active rather than passive verbs, sensory rather than evaluative adjectives, and verbatim rather than summarized dialogue.

Making Jottings: How, Where, and When

Making jottings is not simply a matter of writing words on a notepad or laptop. Since jottings are often written close to or even in the immediate presence of those whose words and deeds are at issue, producing jottings is a social and interactional process.

Specifically, how and when an ethnographer makes jottings may have important implications for how others see and understand who she is and what she is about. There are no hard and fast rules about whether to make jottings and, if so, when and how to do so. But with time spent in a setting and by benefitting from trial and error, a field researcher may evolve a distinctive set of practices to fit writing jottings to the contours and constraints of that setting.

One initial choice involves the selection of writing materials. Traditionally, fieldworkers have relied on pen and paper. Many have used small notepads that fit easily into pocket or purse. Others prefer even less obtrusive materials, using folded sheets of paper to record jottings about different topics on specific sides. Writers also frequently develop idiosyncratic preferences for particular types of pens or pencils. But with the spread and common use of electronic and computer technologies in many contemporary settings, many field researchers now avoid pen and paper entirely and make jottings directly onto laptop computers, netbooks, smartphones, or audio recorders.

Field researchers actually write jottings in different ways. It is time-consuming and cumbersome to write out every word fully. Many fieldworkers use standard systems of abbreviations and symbols (for pen-and-paper ethnographers, a formal transcribing system such as shorthand or speed writing; for those using electronic devices, the evolving codes of texting). Others develop their own private systems for capturing words in shortened form in ways appropriate to their particular setting; in studying highly technical judicial mediation sessions, for example, Burns (2000:22) "developed a system of shorthand notation and abbreviations for commonly used terms" that allowed her to produce minutely detailed accounts of these events. Abbreviations and symbols not only facilitate getting words on a page more quickly; they also make jotted notes incomprehensible to those onlookers who ask to see them and, hence, provide a means for protecting the confidentiality of these writings.

Field researchers must also decide when, where, and how to write jottings. Clearly, looking down to pad or keyboard to write jottings distracts the field researcher (even if only momentarily), making close and continuous observation of what may be complex, rapid, and subtle actions by others very difficult. But beyond limited attention, jotting decisions can have tremendous import for relations with those in the field. The researcher works hard to establish close ties with participants so that she may be included in activities that are central to their lives. In the midst of such activities, however, she may experience deep ambivalence: On the one hand, she may wish to preserve the immediacy of the moment by jotting down words as they are spoken and details of scenes as they are enacted, while, on the other hand, she may feel that taking out a notepad or smartphone will ruin the moment and plant seeds of distrust. Participants may now see her as someone whose primary interest lies in discovering their secrets and turning their most intimate and cherished experiences into objects of scientific inquiry.[12]

Nearly all ethnographers feel torn at times between their research commitments and their desire to engage authentically those people whose worlds they have entered. Attempting to resolve these thorny relational and moral issues, many researchers hold that conducting any aspect of the research without the full and explicit knowledge and consent of those studied violates ethical standards. In this view, those in the setting must be understood as collaborators who actively work with the researcher to tell the outside world about their lives and culture. Such mutual collaboration requires that the researcher ask permission to write about events and also respect people's desire not to reveal aspects of their lives.

Other field researchers feel less strictly bound to seek permission to conduct research or to tell participants about their intention to record events and experiences. Some justify this stance by insisting that the field researcher has no special obligations to disclose his intentions since all social life involves elements of dissembling with no one ever fully revealing all of their deeper purposes and private activities. Other researchers point out that jottings and fieldnotes written for oneself as one's own record will do no direct harm to others. This approach, of course, puts off grappling with the tough moral and personal issues until facing subsequent decisions about whether to publish or otherwise make these writings available to others. Finally, some advocate withholding knowledge of their research purposes from local people on the grounds that the information gained will serve the greater good. For example, if researchers want to describe and publicize the conditions under which undocumented factory workers or the elderly in nursing homes live, they must withhold their intentions from the powerful who control access to such settings.

Many beginning researchers, wanting to avoid open violations of trust and possibly awkward or tense encounters, are tempted to use covert procedures and to try to conceal the fact that they are conducting research; this practice often requires waiting until one leaves the field to jot notes. While these decisions involve both the researcher's conscience and pragmatic considerations, we recommend, as a general policy, that the fieldworker inform people in the setting of the research, especially those with whom he has established some form of personal relationship. In addition to making these relations more direct and honest, openness avoids the risks and likely sense of betrayal that might follow from discovery of what the researcher has actually been up to. Concerns about the consequences—both discovery and ongoing inauthenticity—of even this small secret about research plans might mount and plague the fieldworker as time goes on and relations deepen.

Of course, strained relations and ethical dilemmas are not completely avoided by informing others of one's research purposes. While participants might have consented to the research, they might not know exactly what the research involves or what the researcher will do to carry it out.[13] They might realize that the fieldworker is writing fieldnotes at the end of the day, but they become used to his presence and "forget" that this writing is going on. Furthermore, marginal and transient members of the setting may not be aware of his research identity and purposes despite conscientious efforts to inform them.

By carrying out fieldwork in an overt manner, the researcher gains flexibility in when, where, and how to write jottings. In many field situations, it may be feasible to jot notes openly. In so doing, the fieldworker should act with sensitivity, trying to avoid detracting from or interfering with the ordinary relations and goings-on in the field. If possible, the fieldworker should start open jottings early on in contacts with those studied. If one establishes a "note-taker" role, jotting notes comes to be part of what people expect from the fieldworker. Here, it helps to offer initial explanations of the need to take notes; an ethnographer can stress the importance of accuracy, of getting down exactly what was said. People often understand that such activities are required of students and, therefore, tolerate and accommodate the needs of researchers who, they believe, want to faithfully represent what goes on. When learning a new language in another culture, the field researcher can explain that she is writing down local terms in order to remember them. By saying the word as she writes, people might offer new terms and become further interested in teaching her.

Although taking down jottings may at first seem odd or awkward, after a time, it often becomes a normal and expected part of what the fieldworker does. In the following excerpt from a Housing and Urban Development (HUD) office, the office manager and a worker jokingly enlist the fieldworker as audience for a self-parody of wanting to "help" clients:

> Later I'm in Jean's office and Ramon comes up and waxes melodramatic. Take this down, he says. Jean motions for me to write, so I pull out my notepad. "I only regret that I have but eight hours to devote to saving" … He begins to sing "Impossible Dream," in his thick, goofy Brooklyn accent. … "Feel free to join in," he says. …

Here, the ethnographer and his note-taking provide resources for a spontaneous humorous performance.[14]

Yet even when some people become familiar with open writing in their presence, others may become upset when the researcher turns to a notepad or laptop and begins to write down their words and actions. Ethnographers may try to avoid the likely challenges and facilitate open, extensive note-taking by positioning themselves on the margins of interaction. Even then, they may still encounter questions, as reflected in the following comment by a field researcher observing divorce mediation sessions:

> I tried to take notes that were as complete as possible during the session. My sitting behind the client had probably more to do with wanting to get a lot of written notes as unobtrusively as possible as with any more worthy methodological reason. While taking copious amounts of notes (approximately 50 pages per session) did not seem to bother the clients, a few mediators became quite defensive about it. One mediator wanted to know how I "decided what to write down and what not to write down." At staff meetings, this same mediator would sit next to me and try to glance over to see what I had written in my notebook.

Given the delicacy of this and similar situations, fieldworkers must constantly rely upon interactional skills and tact to judge whether or not taking jottings in the moment is appropriate.[15]

Furthermore, in becoming accustomed to open jotting, people may develop definite expectations about what events and topics should be recorded. People may question why the fieldworker is or is not taking note of particular events: On the one hand, they may feel slighted if she fails to make jottings on what they are doing or see as important; on the other hand, they may react with surprise or indignation when she makes jottings about apparently personal situations. Consider the following exchange, again described by the field researcher studying divorce mediation, which occurred as she openly took notes while interviewing a mediator about a session just completed:

> On one occasion when finishing up a debriefing, … [the mediator] began to apply some eye makeup while I was finishing writing down some observations. She flashed me a mock disgusted look and said, "Are you writing *this* down too!" indicating the activity with her eye pencil.

Open jotting, then, has to be carefully calibrated to the unfolding context of the on-going interaction.[16] Open jottings not only may strain relations with those who notice the writing, but, as noted previously, jottings can also distract the ethnographer from paying close attention to talk and activities occurring in the setting. A field researcher will inevitably miss fleeting expressions, subtle movements, and even key content in interactions if his nose is in his notepad.

Taking open jottings is not always advisable for other reasons as well. In some settings, the fieldworker's participation in ongoing interaction might be so involving as to preclude taking breaks to write down jottings; in such instances, he may have to rely more upon memory, focusing on incidents and key phrases that will later trigger a fuller recollection of the event or scene. For example, in a setting where only a few people write and do so only on rare occasions, an ethnographer who writes instead of participating in an all-night village dance might be perceived as failing to maintain social relationships—a serious offense in a close-knit village.

As a result of these problems, even ethnographers who usually write open jottings may, at other times, make jottings privately and out of sight of those studied. Waiting until just after a scene, incident, or conversation has occurred, the ethnographer can then go to a private place to jot down a memorable phrase. Here, it is often useful for the fieldworker to adopt the ways members of the setting themselves use to carve out a moment of privacy or to "get away." Fieldworkers have reported retreating to private places such as a bathroom (Cahill 1985), deserted lunchroom, stairwell, or supply closet to record such covert jottings. Depending upon circumstances, the fieldworker can visit such places periodically, as often as every half hour or so, or immediately after a particularly important incident. Another option is to identify the natural "time-out" spaces that members of the setting also rely on and use as places to relax and unwind, to be by oneself, and so on. Thus, fieldworkers can often go to the institutional cafeteria or coffee shop, to outside sitting areas, or even to waiting rooms or hallways to make quick jottings about events that have just occurred. Other researchers avoid all overt writing in the field setting but immediately upon leaving the field, pull out a notepad or laptop to jot down reminders of the key incidents, words, or reactions they wish to include in full fieldnotes. A similar procedure is to record jottings or even fuller notes on some kind of recording device while driving home from a distant field site. These procedures allow the fieldworker to signal items that she does not want to forget without being seen as intrusive.

Finally, an ethnographer may write jottings in ways intermediate between open and hidden styles, especially when note-taking becomes a part of her task or role. In settings where writing—whether pen on paper or on a computer or laptop—is a required or accepted activity, fieldworkers can take jottings without attracting special notice. Thus, classrooms, meetings where note-taking is expected, organizational encounters where forms must be filled out (as in domestic violence legal aid clinics), or in public settings such as coffee shops and cafeterias where laptops are common, jottings may be more or less openly written. Those in the field may or may not know explicitly that the fieldworker is writing jottings for research purposes. Though many activities do not so easily lend themselves to writing jottings, fieldworkers can find other naturally occurring means to incorporate jottings. For example, fieldworkers often learn about settings by becoming members. For the fieldworker who assumes the role of a novice, the notes that as a beginner he is permitted or even expected to write may become the jottings for his first fieldnotes.

Strategies for how, where, and when to jot notes change with time spent in the field and with the different relationships formed between fieldworker and people in the setting. Even after the ethnographer has established strong personal ties, situations might arise in fieldwork when visibly recording anything will be taken as inappropriate or out of place; in these situations, taking out a notepad or laptop would generate deep discomfort to both fieldworker and other people in the setting.[17] One student ethnographer studying a campus bookstore who had grown quite friendly with bookstore workers—with whom she had spoken openly about her study—nonetheless reported the following incident:

> One of the younger cashiers came up to me after having seen me during two of my last observation sessions. She approached me tentatively with a question about me being a "spy" from the other campus bookstore or possibly from the administration. Trying to ease the situation with a joke, I told her I was only being a spy for sociology's sake. But she didn't understand the joke, and it only made the situation worse.

Sometimes people may be uncomfortable with a jotting researcher because they have had little experience with writing as a part of everyday life. Especially in oral cultures, watching and writing about people may seem like a strange activity indeed. In other instances, people have unpleasant associations with writing and find jottings intrusive and potentially dangerous. On one occasion, an elder in a Zambian village became very hesitant to continue speaking after the ethnographer jotted down his name on a scrap of paper simply to remember it. She later learned that government officials in colonial times used to come by and record names for tax purposes and to enlist people into government work projects.

Finally, even with permission to write openly, the tactful fieldworker will want to remain sensitive to and avoid jotting down matters that participants regard as secret, embarrassing, too revealing, or that put them in any danger. In other instances, the people themselves might not object and, in fact, urge the researcher to take notes about sensitive matters. Even though she thinks they may be embarrassing or bring them harm if they were to be made public, the researcher might take jottings but then later decide not to use them in any final writing.

All in all, it is a defining moment in field relations when an ethnographer begins to write down what people are saying and doing in the presence of those very people. Therefore, fieldworkers take very different approaches to jottings, their strategies both shaping and being shaped by their setting and by their relationships. Hence, decisions about when and how to take jottings must be considered in the context of the broader set of relations with those in the setting. In some situations and relations, taking open jottings is clearly not advisable. In others, fieldworkers decide to take jottings but must devise their own unique means to avoid or minimize awkward interactions that may arise as a result. When deciding when and where to jot, it is rarely helpful or possible to specify in advance one "best way." Here, as in other aspects of fieldwork, a good rule of thumb is to remain open, flexible, and ready to alter an approach if it adversely affects the people under study.

Reflections: Writing and Ethnographic Marginality

Starting as outsiders to a field setting, many fieldworkers find themselves pulled toward involvement as insiders in ways that make maintaining a research stance difficult. The student-ethnographer working in a bookstore, for example, noted this tension:

> There were times when I wanted to be free to listen to other individuals talk or to watch their activities, but friends and acquaintances were so "distracting" coming up and wanting to talk that I wasn't able to. Also, there was this concern on my part that, as I got to know some of the staff people better, their qualities as human beings would become so endearing that I was afraid that I would lose my sociological perspective—I didn't want to feel like in studying them, I was exploiting them.

Many field researchers similarly find themselves unable to consistently sustain a watching, distancing stance toward people they are drawn to and toward events that compellingly involve them.[18] Indeed, some may eventually decide to completely abandon their commitment to research (a possibility that has long given anxiety to anthropologists concerned about the dangers of "going native"). Others may abandon their research commitment in a more limited, situational fashion, determining not to write fieldnotes about specific incidents or persons on the grounds that such writing would involve betrayals or revelations that the researcher finds personally and/or ethically intolerable (see Warren 2000:189–90).

But more commonly, ethnographers try to maintain a somewhat detached, observational attitude, even toward people whom they like and respect, balancing and combining research commitments with personal attachments in a variety of ways.[19] One way to do so is to take occasional time-outs from research, not observing and/or writing fieldnotes about selected portions of one's field experience while continuing to do so about other portions. When living in a village on a long-term basis, for example, an ethnographer may feel drawn into daily, intimate relations as a neighbor or perhaps even as a part of a family. On these occasions, she may participate "naturally"—without a writing orientation or analytic reflection—in ongoing social life. But on other occasions, she participates in local scenes in ways that are directed toward making observations and collecting data. Here, her actions incorporate an underlying commitment to write down and ultimately transform into "data" the stuff and nuances of that life.

Several practical writing conflicts arise from these opposing pressures toward involvement and distance. The inclination to experience daily events either as a "natural" participant or as a researcher shows up in writing as shifts in point of view as well as in varying kinds of details considered significant for inscription. Even where and when to jot notes depends on the person's involvement, at a particular moment, as a participant or as an observer. Whether a researcher-as-neighbor in the village or as a researcher-as-intern on a job, ethnographers experience tension between the present-oriented, day-to-day role and the future-oriented identity as writer; this tension will shape the practical choices they make in writing both jottings and more complete notes.

While a primary goal of ethnography is immersion in the life-worlds and everyday experiences of others, the ethnographer inevitably remains in significant ways an outsider to these worlds. Immersion is not merging; the ethnographer who seeks to "get close to" others usually does not become one of these others. As long as, and to the extent that, he retains commitment to the exogenous project of studying or understanding the lives of others, as opposed to the indigenous project of simply living a life in one way or another, he stays at least a partial stranger to their worlds, despite sharing many of the ordinary exigencies of life that these others experience and react to (see Bittner 1988; Emerson 1987).

Writing fieldnotes creates and underlies this socially close, but experientially separate, stance. The ethnographer's fieldnote writing practices—writing jottings on what others are doing in their presence, observing in order to write, writing extended fieldnotes outside the immediacy of the field setting—specifically create and sustain separation, marginality, and distance in the midst of personal and social proximity. Overtly writing jottings interactionally reminds others (and the ethnographer herself) that she has priorities and commitments that differ from their own. Observing in order to write generates moments when the fieldworker is visibly and self-consciously an outsider pursuing tasks and purposes that differ from those of members.[20] And going to tent, home, or office to write fieldnotes regularly reminds the ethnographer that she is not simply doing what members are doing but that she has additional and other commitments.

In sum, in most social settings, writing down what is taking place as it occurs is a strange, marginalizing activity that marks the writer as an observer rather than a full, ordinary participant. But independently of the reactions of others, participating in order to write leads one to assume the mind-set of an observer, a mind-set in which one constantly steps outside of scenes and events to assess their "writeable" qualities. It may be for this reason that some ethnographers try to put writing out of mind entirely by opting for the more fully experiential style of fieldwork. But this strategy simply puts off, rather than avoids, the marginalizing consequences of writing, for lived experience must eventually be turned into observations and represented in textual form.

ENDNOTES

1. Jackson (1990b:23), for example, quotes several anthropologists who emphasized the pure "doing" of ethnography as follows: "Fieldnotes get in the way. They interfere with what fieldwork is all about—the doing." And: "*This* is what I would call fieldwork. It is not taking notes in the field but is the interaction between the researcher and the so-called research subjects."

2. Jackson (1990b:25) provides an example of the former, quoting an anthropologist who gained "insight into Australian Aboriginal symbolism about the ground while on the ground": "You notice in any kind of prolonged conversation, people are squatting, or lie on the ground. I came to be quite intrigued by that, partly because I'd have to, too ... endless dust." Emerson and Pollner (2001: 250) present an instance of the latter when a previously marginalized and detached observer is suddenly brought stage center into an in-the-home psychiatric evaluation.

3. Some ethnographers committed to ez xperiencing immersion may put off systematic writing almost indefinitely, often until leaving the field permanently. Given our commitment to more or less contemporaneously written notes, we do not address procedures for writing fieldnotes long after the occurrence of the events of interest.

4. This term is taken from Jackson (1990b:5), who credits it to Simon Ottenberg.

5. Gottlieb and Graham (1993) depict these processes of note-taking in their narrative of the course of their ethnographic research in Africa.

6. However, Catherine's placement of this remark immediately following introductions indicates that she considers it important "news" that should be delivered to Ellen in a timely fashion, And the remark takes on further import since it involves an explicit change in topic that excludes the newcomer by referring to someone she clearly does not know.

7. These jottings were originally written in a version of speed writing that is incomprehensible to most readers. We have translated them into readable form.

8. Wolfinger (2002) notes that fieldworkers rely heavily on tacit social knowledge and taken-for-granted assumptions when they determine what to observe and what to recall in writing jottings and fieldnotes. These emergent and situational decisions vary with the concerns and personal dispositions of the fieldworker.

9. This excerpt,[...], draws on interviews conducted by Linda Shaw in which student fieldworkers were encouraged to "talk out loud" while seated at their computers writing fieldnotes from jottings and headnotes.

10. It is possible, of course, to *interview* those involved in the social world under study and to ask directly about their own inner states and motives as well as about their assessments of those of others. Such interviews, however, do not provide definitive answers to these matters but only another set of observations that the ethnographer must still assess and evaluate. See Emerson and Pollner's (1988) consideration of the contingent, deeply problematic interpretations required to evaluate the interview statements of a mental health clinic worker asked to assess ethnographic writings describing his own work circumstances and decision making.

11. This student ethnographer offered these reflections on this process: "Before, I never could write about it. I just never could remember them [concrete events]. It seemed very small and insignificant because everything with these children is in very small steps, and nothing really outstanding ever happens, but this really stood out in my mind, and I wanted to remember it. At the time, I told myself, 'Remember that.'"

    These notes also reflect this student intern/fieldworker's distinctive *commitments* in this setting as is evident in the point of view implicit in her writing. She not only identifies the incident that has just taken place as "listening to the teacher" and as a change from Nicole's prior pattern of behavior. But reflecting her real teaching responsibilities in the setting, she also *evaluates this change positively as an "accomplishment,"* as something that Nicole *should* learn. An ethnographer without job responsibilities in the setting might well characterize the incident differently (e.g., as an adult staff member's exercise of authority) and withhold immediate evaluation as to whether what Nicole did was "good" or "bad."

12. Indeed, Everett Hughes (1971:505) emphasized that it is less the published report than taking a detached outlook toward the personal and intimate that brings people's wrath down upon the field researcher: "The hatred occasionally visited upon the debunking historian is visited almost daily upon the person who reports on the behavior of people he has lived among; and it is not so much the writing of the report, as the very act of thinking in such objective terms that disturbs the people observed."

13. In part, this lack of knowledge about what the field researcher is doing may result from the latter's evolving analytic purposes and concerns, which are not preestablished but which change with immersion in the setting (see Emerson 2001: 282–95). As Thorne (1980: 287) emphasizes, "fieldworkers usually enter the field with an open-ended sense of purpose; they tend to work inductively and may shift interests and outlooks as the research proceeds; practical exigencies may force extensive change of plans."

14. Similarly, those observed often use humor to comment on the role of the note-taking ethnographer. Again, from the HUD office: "The workers are talking and laughing as Sam decides where to put his desk in his new office. I hear one of the workers say, 'I hope Bob didn't write that down.' I walked up. 'What?' 'Oh, I just told Sam it's good he's got space for his machete behind his desk.' They laugh."

15. Here, further complications arise about whether the ethnographer will write fieldnotes about matters that she avoided making jottings on or was asked not to make jottings on. On the one hand, a fieldworker might feel that her fieldnotes are her personal (as well as scientific) record and that she can write anything and everything in those notes that she desires. Such a practice puts off any decision about whether or not to use these particular fieldnote writings in a paper to be seen by any outside audience. On the other hand, the ethnographer might well feel constrained by an implicit agreement not to take jottings about a particular event and to also avoid writing full fieldnotes about the event, independently of whether anyone would ever read that material. Here, the fieldworker honors the personal, ethical bond with the person observed over any commitment to her fieldnotes as research record.

16. Thus, making jottings "off-phase," recommended by Goffman (1989:130) as a means of minimizing reactive effects (i.e., "don't write your notes on the act you're observing because then people will know what it is you're recording"), may risk offending others when the focus of the jottings appears to be the *current* activity or topic.

17. For example, to have made jottings during a Chokwe initiation ceremony (*mwadi*) when the older women were teaching a young woman how "to dance with a husband" by simulating the sexual act might have appeared inappropriate and might have drawn immediate criticism from participants.

18. The seductions of the field, seductions that impart "liminal" or "betwixt-and-between" qualities to field-notes and the experience of writing them, are strikingly revealed in Jackson's (1990a) interviews with anthropologists. Many reported feeling inclined to let fieldnotes go as they began to fit into the rhythms of local life. For example: "I slowed down. More concerned with the hour by hour. You forget to take notes because you feel this is your life" (Jackson 1990a:18).

19. Field researchers routinely use a number of tactics to maintain research distance in the face of pressures for heightened involvement from those under study (Emerson and Pollner 2001). These practices involve "a variety of distancing practices to manage overtures to deeper involvement," including "interactional efforts to preclude, to finesse, and to decline" such overtures, and "cognitive reminders to retain the 'research' framing of one's experiences in the field" (Emerson and Pollner 2001:248).

20. Many ethnographers also create that same separate stance through photographing or filming events. See Jackson (1987).

Writing Fieldnotes I: At the Desk, Creating Scenes on a Page

◆

From *Writing Ethnographic Fieldnotes* By Robert M. Emerson, Rachel I. Fretz, and Linda L. Shaw

After hours participating in, observing, and perhaps jotting notes about ongoing events in a social setting, most fieldworkers return to their desks and their computers to begin to write up their observations into full fieldnotes. At this point, writing becomes the explicit focus and primary activity of ethnography: Momentarily out of the field, the ethnographer settles at her desk, or other preferred spot, to write up a detailed entry of her day's experiences and observations that will preserve as much as possible what she noticed and now feels is significant. At first glance, such writing up might appear to be a straightforward process to the fieldworker. It might seem that with sufficient time and energy, she can simply record her observations with little attention to her writing process. While having enough time and energy to get her memories on the page is a dominant concern, we suggest that the fieldworker can benefit by considering several kinds of basic writing choices.

To view writing fieldnotes simply as a matter of putting on paper what field researchers have heard and seen suggests that it is a transparent process. In this view, ethnographers "mirror" observed reality in their notes; they aim to write without elaborate rhetoric, intricate metaphors, or complex, suspenseful narration. Writing a detailed entry, this view suggests, requires only a sharp memory and conscientious effort.

A contrasting view insists that all writing, even seemingly straightforward, descriptive writing, is a construction. Through his choice of words, sentence style, and methods of organization, a writer presents a version of the world. As a selective and creative activity, writing always functions more as a filter than a mirror reflecting the "reality" of events. Ethnographers, however, only gradually have deepened their awareness and appreciation of this view; they see how even "realist" ethnographies are constructions that rely upon a variety of stylistic conventions. Van Maanen (1988:47) draws ethnographers' attention to a shift from "studied neutrality" in writing to a construction through narrating conventions. He identified studied neutrality as a core convention in realist ethnography; through this convention, the narrator "poses as an impersonal conduit, who unlike missionaries, administrators, journalists, or unabashed members of the culture themselves, passes on more-or-less objective data in a measured intellectual style that is uncontaminated by personal bias, political goals, or moral judgment" (1988:47). The increasing awareness of writing as a construction, whether in realist or other styles, has led to closer examination of how ethnographers write.

While these analyses of ethnographic writing focus primarily on completed ethnographic texts, fieldnotes also draw on a variety of writing conventions. Ethnographers construct their fieldnote entries from selectively recalled and accented moments. Whether it be an incident, event, routine, interaction, or visual image, ethnographers recreate each moment from selected details and sequences that they remember or have jotted down: words, gestures, body movements, sounds, background setting, and so on. While writing, they further highlight certain actions and statements more than others in order to portray their sense of an experience. In other words, ethnographers create scenes on a page through highly selective and partial recountings of observed and re-evoked details. These scenes—that is, moments re-created on a page—represent ethnographers' perceptions and memories of slices of life, enhanced or blurred by their narrating and descriptive skills in writing. An ethnographer's style of writing (whether describing, recounting/narrating, or analyzing) inevitably draws on conventions in order to express and communicate intelligibly to readers, whether they be simply the ethnographer herself or others.

This reading explores the relations between an ethnographer's attention to people's sayings and doings, processes for recalling these moments, and writing options for presenting and analyzing them. Of course, no writing techniques enable an ethnographer to write up life exactly as it happened or even precisely as she remembers it. At best, the ethnographer "re-creates" her memories as written scenes that authentically depict people's lives through selected, integrated details. But in mastering certain descriptive and narrating techniques, she can write up her notes more easily in that first dash of getting everything down; and she can depict more effectively those scenes that she intuitively selects as especially significant. Whether she writes up key scenes first or goes back to them to fill in details, more explicit awareness and exploration of writing strategies enables her to more vividly and fully create those scenes on the page.

In this reading, we focus on how ethnographers go about the complex tasks of remembering, elaborating, filling in, and commenting upon fieldnotes in order to produce a full written account of witnessed scenes and events. We begin by discussing the process of writing up full fieldnotes as ethnographers move from the field to desk and turn their jottings into detailed entries. Next, we explain various writing strategies that ethnographers often draw on as they depict remembered slices of life in fieldnotes and organize them in sequences using conventions of narrating and describing. Although we discuss depicting and organizing strategies separately, in actual fieldnote writing, one does both at the same time. Finally, we discuss several analytic options for reflecting on fieldnotes through writing *asides* and/or more extended *commentaries* in the midst of or at the end of an entry. Whereas strategies for "getting the scene on the page" create a sense of immediacy that allows readers—whether self or others—to envision a social world, analytic strategies explore the ethnographer's understandings about that world but do not portray it. Thus, these strategies complement each other, assisting the ethnographer both to recall events and also to reflect on them.

Throughout the reading, we make suggestions and offer examples in order to increase fieldworkers' awareness of their options for writing. For example, first-time fieldworkers typically have little difficulty in writing snippets about brief interactions; however, they are often uncertain about how to write about more complex, key scenes by sequencing inter-actions, creating characters, reporting dialogue, and contextualizing an action or incident with vivid, sensory details. Though we offer many concrete suggestions and examples, we do not attempt to prescribe a "correct" style or to cover all the writing options an ethnographer might use. Yet, we do suggest that one's writing style influences how one perceives what can be written. Learning to envision scenes as detailed writing on a page is as much a commitment to a lively style of writing as it is to an intellectual honesty in recording events fully and accurately.

Moving from Field to Desk

In this section, we discuss several practical issues that surround the shift of context from the field to desk (or other preferred writing spot). Here we answer some of the novice ethnographer's most basic questions: How much time should one allow for writing field-notes? How long should one stay in the field before writing fieldnotes? What is the most effective timing for writing fieldnotes after returning from the field? What writing tools and equipment does one need? How does the goal of "getting it down on the page," quickly before forgetting, shape one's writing style?

Writing requires a block of concentrated time. Sometimes, incidents that span a few minutes can take the ethnographer several hours to write up; he tries to recall just who did and said what, in what order, and to put all that into words and coherent paragraphs. Indeed, an ethnographic maxim holds that every hour spent observing requires an addi-tional hour to write up.

Over time, fieldworkers evolve a rhythm that balances time spent in the field and time writing notes. In some situations, the field researcher can put a cap on time devoted to observing in order to allow a substantial write-up period on leaving the field. Limiting time in the field in this way lessens the likelihood that the fieldworker will forget what happened or become overwhelmed by the prospect of hours of composing fieldnotes.

We recommend that beginning ethnographers, when possible, leave the field after three to four hours in order to begin writing fieldnotes.

In other situations, the fieldworker might find it more difficult to withdraw for writing. Anthropologists working in other cultures generally spend whole days observing and devote evenings to writing. Field researchers who fill roles as regular workers must put in a full workday before leaving to write notes. In both cases, longer stretches of observation require larger blocks of write-up time and perhaps different strategies for making note writing more manageable. For example, once having described basic routines and daily rhythms in the first sets of notes, the ethnographer who spends hours in the field might focus subsequent notes on significant incidents that occurred throughout the day. At this stage, longer periods spent in the field might in fact prove advantageous, allowing greater opportunities for observing incidents of interest.

Alternatively, the field researcher with regular workday responsibilities might find it useful to designate certain hours for observing and taking jottings, giving priority to these observations in writing up full fieldnotes. Varying these designated observation periods allows exploration of different patterns of activity throughout the day. Of course, while using this strategy, the fieldworker should still write notes on important incidents that occur at other times.

More crucial than how long the ethnographer spends in the field is the timing of writing up fieldnotes. Over time, people forget and simplify experience; notes composed several days after observation tend to be summarized and stripped of rich, nuanced detail. Hence, we strongly encourage researchers to sit down and write full fieldnotes as soon as possible after the day's (or night's) research is done. Writing fieldnotes *immediately* after leaving the setting produces fresher, more detailed recollections that harness the ethnographer's involvement with and excitement about the day's events. Indeed, writing notes immediately on leaving the field offers a way of releasing the weight of what the researcher has just experienced. It is easier to focus one's thoughts and energies on the taxing work of reviewing, remembering, and writing. In contrast, those who put off writing fieldnotes report that with the passage of time, the immediacy of lived experience fades, and writing fieldnotes becomes a burdensome, even dreaded, experience.

Often, however, it is impossible for an ethnographer to find time to write up notes immediately upon leaving the field. Long or late hours, for example, often leave him too tired to write notes. Under these circumstances, it is best to get a good night's sleep and turn to writing up first thing in the morning. Sometimes, even this rest is impossible: A village event might last through several days and nights, confronting the anthropological researcher with a choice between sleeping outside with the villagers or taking time out periodically to sleep and write notes.

When a researcher has been in the field for a long period and has limited time immediately afterward for writing full fieldnotes, she has several alternatives. First, she could make extensive, handwritten jottings about the day's events, relying on the details of these notes to postpone writing full fieldnotes, often for some time.[1] Second, she could dictate fieldnotes into a tape recorder. One can "talk fieldnotes" relatively quickly and can dictate while driving home from a field setting. But while dictation preserves vivid impressions and observations immediately on leaving the field, dictated notes eventually have to be transcribed, a time-consuming, expensive project. And in the meantime, the field researcher does not have ready access to these dictated notes for review or for planning her next steps in the field.

When writing immediately or soon after returning from the site, the fieldworker should go directly to computer or notebook, not talking with intimates about what happened until full fieldnotes are completed. Such "what happened today" talk can rob note writing of its psychological immediacy and emotional release; writing the day's events becomes a stale recounting rather than a cathartic outpouring.[2]

Ethnographers use a variety of different means to write up full notes. While the typewriter provided the standard tool for many classic ethnographers, some handwrote their full notes on pads or in notebooks. Contemporary ethnographers strongly prefer a computer with a standard word-processing program. Typing notes with a word-processing program not only has the advantage of greater speed (slow typists will soon notice substantial gains in speed and accuracy) but also allows for the modification of words, phrases, and sentences in the midst of writing without producing messy, hard-to-read pages. Fieldnotes written on the computer are also easily reordered; it is possible, for example, to insert incidents or dialogue subsequently recalled at the appropriate place. Finally, composing with a word-processing program facilitates coding and sorting fieldnotes as one later turns to writing finished ethnographic accounts.

In sitting down at a desk or computer, the ethnographer's most urgent task or writing purpose is to record experiences while they are still fresh. Thus, ethnographers write hurriedly, dashing words "down on the page." Their notes read like an outpouring, not like polished, publishable excerpts. Knowing that a memorable event fades and gets confused with following ones as time passes, a fieldworker writes using whatever phrasing and organization seems most accessible, convenient, and doable at the time. He need not worry about being consistent, and he can shift from one style, one topic, or one thought to another as quickly as the fingers can type. In that initial writing, the field researcher concentrates on a remembered scene more than on words and sentences. If the ethnographer focuses too soon on wording, she will produce an "internal editor," distracting her attention from the evoked scene and stopping her outpouring of memory. The goal is to get as much down on paper in as much detail and as quickly as possible, holding off any evaluation and editing until later. But in this process, the ethnographer tries to strike a balance between describing fully and getting down the essentials of what happened. One student explains her struggle to describe an incident:

> Here I'm going to stop and go back later because I know what I'm trying to say, but it isn't coming out. ...So there's a little more to it than that, but I have to think about how to say it, so I'm just going to leave it. When I write my fieldnotes, I just try to get it all down, and I go back through and edit, take time away from it and then come

back and see if that's really what I meant to say or if I could say that in a better way, a clearer way.

Fieldworkers may write down all the words that come to mind and later choose a more evocative and appropriate phrasing. Many writers produce a first round quickly, knowing that they will make additions, polish wording, or reorganize paragraphs at some other time. Thus, in that first rush of writing, finding the absolutely best word or phrase to persuade a future audience should not be of such concern that it slows down the flow of getting words to paper.

Beginning ethnographers should not be surprised to experience ambivalence in writing fieldnotes. On the one hand, the outpouring of thoughts and impressions as the writer reviews and reexperiences the excitement and freshness of the day's events might bring expressive release and reflective insight. Having seen and heard intriguing, surprising things all day long, the fieldworker is finally able to sit down, think about, and relive events while transforming them into a permanent record. On the other hand, after a long, exciting, or draining stint in the field, a busy schedule might inhibit finding enough time to write up notes, turning the writing-up process into an intrusive, humdrum burden. This experience is more likely to occur after the ethnographer has spent weeks or months in the field; writing notes more selectively and/or focusing on new and unexpected developments not described in previous writings can provide some relief to these feelings.

Recalling In Order to Write

In sitting down to compose fieldnotes in a fluid, "get it down quickly" fashion, the fieldworker seeks to recall in as much detail as possible what he observed and experienced earlier that day. This process of recalling in order to write involves reimagining and replaying in one's mind scenes and events that marked the day, actively repicturing and reconstructing these witnessed events in order to get them down on a page. Sometimes replaying and reconstructing are keyed to jottings or lists of topics written earlier; at others, the ethnographer works only with "headnotes" and other memories to reconstruct detailed accounts of the day's events. In both cases, the descriptions that result must make sense as a logical, sensible series of incidents and experiences, even if only to an audience made up of the fieldworker himself.

Ethnographers often use a mix of standard practices for recalling the day's events in order to organize and compose detailed, comprehensive fieldnotes. One strategy is to trace one's own activities and observations in chronological order, recalling noteworthy events in the sequence in which one observed and experienced them. Another strategy is to begin with some "high point" or an incident or event that stands out as particularly vivid or important, to detail that event as thoroughly as possible, and then to consider in some topical fashion other significant events, incidents, or exchanges. Or, the ethnographer can focus more systematically on incidents related to specific topics of interest in order to recall significant events. Often ethnographers combine or alternate between strategies, proceeding back and forth over time in stream-of-consciousness fashion.

As noted, ethnographers often compose full fieldnotes without any prior writings, working strictly from memory and the recollection of what was seen and heard in the field. In other cases, they can work from jottings made in the field or soon after. Some ethnographers also find it useful, on moving to the desk in preparation for writing, to write up a list of topics—brief references to key events that unfolded that day or to the sequence of action that marked a key incident—using the list to get started on and to organize notes on these events. In these later instances, the fieldworker fills in, extends, and integrates these abbreviated bits and pieces of information by visualizing and replaying the events, incidents, and experiences they refer to. Jottings and lists of topics, then, can anchor the writing process, providing links back to the field; the fieldworker simply turns to the start of that day's jottings or topics and moves through in the order recorded, filling in and making connections between segments on the basis of memory.

To explore the process of using memory and abbreviated writings to construct full fieldnotes, we consider how fieldworkers turn brief jottings into extended texts. Looking at the movement back and forth between jottings and the fuller, richer recollection of events in the final fieldnotes provides a grounded way of examining the generic processes of recalling in order to write. Here, we return to the two illustrations of jottings provided in Reading 2.1, examining how each was used to produce sets of full fieldnotes.

1. *"Too Many Sexual References"*

A. Jottings

Sexual Harassment
Andy—too many sexual references
    PE frisbee game "This team has too many sausages"
Reynaldo—(*Carlos—in jail for stealing bicycle, 18 yrs old*) [circled]
Laura—Wants to propose sexual harassment forms
    Thinking about detention for these students but already too much work
    for keeping track of tardies/truancies/tendencies

B. Full Fieldnotes

Next Laura goes off topic and mentions that some of the students keep making sexual comments that are "inappropriate." She says that Andy is particularly bad and recounts an instance where the class was out on the PE field and she split the class into teams for Ultimate Frisbee. I split the boys and girls evenly but you know how the girls tend to just switch teams so they can be together. Most of the boys ended up on one team, and the other team, the team with Andy, had a lot of boys. Andy says, "Jezz, this team has too many cocks!" right in front of me! Then Laura focuses on Reynaldo. Someone used lotion at my desk and it squirted out onto the table in front of my desk. Reynaldo comes in and says, Wow, somebody had an accident over here! Don't worry, Laura, I'll clean it up for you. And he did, he took some Kleenex and cleaned it up, but still, do you really think that it's appropriate to mention to me, someone in her 50s, that someone excreted ejaculatory fluid on my desk?! I mean, I'm in my 50s, I have three sons, and I have a Master's degree!

The other teachers nod their heads and agree this is wrong. Marie says, I feel exactly the same way. She wanted to say something else but Ms. Diaz interrupts her: The other day I was trying to teach Jerry something and he yelled at me, "Get off my nuts!" Can you believe that? The principal mentions, Oh yeah, I remember you came down to tell me about that. Laura then says, We need a system to control this. I think that we should type out a statement that shows exactly what they said and have the student who said it sign and date it. If they have three of those, we punish them somehow. The teachers debate the merits of this system and ask what kinds of punishment they could realistically enforce. Laura says they could give students detention. Rose says, Yeah, but look at how much paperwork we already have to do for the students who are already in detention, so you want to make more work in general for all of us? No, we can't give the students detention, it'd have to be something else. In the end, there is a consensus that this system is good but has kinks to work out. (The punishment of the students is contingent on the workload of the staff.)

Note the contrasts in content, texture, and comprehensibility between the initial jottings and the full fieldnotes. The fieldworker uses the references to Andy and Reynaldo to recollect and reconstruct the teacher's accounts of inappropriate "sexual references" recently made by each boy. Nothing is written here from the jotting about Carlos being in jail for stealing a bicycle; presumably one of the staff mentioned this as a side issue in the midst of this talk. That these words were circled suggests that they have been included elsewhere in the notes, perhaps to document staff plans to dismiss students who were eighteen or older whom the school was not legally mandated to retain. The second paragraph fills in the discussion generated by Laura's proposal to create "sexual harassment forms" and to punish students who accumulate three such forms. Note that it is only here that the school staff use the term "sexual harassment," although the ethnographer has used this heading to mark and recall these exchanges in his jottings.

Furthermore, a discrepancy between the jottings and the full notes is evident: in the former, Andy is reported to have referred to "too many sausages," while in the full notes Laura quotes Andy as having said "too many cocks." The student ethnographer explained what happened here (personal communication): "Reynaldo told me Andy used the words 'too many cocks.' I got mixed up when creating the fieldnotes. It should have been Laura 'too many sausages' and Reynaldo 'too many cocks'."[3]

2.   *"You Can Call His Doctor at UCLA"*

A.   Jottings

[case number]
Snow, Marcia
Thomas

atty—AIDS Mike
Murphy
legal guardian

---

are you prepared to proceed against
the one individual—(both)
massive doses of chemother(apy)
I don't think he's ever going to come in
here
I know he's well enough to walk–
came in (returned heater)—when?
you can call his doctor at UCLA and
he can verify all this
I just don't call people on the
telephone—courts don't operate that way—it has to be on paper or (in
person)

Mr. M returned my heaters–
was walking

Let me be clear
You don't want to proceed against
only one of these individuals?
I want to proceed against (no, but)
—if he is his guardian both—but

---

unravel it
Dept 10—J(udge) Berkoff
Ms. S, hold on just a

B.   Full Fieldnotes

Marcia Snow has longish, curly, dark brown hair, in her 20s, dressed informally in blue blouse and pants. No wedding ring, but with a youngish looking guy with glasses. Robert Thomas is in his 40s, light brown hair, shaggy mustache, jacket with red-black checked lining.

Judge begins by asking RT if he has an atty; he does, but he is not here. He explains that his business partner, Mike Murphy, who is also named in the TRO, is not here today; he has AIDS and is very ill. "I'm his legal guardian," so I can represent his concerns. J asks MS: "Are you prepared to proceed against this one individual?" MS answers that she wants the order against both of them. RT then explains that MM has had AIDS for three years, has had "massive doses of chemotherapy," and adds: "I don't think he's ever going to come in here." J asks MS if from what she knows that MM is this sick. MS hesitates, then says: "I know he's well enough to walk." I saw him walking when he returned the heaters that they stole. J: When was this? (I can't hear her answer.) RT: He's had his AIDS for three years. He's very sick. "You can call his doctor at UCLA, and he can verify this." J: "I just don't call people on the telephone. Courts don't operate that way. It has to be on paper" or testified in person. RT repeats that MM is very ill, that he has to take care of him, and he is not getting better. But MS again counters this, saying again: "Mr. Murphy returned my heaters—he was walking then ..."

J then looks to MS, asking: "Let me be clear—you don't want to proceed against only one of these individuals?" MS: "No, I want to proceed against both. But if he is his guardian," then I can go ahead today with it. J agrees to this, saying he will let another judge "unravel it," and assigns the case to Dept. 10, Judge Berkoff. MS and RT turn to leave, but J says: "Ms. Snow, hold on just a minute until the clerk has your file." MS waits briefly, then gets file and goes out with the guy with her.

Compared to the highly selected, partial, and abbreviated jottings, the full fieldnotes tell a coherent, step-by-step story of what was observed in the courtroom. Most of this story consists of details that have been filled in from memory. The brief "background" of the case provided by the jottings, for example, has been fleshed out into relatively full descriptions of the two litigants (but not of the judge or other regular courtroom personnel). In addition, the notes tell a story about one specific topic—the problems arising from the absence of a codefendant, the questions the judge raises about this absence, and a sequence of responses to this problem by the petitioner and defendant. The story, however, is missing key elements (for example, the fact that this case involves a tenant-landlord dispute) and contains elements of unknown meaning (for example, Marcia's comment about how the absent defendant "returned the heaters that they stole").

Also consider the handling of direct quotations in moving from jottings to fieldnotes. Only those words actually taken down at the time are placed in quotes; a portion of the direct speech missed at the time is paraphrased outside the direct quotes. Thus, the jotted record of the judge's remark, "it has to be on paper or (in person)," is written in fieldnote form as "'It has to be on paper' or testified in person." As a general practice, speech not written down word for word at the time should either be presented as indirect quotation or paraphrased (see discussion of "dialogue" below).

Ethnographers rely upon key words and phrases from their jottings to jog their memories. But writing fieldnotes from jottings is not a straightforward remembering and filling in; rather, it is a much more active process of constructing relatively coherent sequences of action and evocations of scene and character (see below). In turning jottings and headnotes into full notes, the fieldworker is already engaged in a sort of preliminary analysis whereby she orders experience, both creating and discovering patterns of interaction. This process involves deciding not simply *what to include* but also *what to leave out*, both from remembered headnotes and from items included in jottings. Thus, in writing full fieldnotes, the ethnographer might clearly remember or have jottings about particular incidents or impressions but decide, for a variety of reasons, not to incorporate them into the notes. The material might seem to involve matters that are peripheral to major activities in the setting, activities that members appear to find insignificant, or that the ethnographer has no interest in.

However, in continuing to write up the day's fieldnotes or at some later point in the fieldwork, the ethnographer might see significance in jottings or headnotes that initially seemed too unimportant or uninteresting to include in full fieldnotes. The student ethnographer who, in writing full notes, had initially passed over a jotting about the "delivery of three new bags of sand" to the sandbox at a Headstart Program saw relevance and meaning in this incident as she continued to write up and reflect on the day's observations:

> Now that I'm thinking back, when we got the sand, it was a really hot day so that actually that jotting did help me remember because it was so warm out that Karen, the teacher, said that the children could take their shoes off in the sandbox. This became a really tough rule to enforce because the children aren't allowed to have shoes off anywhere else. They would just run out of the sandbox and go into the parking lot, and so it was a really tough rule to enforce. And I have an incident about that.

In the comments made here, the student comes to appreciate (and construct) a linkage between the three new bags of sand included in her jottings and what she sees as significant issues of rule enforcement and control in the setting; with this appreciation, she decides to incorporate the delivery of the sand as an incident in her notes. Moreover, this focus on enforcement and control leads her to review her memory for "relevant" events or "incidents"; here she recollects "an incident about that," signaling her intent to write up this incident in her notes.

In light of the ways "significance" shifts and emerges in the course of writing notes and thinking about their import, we encourage students to write about as many of these "minor" events as possible, even if they seem insubstantial or only vaguely relevant at the moment. They might signal important processes relevant to other incidents or to emerging analytic themes in ways the ethnographer can only appreciate at some later point. Even when writing the story of one rather cohesive event, writers should include apparently tangential activities and comments, for they might turn out to provide key insights into the main action.

Writing Detailed Notes: Depiction of Scenes

The ethnographer's central purpose is to portray a social world and its people. But often beginning researchers produce fieldnotes lacking sufficient and lively detail. Through inadvertent summarizing and evaluative wording, a fieldworker fails to adequately describe what she has observed and experienced. The following strategies—description, dialogue, and characterization—enable a writer to coherently depict an observed moment through striking details. As is evident in several of the included excerpts, ethnographers often merge several strategies. In this section, we explain and provide examples of these writing strategies; in the next section, we discuss various options for organizing a day's entry.

Description

"Description" is a term used in more than one way. Thus far, we have referred to writing fieldnotes as descriptive writing in contrast to analytic argumentation.[4] Here, we refer more specifically to description as a means of picturing through concrete sensory details the basic scenes, settings, objects, people, and actions the fieldworker observed. In this sense, writing descriptive images is just one part of the ethnographer's storytelling about the day's events.

As a writing strategy, description calls for concrete details rather than abstract generalizations, for sensory imagery rather than evaluative labels, and for immediacy through details presented at close range. Goffman (1989:131) advises the fieldworker to write "lushly," making frequent use of adjectives and adverbs to convey details. For example, details present color, shape, and size to create visual images; other details of sound, timbre, loudness, and volume evoke auditory images; those details describing smell or fragrance recreate olfactory images; and details portraying gestures, movements, posture, and facial expression convey kinetic images. While visual images tend to predominate in many descriptions, ethnographers find that they often combine these various kinds of images in a complete description.

When describing a scene, the writer selects those details that most clearly and vividly create an image on the page; consequently, he succeeds best in describing when he selects details according to some purpose and from a definite point of view. For example, the writer acquires a clearer sense of what details to accent if he takes as his project describing, not the office setting in a general sense, but, rather, the office environment as a cluttered place to work, perhaps as seen from the perspective of a secretary who struggles with her boss's disorder every day. However, frequently the fieldworker sits down to write about a setting he does not yet understand. In fact, the beginning ethnographer often faces the dilemma of not knowing what counts as most important; under these circumstances, his purpose is simply to document the impression he has at that time. Wanting to recall the physical characteristics and the sensory impressions of his experience, a fieldworker often describes the setting and social situations, characters' appearances, and even some daily routines.

Ethnographers often select details to describe the ambience of a setting or environment that is important for understanding subsequent action. For example, during initial fieldwork in a village in southeastern Congo (formerly Zaire), an ethnographer might reflect on the spatial arrangement and social relations as she has observed them thus far. In her fieldnotes, she might describe how the houses all face toward an open, cleared area; that the village pavilion where men visit is situated in the center; that the women cook by wood fires in front of their houses, often carrying babies on their backs as they work and are assisted by younger girls; and that some men and boys sit under a tree in the yard near two other men weaving baskets. How she perceives these details and the way she frames them as contextualizing social interactions determines, in part, the details she selects to create this visual image of a small village in the late afternoon.

An ethnographer should also depict the appearance of characters who are part of described scenes in order to contextualize actions and talk. For example, in looking at how residents adapted to conditions in a psychiatric board-and-care home, Linda Shaw described someone who others living in the home thought was especially "crazy":

> Robert and I were sitting by the commissary talking this afternoon when a new resident named Bruce passed by several times. He was a tall, extremely thin man with straggly, shoulder-length, graying hair and a long bushy beard. I had heard that he was only in his thirties, even though he looked prematurely aged in a way that reminded me of the sort of toll that harsh conditions exact from many street people. He wore a long, dirty, gray-brown overcoat with a rainbow sewn to the back near the shoulder over a pair of torn blue jeans and a white tee shirt with what looked like coffee stains down the front. Besides his disheveled appearance, Bruce seemed extremely agitated and restless as he paced from one end of the facility to the other. He walked with a loping gait, taking very long strides, head held bent to his chest and his face expressionless, as his arms swung limply through the air, making a wide arc, as though made of rubber. As Bruce passed by on one of these rounds, Robert remarked, "That guy's really crazy. Don't tell me he's going to be recycled into society."

Here the ethnographer provides a detailed description of a newcomer to the home, providing the context necessary to understand a resident's comment that this person was too crazy to ever live outside of the home. In fact, the final comment, "Don't tell me he's going to be recycled into society," serves as a punch line dramatically linking the observer's detailed description of the new resident with the perceptions and concerns of an established resident.

While describing appearance might initially seem easy, in fact, many observers have difficulty doing so in lively, engaging ways. Part of the problem derives from the fact that when we observe people whom we do not know personally, we initially see them in very stereotyped ways; we normally notice and describe strangers in terms of gender, age, or race, along with other qualities in their physical appearances.[5] Thus, beginning fieldworkers invariably identify characters by gender. They frequently add one or two visible features: "a young woman," "a young guy in a floral shirt," "two Latina women with a small child," "a woman in her forties," "a white male with brown/blond medium length hair." Indeed, many fieldnotes present characters as *visual clichés,* relying on worn-out, frequently used details to describe others, often in ways that invoke common stereotypes: a middle-aged librarian is simplistically described as "a bald man wearing thick glasses," a youth in a juvenile hall as having "slicked back hair," a lawyer as "wearing a pin-striped suit" and "carrying a briefcase." Such clichés not only make for boring writing but also, more dangerously, blind the writer to specific attributes of the person in front of him.

The description of a character's appearance is frequently "categoric" and stereotyped for another reason as well: Fieldworkers rely upon these clichés not so much to convey another's appearance to envisioned readers but to label (and thus provide clarity about) who is doing what within the fieldnote account. For example, a fieldworker used the phrase "the floral shirt guy" a number of times to specify which character he was talking about when he described the complicated comings and goings occurring in a Latino street scene. Thus, the initial description does not provide many details about this character's appearance but merely tags him so that we can identify and follow him in the subsequent account.

However, the ethnographer must train herself both to notice more than these common indicators of general social categories and to capture distinctive qualities that will enable future readers (whether herself in rereading the notes or others who read excerpts) to envision more of what she saw and experienced. A *vivid image* based on actual observation depicts specific details about people and settings so that the image can be clearly visualized. For example, one fieldworker described a man in a skid row mission as "a man in the back who didn't have any front teeth and so spoke with a lisp." Another described a boy in a third-grade classroom as "wiggling his butt and distorting his face for attention" on entering the classroom late. Such images use details to paint more specific, lively portraits and avoid as much as possible vague, stereotypic features.

Ethnographers can also write more vivid descriptions by describing how characters dress. The following excerpt depicts a woman's clothes through concrete and sensory imagery:

> Today Molly, a white female, wore her African motif jacket. It had little squares on the front which contained red, yellow, green, and black colored prints of the African continent. Imposed on top was a gold lion of Judah (symbol of Ethiopian Royal Family). The sleeves were bright—red, yellow, and green striped. The jacket back had a picture of Bob Marley singing into a microphone. He is a black male with long black dreadlocks and a little beard. Written in red at the top was: "Rastafari."

This description advances the ethnographer's concern with ethnic identity and affiliation. The initial sentence, "Today Molly, a white female, wore her African motif jacket," sets up an unexpected contrast: Molly is white, yet she wears an item of clothing that the researcher associates with African American culture. "African motif" directs attention to particular attributes of the jacket (colors, insignia, and symbols) and ignores other observable qualities of the jacket, for example, its material, texture, style, cleanliness, or origins. Consequently, this description frames the jacket as an object publicly announcing its wearer's affiliation with African Americans.[6]

Furthermore, rather than simply *telling* the reader what the ethnographer infers, this passage *shows* affiliation with African Americans in immediate detail through actions and imagery. Contrast this descriptive strategy with the following (hypothetical) abstract and evaluative depiction that generalizes, rather than specifies, details: "Today, Molly, a white girl, *assertively* wore her *bright African* jacket. She always *shows off* in these clothes and *struts* around pretending to act *like a black*." Not only does this summary rely on a vague adjective ("bright"), but it also obscures the actions with evaluative adverbs and verbs ("assertively," "struts," and "shows off") and categorizing labels ("like a black").

Because an ethnographer wishes to depict a scene for a reader, he does not condense details, avoids evaluative adjectives and verbs, and never permits a label to stand for description. While all writing entails grouping and identifying details, the ethnographer resists the impulse to unself-consciously label others according to received categories from his own background. Nonetheless, it is not enough to avoid evaluative wording. In descriptions, the writer's tone of voice unavoidably reflects his personal attitude toward the people described. A better-than-thou attitude or objectifying the other (as odd, a foreigner, from a lower class, from a less civilized culture, from another ethnic group) always "shows" in subtle ways: Tone, like a slip of the tongue, appears in word choice, implicit comparisons, and even in rhythms as in the staccato of a curt dismissal. A self-reflective ethnographer should make his judgments explicit in written asides. But, the best antidote to these evaluative impulses is to keep in mind that the ethnographer's task is to write descriptions that lead to empathetic understanding of the social worlds of others.

In addition to describing people, places, and things, an ethnographer might also depict a scene by including action. For example, she might portray a character's talk, gesture, posture, and movement. In contrast to describing a person's appearance, action sequences highlight a character's agency to affect her world; a character acts within a situation in routine ways or in response to set conditions. The following fieldnote excerpt of a grocery stocker working in a nearly empty store reveals how sensory details about action can create a vivid description of a scene:

> As I conclude my first "lap" [around the store] and begin my second, I find myself slowly making my way through the frozen food aisle when I come across a female "stocker." She seems to be pretty young (college age) and is thin with dark, heavily lined eyes. Although her eyes are dark, the makeup is not to the point where she looks gothic. Her brown hair is pulled back in a loose bun, and she is in the process of restocking TV dinners into the freezer. She is like a robot: she seems to be in her own space as she opens the freezer door and props open the door using her body. She then grabs a few TV dinners from their original boxed container and sorts and loads them into the new and appropriate location within the freezer. As she turns around to reload, she fails to prop open the freezer door with something other than her body. This causes the door to involuntarily close when she shifts her body in order to grab more boxes. This action causes the freezer door to slam shut with a loud "snap" sound. As strange as it may seem, the sound that the door makes is almost as if the freezer is mocking the female stocker. But this does not seem to distress her as she turns around and repeats the whole process, again and again.

Here, the ethnographer sets the scene, using an evocative image (eyes are dark, but the makeup is not gothic-looking) to enable the reader to visualize the stocker's appearance. Notice how she uses a familiar metaphor, for example "robot," as a starting point to call up a visual image, but she avoids creating a stereotyped character by providing the details of actions to create a fuller, in-depth picture of what the stocker is doing. She employs visual images of the stocker's physical movement (using her body to keep the freezer door open), as well as auditory images (the freezer door slams shut with a loud "snap" sound), to give the door a human-like character (the ability to mock the stocker). Thus, she effectively portrays both the physical and emotional effort required to place the TV dinners in the freezer. When ethnographers occasionally use figurative language, such as this robot metaphor, they always should supplement the image with descriptive detail as this ethnographer does. Otherwise, later on when reading her fieldnotes, she might not remember why she chose this metaphor or what actions it represented.

Dialogue

Ethnographers also reproduce dialogue—conversations that occur in their presence or that members report having had with others—as accurately as possible. They reproduce dialogue through direct and indirect quotation, through reported speech, and by paraphrasing. We hold that only those phrases actually quoted verbatim should be placed between quotation marks; all others should be recorded as indirect quotations or paraphrases.

The following example illustrates how direct quotation, indirect quotation, and reported speech work together to convey back-and-forth conversation:

> For a minute or so before I left, I talked with Polly, the black woman who guards the front school entrance. As we were talking, a black girl, wearing dark blue sweats, walked by. Polly pointed to her. "Did you see that girl?" she asked me. I told her I had, and Polly confided that the girl had hassled her. Polly said the girl tried to leave school without permission and had started arguing. She said the principal had been walking by and he had tried to deal with the disturbance. And the girl had answered, "This is my school. You can't control me!" and then she had called the principal a "white MF." Polly told me, "It's usually a black MF, but she changed it." She said that girl had a "bad attitude" and shook her head.

Writing up this conversation as predominately indirect quotation preserves the back-and-forth flow of the spoken interaction. Interspersing quoted fragments livens up the dialogue and lends a sense of immediacy. By clearly marking the direct quotation, indirect quotation, and reported speech, we can see how they work together.

Direct: "Did you see that girl?"

Indirect: I told her I had …

Indirect: … and Polly confided that the girl had hassled her. Polly said that the girl tried to leave school without permission and had started arguing. She said the principal had been walking by and he had tried to deal with the disturbance.

Reported speech, direct: And the girl had answered, "This is my school. You can't control me!" and then she called the principal a "white MF."

Direct: "It's usually a black MF, but she changed it."

Indirect: She said that the girl has a

Direct: "bad attitude" …

Indirect quotation more closely approximates dialogue than paraphrasing does. Paraphrasing this conversation with Polly might have preserved the basic content. But in paraphrasing, a writer translates speech into her own words and too readily starts to summarize. For example, a paraphrase of the last portion of this excerpt might read: "The girl talked back to the principal and called him names. …She has some attitude problems." This paraphrasing obscures the flavor of chatting and offering confidences, and it fails to voice the student's remarks to the principal, which thus would have been unheard.

Clearly, this ethnographer has a lively style that moves easily because the fieldnote varies the phrasing and only uses "she said" as needed. In writing direct or indirect quotations, ethnographers do not need to repeat "she said that …" each time they introduce dialogue. Instead, one can keep the pace of the dialogue moving by immediately stating the verbatim-recalled wording or the approximately recalled phrase. For example, "Polly said that the girl had hassled her," could also be written as, "Polly replied, the girl hassled me," or, sometimes when it is clear who is speaking, simply as "the girl hassled me." Too many repetitions of "she said" or "he said" begin to echo and, thus, detract from the flow of the dialogue.

Members' own descriptions and "stories" of their experiences are invaluable indexes to their views and perceptions of the world and should be documented verbatim when possible. Writing this exchange as a "story" told verbatim to the fieldworker preserves two different kinds of information. First, it shows that "something happened" between a student, a guard, and the principal. Second, the account provides the guard's experience of that something. As the guard's story, this fieldnote conveys more about the teller and her concerns than it does about the girl and her trouble.

Writing up dialogue is more complicated than simply remembering talk or replaying every word. People talk in spurts and fragments. They accentuate or even complete a phrase with a gesture, facial expression, or posture. They send complex messages through incongruent, seemingly contradictory and ironic verbal and nonverbal expression as in sarcasm or polite put-downs. Thus, ethnographers must record the meanings they infer from the bodily expression accompanying words—gesture, movement, facial expression, tone of voice. Furthermore, people do not take turns smoothly in conversations: They interrupt each other, overlap words, talk simultaneously, and respond with ongoing comments and murmurs. Such turn taking can be placed on a linear page by bracketing and overlapping speech.

Although accurately capturing dialogue in jottings and full fieldnotes requires considerable effort, ethnographers have a number of reasons for peppering their notes with verbatim quoted talk. Such dialogue conveys character traits, advances action, and provides clues to the speaker's social status, identity, personal style, and interests. Dialogue allows the field researcher to capture members' terms and expressions as they are actually used in specific situations. In addition, dialogue can point to key features of a cultural worldview. The following excerpt comes from a discussion in an African American history course:

> Deston, a black male with Jheri curls, asked Ms. Dubois, "What's a sellout? I hear that if you talk to a white person—you sell out. If you go out with a white girl—you sell out." She replied that some

people "take it to the extreme." She said that a sellout could even be a teacher or someone who works at McDonalds. Then she defined a sellout as "someone who is more concerned about making it … who has no racial loyalty, no allegiance to people."

The writer uses direct quotation to capture an ongoing exchange about racial identity and to retain a key member's term.

The use of indirect, along with direct, quotation also allows an ethnographer to represent the back-and-forth character of everyday interaction in accurate and effective ways. In the following excerpt from a swap meet, for example, directly quoting the actual negotiations over price highlights and focuses the reader's attention on this aspect of the interaction.

> She (swap meet vendor) had many different items including a Sparkletts water dispenser, some big outdoor Christmas lighted decorations, a blanket, wooden shoes from China, salt and pepper shakers, a vacuum cleaner, mini wooden mantels, clothes, small pieces of furniture, and shoes. I see a beaded curtain jumbled up on the tarp and walk toward it. I point to it and ask the vendor how much she wants for it. She takes a moment to think and then says, "Ummm, five dollars." She stands up slowly and walks over to it. She picks it up off the ground. She shows us that it is in good condition by holding it up high and letting all the bead strands hang down. "Will you take three?" I ask as I look it over. It has a fancy top that the beads hang off of. It is all one color—ivory or light brown. "How about four?" she says. "Alright, I'll take it," I say. She tells me that she will bag it up for me, and she turns around to get a plastic bag from the inside of the van. I rummage through my pockets looking for the one dollar bills. All I have left are three ones and a five. I hand her the five and she gives me the bag. She puts the five dollar bill into her fanny pack and withdraws a one dollar bill. She hands it to me and says thank you. I say thank you back and turn to leave.

In addition to contributing to a lively description of a scene at the swap meet, the presentation of dialogue furthers sensitivity to the interactional processes through which members construct meanings and local social worlds in such routine exchanges.

These issues and choices in writing dialogue become even more complex when the local language differs from the researcher's. How well the researcher knows the language certainly determines the extent of verbatim quoting. When the ethnographer hears slang, nonstandard English, or grammatically incorrect phrasing, she should resist correcting this wording but, instead, put such expressions in quotation marks. In addition, when a fieldworker does research in a second language, not only will she frequently miss what someone said because she did not understand a particular word, but she also will have difficulty capturing the verbatim flow of a dialogue even when she does understand. By working with a local assistant and checking to make sure she understands correctly what people are saying, she can compensate for some of her difficulty. Similar problems arise when working in English in a setting with much technical lingo or other in-group expressions such as slang. Unable to follow all the talk, the researcher paraphrases as much as she can and occasionally includes the snippets of verbatim talk she heard and remembered clearly.

In response to these language difficulties, many ethnographers supplement their fieldnotes by tape recordings. They might also make recordings in order to preserve as detailed a record of naturally occurring talk as possible so that they can pursue particular theoretical issues. For example, field researchers interested in recurrent patterns of interaction in institutional settings might make special efforts to tape-record at least some such encounters.[7] Still, most ethnographers do not regard recordings as their primary or exclusive form of data; rather, they use them as one way among others for closely examining the meaning events and experiences have for those studied.

By way of illustration, consider how Rachel Fretz worked with recordings of storytelling performances among the Chokwe people in Bandundu, Congo (formerly Zaire). She recorded and carefully transcribed all verbal expressions of both narrators and audience, since listeners actively participate in the storytelling session. The following is an excerpt from the beginning of one such performance; the narrator (N), a young man, performs to an audience (A) of women, men, and children one evening around the fire (Fretz 1995a).

N: Once upon a time, there were some young boys, myself and Fernando and Funga and Shamuna.

A: Is it a story with a good song?

N: They were four persons. They said, "Ah. Let's go hunting."

Pia they went everywhere. *Pia* they went everywhere.

A: Good.

N: They went this way and that way, this way and that way. No game. "Let's return.

Let's go." They saw a large hut.

Inside there was a container with honey in it.

"My friends, this honey, *mba*, who put it here?"

He said, "Who?"

Another said, "Who?"

[Another said,] "Let's go. We can't eat this."

Then, *fwapu*, Funga came forward and said, "Ah! You're just troubled. Even though you're so hungry, you won't eat this honey?"

"Child. The man who put the honey here is not present. You see that this house was built with human ribs, and you decide to eat this honey."

He [Funga] said, "Get out of here. I'll eat it. Go on ahead. Go now." He took some honey; he ate it.

"Shall we wait for him? We'll wait for him."

He came soon. "Let's go."

Liata, liata, liata, they walked along. "We're going a long way. We came from a great distance." They arrived and found, ah! *Kayanda* [my goodness], a large river.

"My friends, what is this?"

"My friends, such a large river. Where did it come from?"

He said, "Ah! Who can explain it?"

"We can't see its source or where it's going."

"Let's cross the river. I'll go first.

First Singing

N: Oh Papa. Eee, Papa, it's I who ate the honey.

A: This large river God created, I must cross it.

N: Papa! Eee, Papa, I'm going into the water.

A: This large river God created, I must cross it.

N: Papa! Eee, Papa, I didn't it.

A: This large river God created, I must cross it.

N: Papa! Eee, Papa, I'm crossing to the other side.

A: This large river God created, I must cross it.

Transcribing a performance involves catching all the teller's words and audience responses (often requiring the help of a native speaker) despite such interfering sounds as a dog barking and children crying. Accurate transcription also requires close attention to the rhythm and pauses in speaking so that the punctuation and line breaks reflect the storytelling style (cf. Hymes 1991; Tedlock 1983).

But transcribing and translating the tape is only one part of the ethnographer's efforts to learn about and understand storytelling performances. She also wrote extensive fieldnotes describing the situation and participants.[8] For example, she noted that the storytelling session took place by the fire in the chief's pavilion at an informal family gathering including the chief, his seven wives, and their children and grandchildren. She observed that the women participated primarily by singing the story-songs and by answering with exclamations and remarks. The ethnographer also recorded her conversations with these participants and the general comments Chokwe people offered about telling such stories, called *yishima.* She found out that in this performance, listeners know that the house-made-of-human-ribs probably belongs to a sorcerer, that eating his honey is dangerous because it will cast a spell over them, that the river that appeared from nowhere across their path had been created by the sorcerer, and that Funga who ate the honey most likely will drown as a consequence of not listening to his older brother. She learned that the recurring song, sung four times during the performance, created a tension between hope and panic about the consequences of eating the honey and between trusting that it was a natural river created by God ("This large river God created") and fearing that it was a sorcerer's invention ("Eee, Papa, it's I who ate the honey").

Thus, a transcription of recorded speech is not a straightforward and simple means of documenting an event. The ethnographer needs to observe and listen to more than the words; she needs to ask many follow-up questions and write down what she learns. As a result, much field research uses a variety of recording and encoding processes, combining fieldnotes with audio and video recording.[9]

Characterization

Ethnographers describe the persons they encounter through a strategy known as *characterization*. While a simple description of a person's dress and movements conveys some minimal sense of that individual, the writer more fully characterizes a human being through also showing how that person talks, acts, and relates to others. An ethnographer most effectively characterizes individuals in context as they go about their daily activities rather than by simply listing their characteristics. Telling about a person's traits never is as effective as *showing* how they act and live. This entails presenting characters as fully social beings through descriptions of dress, speech, gestures, and facial expressions, which allow the reader to infer traits. Traits and characteristics thus appear in and through interaction with others rather than by being presented as isolated qualities of individuals. Thus, characterization draws on a writer's skills in describing, reporting action, and presenting dialogue.

In the following set of fieldnotes, Linda Shaw describes an encounter with a couple living in the kitchen area of an apartment in a psychiatric board-and-care facility. The woman, in particular, emphasizes the efforts they have made to create a "normal" living environment and the futility they feel in doing so:[10]

> I went with Terri and Jay today as they offered to show me the "apartment" they had created out of the small converted kitchen area that was their room. Terri escorted me from one space to another, taking great pride in showing me how they had made a bedroom area at one end, a living room next to it, and a kitchen area next to that. They had approximated an entire apartment in this tiny space, and she showed me features of each "room" in detail. The bed, they said, had a real mattress, not like the foam pads on all the other

beds. There was a rug on the living room floor and a TV at the foot of the bed. Then Terri opened the cupboards. She pointed out the spice rack and counted each glass out loud. She took particular pride in the coffeepot she uses to fix Jay's morning coffee and a warmer oven where they sometimes heat take-out pizza.

Terri tried very hard to demonstrate all they had done to make their apartment like one that any married couple might have; yet, the harder she tried, the more apparent it became how different their lives really were. Terri spoke of the futility she felt in spite of all these efforts: "All the noise, the screaming, the tension really bothers me. I'm married, and I can't even be a normal wife here. I want to get up in the morning, fix my husband breakfast—a cup of coffee, eggs, bacon, orange juice—before he goes to work, clean the house, take care of the kids and then fix him a nice dinner and drink or whatever he wants when he gets home. Here, I get up and can fix him a cup of instant coffee. You know, it's not as good to just pick up the apartment, but then there's nothing else to do."

Terri comes across as a fully human individual whose actions and talk reveal her character. She has done her best to create the normal way of life she wishes for but cannot sustain in this quasi-institutional setting. Through her actions and words, we see her struggle in vain to construct this private space as a refuge against the debilitating forces of institutional life.

Pressed to finish his notes, a writer might be tempted to characterize by using some convenient label ("a retarded person," "a homeless person," a black/white/Asian, etc.) rather than looking closely at that person's actual appearance and behavior. Such quick characterization, however, produces a stock character who, at best, comes across as less than fully human and, at worst, appears as a negative stereotype. For example, one student, in describing people in a shopping mall, characterized an older woman as a "senile bag lady" after noting that she muttered to herself while fumbling absentmindedly in a shabby, oversized purse. Such labeling sketches only a pale type and closes the writer's attention to other relevant details and actions.

While ethnographers try to avoid characterizing people by stock characters, they do include members' remarks and actions that stereotype or mock others. The following excerpt describes a student who mockingly acts out typical gestures and postures of a Latino "cholo" before some classmates:

> As the white male and his friend walked away, he said "chale homes" [eh! homies] in a mock Spanish accent. Then he exaggerated his walking style: he stuck his shoes out diagonally, placed his arms at

> a curved popeye angle, and leaned back. ...Someone watching said, "Look at you fools."

In this group of bantering young men, the white teenage male enacts a ludicrous caricature of a Latino "cholo." Ethnographers take care to distinguish members' characterizations from their own by providing details that clearly contextualize the talk and behavior as delivered from a member's point of view.

An ethnographer usually characterizes in detail those persons who act centrally in a scene. Although the full picture of any person develops through time in a series of fieldnotes, each description presents lively and significant details that show a primary character as completely as possible through appearance, body posture, gesture, words, and actions. In contrast, a peripheral figure might indeed be referred to simply with as few details as necessary for that person to be seen doing his small part in the scene.

A number of criteria shape the field researcher's decision about who is central and who is peripheral. First, the researcher's theoretical interests will focus his attention toward particular people. For example, the central characters in a study of teamwork among "support staff" in a courtroom were courtroom clerks and bailiffs rather than attorneys, witnesses, or the judge. Second, methodological strategies also focus the ethnographer's attention. For example, a strategy for depicting a social world by describing distinctive interactional patterns might shape his decision to focus on someone who presents a particularly vivid illustration of such a pattern. Finally, if members in a scene orient to a particular person, then a description that makes that person central to the scene is called for. Conversely, even those who are central figures in a setting might get slight attention from the field researcher if they are so treated by those in the scene. For example, in a scene focusing on students talking in the quad at lunchtime, the "principal walking across the courtyard and looking from side to side" might not be described in much more detail if no one seems to notice him.

As a practical matter, an individual already well known through previous entries does not need to have a full introduction each time he enters a scene. Even for a main character, one describes only those actions and traits relevant to the current interaction or those that were previously unnoted. But continuing contacts with people greatly expand the field researcher's resources for writing fuller, richer characterizations; greater familiarity enables the researcher to note and to write about qualities that are harder to detect. Yet many ethnographers tend to describe even main characters only upon first encountering them, leaving that first characterization unchanged despite coming to know more about that person. Hence, we suggest taking time as research progresses to periodically reflect on and try to capture on paper the appearance and feel of major characters, now known as persons with unique features and special qualities. Each entry is only a partial record, and as notes accumulate, fieldworkers notice that they have assembled enough observations to present some persons as full-fledged individuals ("rounded" characters), leaving others as less well-known figures ("flat" characters), and a few individuals as types such as a bus driver or a policeman ("stock" characters).

Fieldnotes should also include the ethnographer as a character in the interactions. The presence of the ethnographer who truly stands at the side watching might only be noted to identify the position from which the event is seen. But an ethnographer who directly participates in the action becomes a relevant character in the fieldnote, especially when a member clearly interacts with him. Indeed, a researcher might act as a central character in the incident in unanticipated ways. He might shift from his stance as an outside observer and become fully engaged in the interactions. In the following excerpt, students in a deaf-and-hard-of-hearing class encourage each other to speak while playing an educational game. The fieldworker, having had a stuttering problem all of his life, clearly empathizes with the students. Though essentially an outsider in the class, he becomes a pivotal figure at one juncture:

> Lynn keeps on telling Caesar to say what the answers are by speaking (rather than through sign language). The teacher says, "Very good Lynn. ... That's right, Caesar, you should try to speak what the answers are as well so that we can all understand you." Caesar looks over at me a little red in the face and looks down at his desk with a half smile. The teacher asks him (while pointing at me), "Are you afraid of speaking because he is here?" Lynn and Jackie and Caesar all seem to answer at once in sign that he is afraid of having me hear him speak. I tell Caesar, "You don't have to be afraid of what I think. I have a hard time speaking too."
>
> Caesar seems interested by my statements and points a finger at me questioningly. The teacher says, "Yes, it's okay, you speak fine. You don't have to be afraid of what anybody thinks about you. Just say one sentence, and he'll tell you if he can understand you."
>
> Caesar reluctantly says something and then looks at me, his head still slightly down and his face still red. A faint smile lines his lips as he waits for my answer. I had not understood a single word and was feeling desperate. What if they asked me to repeat what he had said? I reply, "Yes, that was fine. I understood you." The teacher quickly turns to Caesar and gives him the appropriate signs for my answer and goes directly into saying that he shouldn't be so intimidated by what other people think. Caesar looks at me and smiles. The game continues, and Caesar starts answering in both sign and speech. And I began to understand some of the things they were saying.

Clearly, this ethnographer's past experiences and presence played a central role in this scene, and his empathetic responses color the description in essential ways. Had he tried to write up these notes without including himself—his own interactions and feelings—the scene would have been deeply distorted.

When describing their own participation in scenes, field researchers generally write in the first person. If this observer had described the scene in the third person, referring to himself by name, much of the impact would have been lost:

> Caesar reluctantly says something and looks at Paul, his head still slightly down and his face still red. A faint smile lines his lips as he waits for his answer. ... He replies, "Yes, that's fine. I understood you." The teacher quickly turns to Caesar and gives him the appropriate signs for Paul's answer and goes directly into saying that he shouldn't be so intimidated by what other people think. Caesar looks at Paul and smiles. The game continues, and Caesar starts answering in both sign and speech.

In the original segment, the writer carefully stuck to Caesar's observable behavior ("looks over at me with a red face" and "looks down at his desk with a half smile") and did not attribute nervousness. But in the third-person account, we miss an essential part of Caesar's struggle to speak. This struggle was conveyed through the ethnographer's empathetic and self-revealing comment, "I had not understood a single word ... ," and by his closing observation, "And I began to understand some of the things they were saying." Through the writer's careful attention to details of behavior and talk, as well as through his own revealed personal feelings, readers can sense the fear and later the relief in speaking and in being understood.

Finally, along with writing in the first person, we also recommend that ethnographers use active rather than passive verbs. Some researchers use passive verbs because they think that it makes their writing more objective (Booth, Colomb, and Williams 2008). Yet, ethnographers prefer active verbs to show how people act together to construct their social worlds (Becker 2007). Consider, for example, the loss of crucial detail about the unfolding interaction among actors in the classroom scene above had the ethnographer used passive rather than active verbs.

> Something is said by Caesar to Paul, his head still slightly down and his face still red. His lips are lined with a faint smile as he waits for his answer. ... He replies, "Yes, that's fine. I understood you." Caesar is given the appropriate signs and is told he shouldn't be so intimidated by what other people think. A smile is received by him. The game is continued, and answers are given in both sign and speech.

The use of passive verbs obscures the agency of those in the setting and the clarity of the moment-by-moment sense of who did what with/to whom that the ethnographer portrayed so effectively in the original excerpt. Hence, we recommend the use of active verbs to show more vividly, clearly, and directly who is engaged in an activity, the meanings that others in the setting give to it, and how they use meanings to shape subsequent interactions.

Narrating a Day's Entry: Organizational Strategies

When first returning from the field to her desk, an ethnographer, worried about getting everything down, writes spontaneously, hurriedly, and in fragments. But at the same time, in order to describe scenes and actions effectively, she needs to balance speed and clarity by organizing her writing into *units* that create coherence and mark beginnings and endings. While some ethnographers consider these units as descriptive writing (in contrast to analytic writing), we find it beneficial to discuss these units as narrating or recounting the day's experiences. By drawing on narrating conventions, ethnographers can sustain their memories by grouping and sequencing details and interactions into coherent units. When they remember observed interactions as a series of moments to be narrated, they can more easily sustain that memory as a perceived whole or unit.

Perhaps the most general unit of writing is simply the day's entry—the ethnographer's telling of the day's experiences and observations in the field. Seeking to document fully all remembered interactions with no specific point or theme in mind, the ethnographer relates his experiences in the field, implicitly drawing on narrating conventions. In this sense, the day's entry is an episodic tale with many segments—perhaps telling about an interaction, next transitioning to a different location, now sketching in the scene of the new context, then recounting another episode of action—on and on until finishing by returning from the field as the tale's ending. Within this overall narrative of the day's entry, the ethnographer might also create other tales that stand out as more focused sequences of interconnected actions and episodes.

The most basic unit within the day's entry is the paragraph, used to coherently depict one brief moment or idea. By convention, a *paragraph* coheres because the writer's attention focuses on one idea or insight.[11] When he perceives some actions as a gestalt and concentrates on them, he writes about them in a paragraph. While continuing to write, he also shifts attention from one recalled moment to another, for example, from one person or activity to another within a classroom. These slight shifts are often indicated by paragraph breaks.

In narrating an entry, ethnographers work with a number of different organizing units that build on the paragraph. Sketches and episodes, which may be several paragraphs, create larger units of detailed scenes and interactions within that day's fieldnotes. In this way, the writer coherently sequences moments—those remembered interactions and specific contexts. Though these units or segments have no explicit connections between them, the ethnographer might write a few transitional sentences, briefly summarizing what happened in the interim or explaining that he shifted his focus to another activity or person to observe.

Sketches

In a sketch, the fieldworker, struck by a vivid sensory impression, *describes* a scene primarily through detailed imagery. Much as in a photograph, sequencing of actions does not dominate. Rather, the writer, as a more distanced observer looking out on a scene, describes what she senses, pausing for a moment in recounting the action to create a descriptive snapshot of a character or a setting. As a result, sketches might be short paragraphs or a few sentences within the overall narrative. Such static snapshots help orient the reader to the relevant details of the contexts in which actions take place.

While the term "sketch" employs a visual metaphor, this form of organizing writing need not rely only on visual details but can also incorporate auditory or kinetic details as well. For example, not appearance but the sense of smell might be the primary criterion for recalling and conveying the merits of a particular food. In describing people, settings, objects, and so forth, the writer must evoke all those senses that recall that moment as she perceived it. Often, the sense of vision dominates, however, simply because the fieldworker observes at a distance or aims to give a brief overview of the setting. It also dominates, in part, because the English language for vision is much more detailed and developed than it is for the other senses.[12] Hence, the ethnographic writer might have to expend special effort to evoke and write about nonvisual sensory images.

A sketch typically is a brief segment, which unifies descriptive details about a setting, an individual, or a single incident. Because it is primarily static, it lacks any sense of consequential action (of plot) and any full characterization of people. Consider the following sketch of a Latino street market that presents a close-up picture of one particular character's momentary behavior at a stall with toys:

> An older Latina woman is bent over looking at the toys on the ground. Behind her she holds two plastic bags of something, which she uses to balance as she leans over. She picks up several toys in succession from the ground, lifting them up several inches to turn them over and around in her hand, and then putting them down. After a minute, she straightens up and walks slowly away.

Organizing details into a sketch in this way permits the writer to give a quick sense of the setting by presenting a close-up picture of one particular character's engagement with it.

Often, sketches contextualize subsequent interactions, placing them into a larger framework of events or incidents and allow the reader to visualize more readily the setting or participants involved. On some occasions, however, these entries might stand as independent units of writing. In the following sketch, for example, an ethnographer describes the scene in a high school during an uneventful, uncrowded lunch hour in a way that documents how students group themselves:

> Even though it was cold and windy, there were still about one hun-
> dred black students clustered in the central quad. On the far left, one
> short black male wearing a black starter jacket was bouncing a ball.
> Next to him, seven black females and two black males were sitting
> on a bench. Further to the right stood a concentrated group of about
> thirty or forty black students. I counted about twenty who were
> wearing different kinds of starter jackets. Further up the quad stood
> another group of fifteen blacks, mostly females. At the foot of quad,
> on the far right, was another group of maybe twenty black students,
> about equally male and female. Some were standing, while others
> were sitting on a short concrete wall against the auditorium. To the
> right of this group, I noticed one male, listening to a yellow walkman,
> dancing by himself. His arms were flung out, pulling as though he
> were skiing, while his feet ran in place.

This ethnographer was especially concerned with ethnic relations and wanted to track how, when, and where students socialized and with whom. Even when he could not hear or see exactly what the students were doing, he depicted these groupings in an almost snapshot fashion. Although the paragraph includes visual and kinetic details, it creates the scene as a still life rather than as an event in which actions could be sequenced.

In general, sketches are useful for providing an overall sense of places and people that sometimes stand as a background for other fieldnote descriptions. Descriptive sketches of people standing around or of a person's expression and posture as she looks at some-one, for example, can reveal qualities of social relations even when apparently nothing much is happening.

Episodes

Unlike a sketch, which depicts a "still life" in one place, an episode recounts action and moves in time to narrate a slice of life. In an episode, a writer constructs a brief incident as a more or less unified depiction of one continuous action or interaction. Consequently, when recalling an incident that does not extend over a long period of time or involve many characters, ethnographers often write up that memory as a one- or two-paragraph episode.[13]

The following excerpt consists of a one-paragraph episode in which the writer de-scribes an interaction between two students during the beginning of class time:

> A black female came in. She was wearing a white puffy jacket, had
> glasses and straight feathered black hair. She sat down to my right.
> Robert and another male (both black) came in and sat down. They

were eating Kentucky Fried Chicken which they took out of little red and white boxes. Robert's friend kept swiping at the black female, trying to slap her. She kept telling him in an annoyed voice to leave her alone. After a minute of this exchange, the black teacher said to the guy, "Leave her alone, brother." He answered Ms. Dubois with a grin on his face, "Don't worry. She's my sistah." The girl said "Chhh," looking briefly at him. He had gone back to eating his chicken.

Here, the students' and teacher's actions are presented as a sequence, each seeming to trigger the next; the girl responds to the boy's swiping, and the teacher responds to him, and so on. Thus, these actions are linked and appear as one continuous interaction, producing a unified episode.

Not every episode needs to build to a climax as the one above does. Many fieldnote episodes minutely recount one character's routine, everyday actions. In fact, in many entries, ethnographers find themselves writing primarily about mundane activities. In the following excerpt, for example, the ethnographer recounts how several students in an ESL class worked together to complete a group activity:

One group consisted of six people: two Korean girls, one Korean boy, two Mexican boys, and one Russian girl. Like all of the other groups, they arranged their chairs in a small circle for the assigned activity. Ishmael, a Mexican boy, held the question card in his hand and read it to the rest of the group: "List five things that you can do on a date for less than $10.00 in Los Angeles." (His English was heavily marked by his Mexican accent, but they could understand him.) Placing his elbows on the desk and looking directly at the group, he said, "Well?" He watched them for a minute or two; then he suggested that one could go for drinks at Hard Rock Café. The others agreed by nodding their heads. Ishmael again waited for suggestions from the group. The other Mexican boy said "going to the beach" and the Russian girl said "roller skating." The Koreans nodded their heads, but offered no other suggestions. (I think that Ishmael waited for others to respond, even though he seemed to know the answers.)

In describing this classroom scene, the ethnographer filled six pages with a series of such more or less isolated episodes occurring during that hour. Thus, she was able to present the small groups as working simultaneously on various activities. The episodes belong together only because they are situated in the same class during one period. Fieldworkers often write up such concurrent actions, loosely linked by time and place, as a series of discrete episodes.

Since episodes present action as progressing through time, a writer should orient the reader to shifts in time, place, and person as the action unfolds, particularly in longer scenes or those without obviously interconnected actions. Writers sequence actions in an order (e.g., first, second, third) and mark action shifts with transitions (e.g., now, then, next, afterward, the next morning). They also locate action with situational markers (e.g., here, there, beyond, behind). In the following excerpt, a researcher studying an outpatient psychiatric treatment facility connects actions through transitional phrases ("as he continues talking" and transitional words ("then," "as"):

> I sat down on the bench in the middle of the hall. And as I sat waiting for something to gain my attention, I heard the director yell out, "Take off your clothes in the shower!" as he shuts the door to the shower room. …Remaining outside the door of the shower room, the director speaks with Roberta, one of the staff members assigned to look after the clients. Then Karen approaches them with a small, dirty Smurf that she found outside. "Look at it, how pretty, kiss it," she says talking to the director, but he doesn't pay any attention to her. As he continues talking to Roberta, he glances over and notices that I am observing them. As our eyes lock, he opens up his arm toward Karen and requests a hug. Karen, in her usual bashful way, giggles as she responds to his hug.

In this episode, the writer focuses on movement—sat, shuts, approaches, glances, opens—interspersed with talk: "the director yell(s) out, 'Take off your clothes in the shower!'" In observing and reporting actions, ethnographers interested in social interactions view action and talk as interconnected features of what people "do." They write about "talk" as part of people's actions.

Ethnographers often write episodic rather than more extended entries because they cannot track a sequence of actions and learn all the outcomes within one day. They may write an episode about an interaction simply because it bears upon a topic they are interested in. They often write without knowing whether that fieldnote will later be important in the full analysis. Yet, writing these episodes over time might enable the ethnographer to find patterns of behavior and connections between people's actions through different fieldnotes.

Many fieldnote episodes stand on their own, barely associated with others. Particularly in initial entries organized as narratives of the researcher's activities and observations for the day, writing *transitional summaries* can link different episodes. A transitional summary provides a succinct bridge between detailed episodes, enabling a reader to understand how the ethnographer got from one event or episode to another. How the ethnographer got from the school office to the classroom with a brief personal stop in the bathroom, for example, can simply be noted in this summary fashion if there is a need to show continuity. Of course, if something interesting occurred during this movement—a student stopped her to talk about a school fight—then writing detailed notes is advisable.

In-Process Analytic Writing: Asides and Commentaries

As the field researcher participates in the field, she inevitably begins to reflect on and interpret what she has experienced and observed. Writing fieldnotes heightens and focuses these interpretive and analytic processes; writing up the day's observations generates new appreciation and deeper understanding of witnessed scenes and events. In writing, a field researcher assimilates and thereby starts to understand an experience. She makes sense of the moment by intuitively selecting, highlighting, and ordering details and by beginning to appreciate linkages with, or contrasts to, previously observed and written-about experiences. Furthermore, she can begin to reflect on how she has presented and ordered events and actions in her notes, rereading selected episodes and tales with an eye to their structuring effects.

To capture these ruminations, reflections, and insights and to make them available for further thought and analysis, field researchers pursue several kinds of analytical writing that stand in stark contrast to the descriptive writing we have emphasized to this point. As the result of such writings, the researcher can bring a more probing glance to further observations and descriptive writing and consequently become more selective and in depth in his descriptions.

The most immediate forms of analytic writing are asides and commentaries, interpretive writings composed while the ethnographer is actively composing fieldnotes.[14] Asides and commentaries consist of brief questions, ideas, or reactions the researcher writes into the body of the notes as he recalls and puts on paper the details of a specific observation or incident. The lines between asides and commentaries (and in-process memos) are often blurred; we offer them as heuristic devices that can sensitize the fieldworker to both momentary and more sustained concentration on analytic writing while actively producing fieldnotes.

Asides are brief, reflective bits of analytic writing that succinctly clarify, explain, interpret, or raise questions about some specific happening or process described in a fieldnote. The ethnographer dashes off asides in the midst of descriptive writing, taking a moment to react personally or theoretically to something she has just recounted on paper and then immediately turns back to the work of description. These remarks may be inserted in the midst of descriptive paragraphs and set off by parentheses. In the following example, the ethnographer uses a personal aside to note his uneasy feeling that someone is watching him:

> I turn around, away from the office, and face the woman with the blondish hair who is still smiling. (I can't shake the feeling that she's gazing at me.) "I'll see you Friday," I say to her as I walk by her and out the front door.

Fieldworkers often write somewhat more elaborate asides, several phrases in length, again triggered by some immediate piece of writing and closely tied to the events or scenes depicted in that writing. In the fieldnote below, the fieldworker describes a moment during her first day at a crisis drop-in center and then reacts to that experience in a more extended aside:

> Walking up the stairs to the agency office, I noticed that almost every step creaked or moaned. At the top stands an old pine coat hanger, piled high with coats. Behind it is a bulletin board containing numerous flyers with information about organizations and services of various kinds. (Thinking about the scene as I climbed those stairs, I think that if I were an upset, distraught client, I would most probably find it difficult to find helpful information in that disorganized mass.)

In providing her own "lived sense" of the agency, the student incorporates in her description the meaning of physical space, while allowing for the possibility that others might perceive it differently. Asides may also be used to explain something that would otherwise not be apparent or to offer some sort of personal reflection or interpretive remark on a matter just considered. Ethnographers frequently use asides, for example, to convey their explicit "feel" for or emotional reactions to events; putting these remarks in asides keeps them from intruding into the descriptive account.

The ethnographer may also use brief asides to offer tentative hunches when the meaning of an incident to members is not clear or may only be inferred. In the following excerpt, the ethnographer asks questions about the meaning and import of an incident at a food bank in which a shopper rejects an item given to her as part of a preselected grocery cart full of food.

> She had a package of frozen turkey meatballs in her hand and said that she didn't want the package because the contents were expired. The meatballs had apparently expired two days prior to today, and she said that she did not like taking expired food to her house. (Why the emphasis on "my house?" Self-respect? Could it be that if she took the expired meatballs, she was somehow accepting hand-me-downs? Just because she is not paying full price doesn't mean she can't receive up-to-par food?)

Using a question in this brief aside to reflect upon the possible meaning of the incident helps the ethnographer avoid reaching premature or unsupported conclusions. The aside also marks the incident as important, reminding her to look for further examples that will clarify and deepen her understanding of similar or contrasting examples.

A *commentary* is a more elaborate reflection, either on some specific event or issue or on the day's experiences and fieldnotes. Focused commentaries of the first sort are placed just after the fieldnote account of the event or issue in a separate paragraph set off with parentheses. A paragraph-long summary commentary of the second sort should conclude each set of fieldnotes, reflecting on and raising issues and questions about that day's observations. Both types of commentaries involve a shift of attention from events in the field to outside audiences imagined as having an interest in something the fieldworker has observed and written up. Again, in contrast to descriptive fieldnotes, commentaries might explore problems of access or emotional reactions to events in the field, suggest ongoing probes into likely connections with other events, or offer tentative interpretations. Putting a commentary in a separate paragraph helps avoid writing up details as evidence for preconceived categories or interpretations.

Focused commentaries can raise issues of what terms and events mean to members, make initial connections between some current observation and prior fieldnotes, and suggest points or places for further observation, as in the following excerpt:

> M called over to Richard. He said, "C'm here lil' Homey." Richard came over to sit closer to M. He asked Richard about something Richard said earlier (I couldn't completely hear it) … something to do with weight lifting. Richard replied, "Oh, I could talk about it for hours …" M asked Richard if there was a place where he could lift weights on campus. Richard said there was a weight room, but only "hoops" could use it today. M then asked Richard what "hoops" was. Richard answered that "hoops" was basketball. (Is the word "homey," possibly derived from homeboy, somebody who is down or cool with another person? It seems to me that M, who apparently didn't know Richard, wanted to talk to him. In order to do that, he tried to let Richard know M thought he was a cool person? "Homey" appears to be applied regardless of ethnicity. … Their interaction appeared to be organized around interest in a common activity, weight lifting. Judging by the size of M's muscles, this was something he excelled in.)

This ethnographer has been noticing the ways blacks use the terms "cool" and "down" to refer to inclusion of nonblacks in their otherwise black groupings. In this commentary, he reflects on other terms that also seem to be inclusive.

Focused commentaries can also be used to create a record of the ethnographer's own doings, experiences, and reactions during fieldwork, both in observing-participating and in writing up. A researcher-intern in a social service agency, after describing an incident with staff, wrote the following commentary about this moment as a turning point in her relationship with staff members:

> Entering the kitchen, where staff often go to socialize alone, I began to prepare my lunch. Soon, several staff had come in, and they began to talk among one another. I stood around awkwardly, not

quite knowing what to do with myself. I exchanged small talk for a while until D, the director, asked in her typically dramatic tone loud enough for everyone to hear: "Guess where A (a staff member who was also present) is going for her birthday?" There was silence in the room. Turning in her direction, I realized that she was speaking to me. "Where?" I asked, somewhat surprised that she was talking to me. "To Hershey Park!" she exclaimed. "No way!" I said, and feeling embarrassed, I started laughing. "Yeah," D exclaimed. "She's gonna dip her whole body in chocolate so R (lover) can eat her!" The room filled up with laughter, and I, too, could not restrain my giggles.

(With that, the group broke up, and as I walked back to my desk, I began to feel that for the first time, I had been an active participant in one of their kitchen get-togethers. This experience made me believe that I was being viewed as more than just an outsider. I have been trying to figure out what it takes to belong here, and one aspect undoubtedly is to partake in an occasional kitchen get-together and not to appear above such practices.)

In this commentary, the researcher not only reports her increased feeling of acceptance in the scene but also reflects on the likely importance of these informal, sometimes ribald "get-togethers" for creating a general sense of belonging in the organization.

In writing a summary commentary, the fieldworker takes a few moments to mentally review the whole day's experiences, selecting an important, memorable, or confusing issue to raise and briefly explore. Here, ethnographers have found it useful to ask themselves questions like the following: What did I learn today? What did I observe that was particularly interesting or significant? What was confusing or uncertain? Did something happen today that was similar to or radically different from things that I have previously observed? In the following excerpt, an ethnographer used commentary at the end of his day in the field to reflect his growing understanding of largely Spanish-speaking day laborers' interactions with employers in their efforts to get work.

English seems to be an important resource to acquire work, but even more interesting is the *illusion of knowing English* because even though Jorge does not speak English, he goes about acting to employers as if he does [know English] to increase his chances for hire. Something that was also intriguing was the employer searching for day laborers with legal documentation. It is interesting because day laborers are stigmatized as all being undocumented but employers seem to know that there are many that are documented ... Jorge believes that when folks are undocumented, employers threaten them with Immigration. Jorge seems to be at odds with this dynamic because as a person with documentation, he is held responsible [by employers] for information on others who may not be documented. And, due to his documentation, he seems to have a sense of entitlement [to work] due to his legal status.

The ethnographer uses this day's commentary to build on his growing understanding of both the strategic ways that day laborers use their knowledge of characteristics desired by employers to compete among themselves for work and day laborers' sense that legal status bring with it extra entitlement to work.

Summary commentaries are also useful for comparing and contrasting incidents that occurred on the same day or earlier in the field experience. In the following commentary, the ethnographer compares two incidents that occurred during the day's observations to further understand parent-child interactions in a public setting, in this case a grocery store:

> Both of these incidents help illustrate how two very different parents choose to deal with their children in a public setting. Both children showed "bratty" behavior in two different ways: the first by illustrating his discontent in being forced to go shopping when he would have preferred staying home and the second by making the need to purchase an item within the store known. In both situations, the moms tried to ignore their children in what seemed to be the hope that their kids would realize that they were in a public setting and consequently stop their behavior. However, this was not the case. I believe that just as the moms knew that they were in a location where outside forces (i.e., limits on the ways that they could exercise control of their kids within a public store setting) influenced their ability to discipline the behavior of their children, the children knew this as well. This is all hypothetical, but the children also seem to know that they could continue to push their moms' buttons because the course of action that their parents could have taken at home would not occur in this public place. The first mom's response of "unbelievable" to her son is an indication that she is fully aware that her motherly duties are limited when considering the environment and the forces within it.

The ethnographer uses commentary to suggest possible patterns of parent-child interactions in public places, taking care to avoid "overinterpreting" and drawing conclusions too quickly based on meanings she attributes to just two examples. The understandings gleaned from these incidents should remain suggestive of avenues for further investigation and ongoing comparison.

Finally, daily summary commentaries might identify an issue that came up in the course of the current set of fieldnotes and suggest practical, methodological steps for exploring that issue in future observations. Indeed, it is often useful simply to ask: What more do I need to know to follow up on a particular issue or event? Asking such questions helped a researcher in a battered women's shelter identify gaps in her understanding of how staff viewed and accomplished their work:

> The goals staff have talked about so far of "conveying unconditional positive regard" for clients and "increasing their self-esteem" seem rather vague. How does the staff know when they have achieved unconditional positive regard? Is it based on their interaction with the client or by their refraining from being judgmental or critical of them during staff meetings? I will attempt to discover how they define and attempt to achieve the goal of "increasing a woman's self-esteem." It has been made clear that this goal is not only seen to be achieved when women leave their abusive relationships. If leaving their abusive partners were the primary indicator of achieving raised self-esteem, the organization would be largely unsuccessful, since most of these women go back to their abusive relationships. Yet, while I have learned what raising self-esteem is not, I have yet to learn what it is.

In this series of comments and questions, the fieldworker identifies two matters that shelter staff members emphasize as goals in their relations with clients: "conveying unconditional positive regard" and increasing client "self-esteem." She then considers ways she might look to understand how these general policies/values are actually implemented and how their success or failure is practically assessed in interactions within the shelter. These questions and tentative answers helped direct the ethnographer's attention, focusing and guiding future observations and analysis.

Reflections: "Writing" and "Reading" Modes

To characterize fieldnotes as descriptions initially conveys the prospect of simple, straightforward writing. But once we recognize that description involves more than a one-to-one correspondence between written accounts and what is going on, writing fieldnotes raises complex, perplexing problems. Descriptions are grounded on the observer-writer's participation in the setting, but no two persons participate in and experience a setting in exactly the same way. Moreover, there is always more going on than the ethnographer can notice, and it is impossible to record all that can be noticed. Description inevitably involves different theories, purposes, interests, and points of view. Hence, fieldnotes contain descriptions that are more akin to a series of stories portraying slices of life in vivid detail than to a comprehensive, literal, or objective rendering.[15]

The ethnographer, however, needs to avoid getting drawn into the complexities of fieldnote descriptions while actually writing fieldnotes. She must initially work in a *writing mode,* putting into words and on paper what she has seen and heard as quickly and efficiently as possible. In this text-producing mode, the ethnographer tries to "get it down" as accurately and completely as possible, avoiding too much self-consciousness about the writing process itself. She stays close to the events at issue, rekindling her excitement about these events and inscribing them before memory fades. The writing ethnographer tries to "capture what is out there," or more accurately, to construct detailed accounts of her own observations and experience of what is "out there." At this point, too much reflection distracts or even paralyzes; one tries to write without editing, to produce detailed descriptions without worry about analytic import and connections, and to describe what happened without too much self-conscious reflection.

Only subsequently, once a text has actually been produced, can the ethnographer really step back and begin to consider the complexities that permeate fieldnote descriptions; only with fully detailed fieldnotes can the ethnographer adopt a *reading mode* and begin to reflect on how these accounts are products of his own, often implicit, decisions about how to participate in and describe events. That is, only with full notes in hand does it make sense to view these writings as texts that are truncated, partial, and perspectival products of the ethnographer's own styles of participating, orienting, and writing. It is at this point that the ethnographer can begin to treat fieldnotes as constructions and read them for the ways they *create* rather than simply record reality.

One key difference between initially working in a writing mode and subsequently in a reflective reading mode lies in how the ethnographer orients to issues of "accuracy," to "correspondence" between a written account and what it is an account of. In the moment of writing, the ethnographer must try to create some close correspondence between the written account and his experiences and observations of "what happened." The immediate task in writing fieldnote descriptions is to create a detailed, accurate, and comprehensive account of what has been experienced. But once notes have been written, this correspondence criterion loses salience. This shift occurs because "what happened" has been filtered through the person and writing of the observer as it was written onto the page. The resulting text "fixes" a social reality in place but does so in a way that makes it difficult to determine its relationship with realities outside that text. Readers might attempt to do so by invoking what they know from having "been there" or from experience with a similar reality. But readers are heavily constrained by what is on the page; they usually lack any effective means of gaining access to "what actually happened" independently of the written account. In such a reading mode, then, conscious, critical reflection on how writing choices have helped construct specific texts and textual realities becomes both possible and appropriate.

ENDNOTES

1. Sanjek (1990b), for example, reports a full year passed before he went from notebook to full fieldnotes; obviously, he spent a great deal of time and care in writing up descriptions and events in these handwritten notebooks.

2. Along these lines, Goffman (1989:127) advises against bringing spouses into the field because "it does give you a way out. You can talk to that person, and all that, and that's no way to make a world."

3. As a general rule, it is important to preserve discrepant reports about the same event to avoid deciding what "really happened" in accepting one account over the other. Here, for example, we can now understand the difference as a likely product of Laura's self-expressed uneasiness with explicit, earthy sexual references.

4. Description is often referred to as one of the four chief types of composition—along with argumentation, exposition, and narration. But here we consider describing as a key strategy for picturing settings, people, objects, and actions as a part of the larger ethnographic narrative that the ethnographer tells throughout her fieldnotes, beginning with the first day that she enters the site and closing when she leaves and writes her last notes.

5. Lofland (1985:15) terms this "categoric knowing" in which "one knows who the other is only in the sense that one knows he can be placed into some category," particularly gender, age, and race, since these categories are readily gleaned from appearance only. In contrast, "personal knowing" involves knowledge of at least some aspects of the other's actual biography.

6. In this sense, this description might be a product of, as well as advance, the ethnographer's theoretical interest in ethnic identity. That is, the observer might have come upon this scene with a preexisting interest in how white students affiliate with African Americans, this sensitivity leading him to appreciate the ironic symbolism and to write so vividly about the jacket. Alternatively, writing a description of something that made an immediate impression on him might have made him begin to think about issues of cross-cultural affiliation. In either case, in subsequent fieldnotes, this ethnographer continued to focus on this woman and other white students who hung out with blacks, describing other instances of ethnically distinct clothes, whites' use of black conversational styles, etc.

7. A combination of field observations and tape recordings of specific interactions marks many ethnographic studies of institutional settings, including medical clinics (Maynard 2003), lawyers' offices (Sarat and Felstiner 1995), and public schools (Garot 2010). However, a number of ethnographers found that tape recorders inhibited and distorted talk in informal settings and exchanges; e.g., see Desmond (2007:291–93) on the problems of attempting to tape-record daily activities among wildland firefighters.

8. Often her fieldnotes were written in English, though she listened in another language; she therefore included many non-English terms to preserve local meanings.

9. For a discussion of how researchers working in second languages or explicitly focusing on verbal expression combine and integrate these methods, see Stone and Stone (1981). Some sociological field researchers advocate the use of similar sorts of "triangulation" procedures—for example, conducting later interviews with participants about what they were thinking and doing during a recorded exchange; see Cicourel (1974: 124ff).

10. Shaw (1991) explores a number of other expressions of this feeling of falling short of achieving a "normal" life, and the resulting pervasive sense of stigma, that afflicts ex–mental patients in their dealings with more conventional people.

11. Grouping details not only makes writing up easier, but the habit of marking paragraph breaks also speeds up reading and making sense of fieldnotes later on.

12. Stoller (1989) suggests that many ethnographers, reflecting their Western culture, have a bias for visual detail even though members might be attending more to other sensory impressions, such as smell, sound, or movement. In this respect, the kinds of sensory details that are dominant vary from one culture to another.

13. Lederman (1990:84) emphasizes that units such as "events" have "an apparent 'wholeness'" that makes them "good modes of entry into fieldnotes" and useful analytic units in her ethnography. One can write up an event as a brief episode or more fully describe it in a tale.

14. Schatzman and Strauss (1973:99–101) recommend tagging each fieldnote segment with an initial label, either "Observational Notes" (ON), "Theoretical Notes" (TN), or "Methodological Notes" (MN). Many field researchers find this procedure helpful in marking transitions in writing focus and intent. We generally avoid using these tags because we think that the distinctions are not only theoretically problematic but also practically difficult to apply in many instances.

15. Although not focused specifically on fieldnote descriptions, Wolf (1992) provides a provocative illustration of the potential variation in how ethnography can portray different slices of life; she presents the "same" series of events in three different story formats—original fieldnotes, a more formal analytic account, and a fictional short story.

chapter *three*

Introduction

The readings in this section introduce the reasons diversity is important in our professional lives as well as some common communications pitfalls that result from unexamined interactions in diverse settings. As you read through *The Intercultural Communication Guidebook: Research-Based Strategies for Successful Interactions*, consider where you fall in the categories described and try to think of instances in which your interactions with, or even your observations of, those with different cultural perspectives in these areas have led to misunderstandings. How can we remember that differences in these perspectives are not "wrong" but instead opportunities to learn from someone else?

READING 3.1

Diversity in a Box

◆

From *Inclusion Breakthrough: Unleashing the Real Power of Diversity* By Judith Katz

E ach person is a unique individual who also belongs to several different social identity groups. A wide range of differences can exist even among people who look, sound, and act alike. This *Paradox of Diversity* is a way of framing diversity that captures one's similarities and differences.

We are like all people: As human beings we share similar needs and wants—to experience joy and love, to be safe, etc.

We are like some people: We share culture and experience.

We are like no other people: We are each unique unto ourselves.

The aspects of ourselves that are like some other people constitute our connection to specific social identity groups, those with which we share similarities, such as age or living in a particular region. But we don't necessarily identify with each group to which we belong, such as—"people with red hair" or "people who drive a Toyota convertible." Regardless of whether or not we identify with a particular group, others might put us in it because the identification has meaning to them, such as—"people who attended Cornell" or "people who live in the Bronx." Bailey Jackson was one of the first people to identify that some differences matter more than others. Those that make the biggest difference are ethnicity, gender, marital status (and children), race, sexual orientation, language, physical ability, socioeconomic status, religion, and mental ability.

These differences can affect the hiring process. Many people and organizations claim they are color blind, gender blind or blind to differences. Although they consider this stance to be a positive attribute, it implies a disregard for differences. Many people have been raised to see differences as a deficit and therefore assume that differences will cease to be problematic if they are ignored.

Also, organizations that used to pride themselves on growing their own, hiring new people for only entry-level jobs and promoting from within, now find themselves needing to bring new and different talent into the organization at all levels. Many leaders have been surprised at how difficult it is to keep these new people. They are often rejected like a virus by both the organizational culture and the people who have been raised in the organization. Most "old timers" wonder why these newcomers were even brought in. The new people are never able to fit in, never able to fully participate and contribute. The organization's inability to include these new hires is often the reason for their leaving.

When a new hire is a person of color or a white woman, another issue may be played out. People often suspect that the person was hired primarily because of Affirmative Action goals to counter past discrimination. A common perception is that individuals of color or white women are hired based on lower standards or fewer qualifications and will therefore be a detriment to the organization.

These issues can be addressed by explaining a basic philosophical tenet: The intent of Affirmative Action is the hiring of competent people. The fact that Affirmative Action hires continue to be commonly perceived as "less-qualified" hires speaks to the bias that remains in many individuals and systems. Lingering in many organizations is an entrenched prejudice that can accept the promotion of some people only as being the result of Affirmative Action, rather than arising from the person's own competencies and abilities.

Another assumption about Affirmative Action that needs to be addressed is the notion that it gives an unfair advantage to certain people. For those who believe that a level playing field now exists for all involved, Affirmative Action looks like preferential treatment for particular underrepresented groups—those who have more suddenly will have less. To those who see the playing field as uneven, Affirmative Action is a means for everyone to have a chance at the opportunities.

Too often, people mistakenly use the terms Affirmative Action, Diversity and Inclusion interchangeably, reflecting the fallacy that they are equivalent. They are not. In most people's minds, diversity programs refer to people of color and women struggling to achieve a place in society. In reality, diversity is an attribute embodied in every individual.

Some organizations increase their diversity in an effort to meet Affirmative Action goals. However, this increase is superficial if the organization is not prepared to *include* an increased range of differences in its day-to-day activities and interactions.

Unfortunately, most organizations end up with a *diversity in a box* strategy. They see diversity as getting in the way of success by forcing the organization to do something it doesn't want to do. Or they see it as an issue to be managed, shaping it and getting it to "fit" in the existing structure of the organization. Still other organizations see diversity as a value and end in itself, unrelated to the mission, vision and purpose of the organization. The result: either a singular focus on representation and awareness or ignoring the issue altogether.

Regardless of the reasons why organizations begin the diversity effort, it is often thought of as an extra—a package of programs and policies run by the Human Resources or in-house training department and never tied to the bottom line. Efforts to change the representation of the organization are taken on with good intentions but are easily side-tracked or minimized when other priorities call.

When diversity is not leveraged, potential benefits to the organization and the individual are lost. For example, a Latina who is an engineer might be hired by an automotive design team to provide insight into preferences of Latinos or Latinas, while being overlooked as a potential contributor to broader engineering expertise. She ends up boxed in by her co-workers, who see her value limited to her apparent difference from the rest of the team. Her technical and design skills may not be fully recognized or utilized. Her diversity isn't fully leveraged for the common goal of the team—new and better ways of doing business. The organization loses an opportunity to tap her varied abilities and perspectives. The individual feels marginalized, leading to dissatisfaction with the work and the organization. Due to the cultural emphasis on community and higher needs for social inclusion, the impact of social exclusion is greater on many Latinos and Latinas than for people from groups that value individualism and independent action.

Hiring people of different backgrounds is no longer enough. Their presence in the organization is a start, but until it moves beyond diversity in a box, it will not unleash the full power of diversity and create fertile ground for everyone's growth in the organization and beyond.

In the current business climate, an organizational culture that *leverages diversity and builds inclusion* is essential for achieving and sustaining higher performance—and is therefore critical to an organization's long-term mission success and financial gain. This is true of international Fortune 100 companies, entrepreneurial start-ups, nonprofit organizations, government agencies, unions, and educational institutions.

When an organization leverages diversity, it sees things that cannot be seen when working from the basis of sameness. Leveraging diversity results in greater innovation and greater capacity for change. However, just *having* diversity does not result in *leveraging* diversity. Leveraging diversity taps into people's unique power and potential, thus unleashing the talent that exists.

There is a need for radical change. An organization that understands that need opens up the playing field and changes the rules of the game for success. An inclusion breakthrough is required—to leverage the diversity of all people and build an inclusive culture—because old assumptions, old styles, old approaches to problem solving and old line-ups are insufficient to help an organization survive and thrive in a turbulent environment.

An inclusion breakthrough is a process to transform the organization from a monocultural organization that values and supports sameness in style and approach, to a culture of inclusion that leverages diversity in all its many dimensions. It also is an approach for any organization that wants to transform their efforts from a diversity in a box approach to one that truly unleashes the power of diversity. An inclusion breakthrough necessitates a whole new way of life.

Barriers to Inclusion

Most organizations are filled with barriers—rigid structures, poor training processes, outmoded equipment, misguided incentive programs, and discriminatory promotion and assignment practices that keep people from contributing the full breadth of their skills, ideas, and energies to the organization's success. Expressed in conscious and unconscious behaviors, as well as routine practices, procedures, and bylaws, these barriers are typically rooted in the very culture of an organization. They favor people who are most like the founders or senior leaders of the organization. These barriers can be as invisible as air to those they favor but demeaning, discouraging, distracting, exhausting and seemingly insurmountable to those who bump up against them every day.

Barriers can be as tangible as stairways that block access to people in wheelchairs, the sign that reads MEN on the door of the only bathroom on the executive floor, or the lack of domestic partner benefits for the partners of people who are lesbian or gay. Barriers can also be subtle: being excluded from the lunch bunch or the golf outing, being seen as not ready for that leadership position, even people not hearing or remembering your ideas or name.

These barriers are reinforced by common negative beliefs about diversity and inclusion. Following are some negative beliefs:

- Differences create a barrier to higher performance because they bog down the process and lead to conflict.
- Diversity means that white men will lose.
- Only a few can succeed.
- It is too challenging to bring in people from diverse backgrounds.
- People who are different should conform.

A diversity in a box approach does not adequately address these barriers. Organizations often turn a blind eye to these barriers, only to discover that they are reinforced by a policy of diversity without inclusion.

Disadvantages of Not Including All People

Some organizations are making concerted efforts to address issues of exclusion and monoculturalism. Few, however, understand the scope of change needed. Even demographically diverse organizations often lack the basic skills and workplace environment required to leverage that diversity. In the absence of effective skills for communicating and partnering across differences, organizations tend to marginalize the people who are most different from the dominant group. These people often feel unheard, devalued, and ignored.

Without effective conflict-management skills, even organizations that are more diverse are unable to capitalize on the wealth of perspectives offered by their members. Instead of basing decisions on careful analysis and synthesis of differing viewpoints or on an informed debate on the relative merits of various people's proposals, many groups base decisions on who has the most seniority, is the most popular, or has the best track record, thereby excluding potentially significant voices and insights. Organizations without conflict-management skills may not be able to address the needs of an increasingly diverse marketplace and workforce.

For example, an advertising agency hired by one organization created two ads that were demeaning to Asian Americans. Because white people in the marketing department lacked competence and no people of color were in the group, the ad was disseminated without the organization's awareness of its offensiveness. Asian American employees and customers were upset and disappointed. At great cost and with great embarrassment, the organization was forced to pull the ads, but the damage had already occurred. This fiasco could have been avoided if the organization had acquired the competencies to understand what might be offensive.

Organizations almost always start out as exclusive, monocultural clubs (Katz & Miller, 1995). And most stay that way—even organizations that make sincere and well-meaning efforts to value diversity or become an Equal Opportunity Employer or an Affirmative Action Employer—unless an aggressive campaign is undertaken to change that condition. The people who start an organization, and then the people they hire, are usually closely matched in terms of one or more of the following: race, gender, ethnicity, age, nationality, and education. This is not an indictment. In organizations, as in life, people tend to associate with those with whom they feel most comfortable.

Although this approach might be reasonable and useful initially, its advantages fade over time. The monocultural values that result tend to reinforce a way of thinking and an approach to problem solving that may, at times, discourage people from suggesting changes, especially when anticipating the needs and wants of the leader is career-enhancing. Also, when work relationships are built upon the unwritten agreement that helping to maintain the status quo is the price of admission, causing conflict means stepping outside the relationship contract.

Extend this monocultural tendency to career advancement opportunities, mentoring and day-to-day workplace activities, and it becomes clear why most of today's organizations look the way they do, especially at the top. In the absence of specific policies, practices, and accountabilities to the contrary, most managers hire and promote the people who seem to require the least amount of maintenance. The outcome of this comfort factor is a truly remarkable statistic: Although women comprise 51 percent of the adult population of the United States and people of color comprise 40 percent (Census 2000), 95 percent of the senior leaders of businesses are white men (Equal Rights Advocates).

For many organizations, the historical belief and practice is that an efficient and successful organization requires people who fit in with and unquestioningly follow their supervisors and leaders. The age-old strategy of hiring individuals drawn from the founders' network of schoolmates, friends, colleagues, and family was acceptable and common. Today's reality makes that far too limited. The collective brainpower needed today in order to create visions beyond the abilities of one or a few requires the inclusion of people from a variety of backgrounds. The phrase "no one of us is as smart as all of us" has never been as true as it is today.

To leverage diversity for greater productivity, one organization reorganized itself into self-managed teams that were diverse in race and gender. Over a period of two years, these teams became significantly less diverse. Turnover rates were highest among the people who were least like the majority members of each group. As time went on, the diversity of the teams diminished until each team was homogenous in its race and gender. Productivity suffered as a result, with few new ideas filtering across to the organization.

This process failed because the teams didn't find the necessary support structures and accountabilities in the larger organization to effectively leverage their diversity. Members trusted only those team members they knew and associated with outside work. They tended to vote and make decisions based on what their social-network members or friends wanted or thought was best. They tended to help coworkers with whom they felt most comfortable. The team did not coalesce because people were most supportive of members of their own racial and gender group and least supportive of those outside those groups. This happened because many people found scant connection between diversity and task accomplishment. The organization's culture still supported and valued sameness and, because there was no education as to why the diversity of the teams would enable greater productivity, the teams eventually reflected the embedded and historic values of the organization. Because there were no new processes to keep the teams diverse or to help them see any benefit from diversity, they went back to what they knew best.

Flawed Foundations and Assumptions

Far too many diversity efforts fail because they are built upon a flawed underlying philosophy, strategy, or approach. One belief that some diversity programs have explicitly or implicitly built into their approach is that everything would be fine if everyone would behave like those who have historically been successful. People are encouraged to find a mentor or role model and learn from their behavior and experiences. Those who speak, look, or behave differently are sent to accent reduction or etiquette classes or are coached in performance-feedback meetings about their attitude or communication problems. This is based on the assumption that people at the top are both happy and successful, and that the goal of each individual should be to do whatever it takes to be like them.

This approach also includes the flawed assumptions that the road which led senior leaders to success is the same for people coming into the organization and that the organization and its challenges are static.

But, of course, people at the top are not always happy and not always prepared for the challenges ahead. For many, their ability to reach the top stemmed from the strong relationships they had established with others who were just like them. Because of those relationships, they were often given much latitude to struggle and fail (latitude that others—those who were so-called different—were not offered). They had people who believed in them, who did not second-guess or scrutinize their every move.

Another variation of the "be like the leaders" model aspires to assimilate those who are different from the dominant group—in United States corporations, this is usually white men. Based on the assumption that the organization is essentially fine, this strategy holds that after women of color, men of color, white women, and others outside the traditional group learn to succeed in the existing organization by behaving like the leaders—to gain equal access to hiring and promotion—all will be fine. The "be like us" attitude implies that you cannot fit in or be successful until you act like the dominant group. For most, this approach is simply not an option because their difference is their nationality, age, sexual orientation, physical ability, ethnic origin, gender, or race.

One of the biggest barriers to success for diversity efforts is the basic assumption that diversity is a problem that must be solved. This "problem-to-be-solved" approach leads to organizational blindness to the valuable resources offered by a diversity of skills, perspectives and problem-solving styles. It keeps organizations from noticing when they are actually practicing inclusion, and so impairs their ability to replicate successes, avoid mistakes, and communicate best practices to the organization as a whole. By reinforcing the message that differences are not really wanted, this approach also prevents organizations from tapping into the potential energy available to support the change process.

Some organizations build their diversity efforts around the belief that the dominant group must be torn down to build up other groups that have historically faced discrimination. As diversity programs are being instituted in organizations, the dominant group may feel that the program does not include them. They may perceive themselves being cast as the problem. They may come to believe that the only way they can be part of the solution is to get out of the way and out of the organization. The dominant group often voices concern that there is no longer a place in the organization's future for them, especially where promotions are concerned. They feel that they are being blamed for the organization's diversity-related problems. For these individuals and others, diversity leads to divisiveness. Their view is that instead of building partnerships and teamwork for higher performance, diversity tears people and the organization apart.

Some organizations make the mistake of devising a disparate smorgasbord of programs unrelated to the organization's mission, core business activities and needs. The best of these strategies read like a top-ten list of nationally benchmarked best practices, addressing such areas as training, support networks, mentoring, celebration of ethnic and cultural holidays, volunteerism, professional and career development, domestic partner benefits, telecommuting, and flextime. When performance continues to stagnate, when turnover rises, when lawsuits are filed, some organizations add another program. But until the diversity effort is understood as being mission critical and not merely diversity in a box, none of these measures will result in the desired outcome.

The motive behind the diversity effort can also doom it to failure. Some organizations implement a diversity effort based on the fact that diversity is simply the right thing to do. However, these organizations find that not everyone holds to the same moral imperative, includes the same people in groups that have been discriminated against, or believes the same volume of organizational resources should be applied to create equity. Some people fervently disagree with the need for an organization to fulfill anyone's moral imperative. Further, efforts based on a moral imperative are often abandoned when a crisis threatens the bottom line or the leaders of the moral imperative leave or change priorities.

Demographic changes in the United States and the global nature of organizations demand that leveraging diversity be considered a core success strategy. The behaviors and thinking of the past are no longer appropriate. Since the 1980s, people have been called upon to expand their behaviors and skills at an accelerated pace. No one group has a corner on the skill set for success. In fact, organizations that previously allowed entry to its middle and top levels only to people who looked and thought a certain way are now realizing that the talent required for success is found in individuals of every background. These organizations are beginning to see that the very differences people bring to the table contribute to an organization's success.

Leveling and Raising the Playing Field

Many organizations are currently involved in the difficult but crucial work of creating a more level playing field in their walls. The work is difficult because all organizations operate within the wider society, whose biases and discriminatory beliefs seep in through every crack and crevice.

Leveling the playing field allows an organization to reap the contributions of all of its people, as well as the synergies and innovations that flow from successful cross-difference partnerships and teams. However, simply seeking a level playing field is not enough. Any plan that aims only to bring the rest of the organization up to the standards applied to its dominant group is missing some fundamental factors and requirements for generating higher performance.

Because many organizations have historically treated their people as replaceable cogs or necessary overhead, the dominant group is often merely the least-abused segment of the population. When disrespecting people, including the dominant group, is standard practice, elevating everyone up to that level is not the answer.

The goal, after all, should be to create an environment in which all people are treated as irreplaceable assets. The most productive environment is the one in which *all* are enabled to do their best work and to continually improve their skills so that they can do even better work tomorrow. Organizations need higher levels of performance from everyone, not just from those who were previously under-contributing or running into barriers to their contributions.

In an environment tilted in their favor, the dominant group (again, traditionally white men) is expected not to complain or make waves. But to achieve higher performance and continuous improvement, all people must constantly challenge the status quo, examine and re-examine their processes, and become the chief operating officers of their jobs and teams. The challenge, therefore, is not to merely level the playing field, but to *raise* the field for everyone.

To level and then raise the playing field and achieve higher performance, organizations must include *everyone.* They need everyone to bring all their talents and energies to the workplace, working together to create something greater than any individual or mono-cultural group could do alone. An effort directed at a single group or a narrow band of groups will not create the synergy, creativity, innovation, and competitive advantage required for the highest performance and sustainability. Making the workplace more productive and rewarding for everyone in it must be a two-step process, with the two pursued simultaneously.

The first step (see Figure 3.1.1) is to level the playing field to ensure that the differences between a social identity group and the traditionally dominant group do not pose barriers to anyone's ability to do her or his best work.

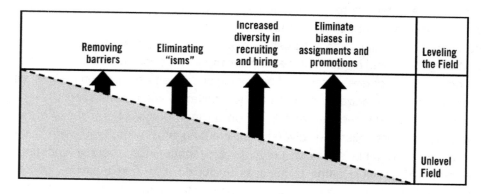

Figure 3.1.1. Leveling the playing field

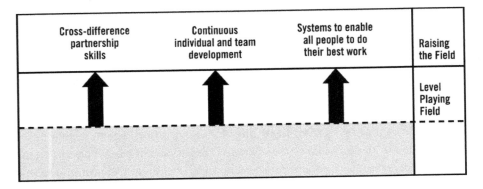

Figure 3.1.2. Raising the playing field

The second step (see Figure 3.1.2) is to raise the entire playing field so that all people and the organization itself are equipped for maximum performance, and each person and every social identity group are leveraged as assets, resources, and organizational strengths.

Enabling All People to Contribute

A culture of inclusion requires a radical shift in thinking and operating—a new set of actions, attitudes, policies, and practices designed to enable all people to contribute their energies and talents to the organization's success. Conflict becomes constructive debate. People are sought because they are different.

Inclusion is a way of joining in a positive manner in the interest of a positive outcome, not a strategy for avoiding conflict, settling for the lowest common denominator, or assimilation. Inclusion creates a sense of belonging and when each person realizes a sense of belonging to the organizational community, motivation and morale soar.

Leveraging diversity means capitalizing on an individual's differences. An inclusive organizational culture leverages diversity by creating an environment with a broader bandwidth of acceptable styles of behavior and appearance, thereby encouraging a greater range of available paths to success. Inclusion also increases the total human energy available to the organization. People can bring far more of themselves to their jobs because they are required to suppress far less.

In fact, when individual and group differences are regarded as valued resources, as in an inclusive environment, differences no longer need to be suppressed. Those who cannot fit into the old monocultural model no longer need waste their energy trying to be what they are not, and those who can successfully suppress or hide their differences no longer need waste their energy doing so.

Only when all people, with their differences and similarities acknowledged and included, are involved in decision making, problem identification, and problem solving can the individual and collective productivity of a diverse workforce be fully engaged.

If an organization brings in new people but doesn't enable them to contribute, those new people are bound to fail, no matter how talented they are. *Diversity without inclusion does not work.*

Although the concept of diversity as an organizational imperative is spoken about at length, few management practices, policies and accountabilities have been changed to make leveraging diversity and creating a culture of inclusion a core success strategy. If they were changed, most organizations would have very different organizational landscapes. What is needed is not mere lip service to a vague business imperative, but a structured, systematic inclusion breakthrough, supported by a shared understanding that such a breakthrough is a mission-critical imperative.

Competing for and Retaining Talent

To become attractive to talented people—to become a *talent magnet*—an organization must consider enhancement of its people a primary business strategy to be integrated into all day-to-day interactions, decisions and activities.

During the Industrial Revolution in the late eighteenth century, people were expected to bring their hands and feet to work. But the old assembly-line model no longer works. For organizations to be competitive today, they must inspire people to bring their brains to work too.

When an organization asks for a person's thinking, it is asking for the whole person—including the person's dreams, hopes and aspirations. This encourages each individual over time to become a knowledge worker, adding thought and value to everything she or he sees and touches. Organizations that create environments in which knowledge workers can thrive gain a competitive advantage in retaining and recruiting these valuable organizational assets. Organizations whose work environments are not as inviting may find themselves becoming training academies for their competitors. Preventing this calls for a radical change in every aspect of an organization's operations and policies.

Today's organizations are also being forced to reassess their assumptions about which talents they need most and who are their *most* valuable people. The definition of the best and brightest has changed. To meet the challenges of a global economy that is ever more focused on customized delivery of products and services, the definition of talent must be expanded to include people of different ages, genders, nationalities, colors, sexual orientations, religions, physical abilities, and other identity groups. The value of today's workforce will be measured not only by its technical skills, but also by how well individuals understand, communicate, and partner with a diverse range of customers, suppliers, colleagues, and team members.

Organizations that treat all their people as valuable resources to be nurtured, developed, recognized, and rewarded will be sought out. The constant need for fresh minds creates an interesting challenge. Over time, even organizations that have diverse work teams tend to evolve a unified point of view. Sometimes they develop a closeness that resembles exclusivity. They become too agreeable and stop questioning what is, thereby limiting their vision of *what can be.*

To ensure the ever-expanding perspective required for continuous improvement and 360-degree vision—to see around all corners and have multiple points of view for decision making and problem solving—every organization and every team in it must continuously expand its range of diversity. This effort cannot be a one-shot deal. The organization must constantly seek out, connect with, and include new dimensions of difference: lesbians and gays; people with disabilities; people of different nationalities and language groups; and on and on. It must drive the team and the organizational culture toward ever-greater inclusion. Taking the action necessary to create the workforce best able to accomplish the work of the organization cannot be viewed as a dreaded, top-down social program. It must be viewed simply as good business.

A New Way of Doing Business

Organizations are transitory entities. As the circumstances and opportunities that fueled their success fade into the past, many successful organizations come to an end. Most businesses fail in their first seven years, and in today's fast-paced environment, failure frequently happens sooner rather than later. Experts predict that 90 percent of the companies doing business today will no longer exist 20 years from now. In today's competitive environment, many organizations will not survive.

Because of the changes organizations are facing, many people and organizations are operating in crisis mode. People are postponing life-critical and life-enhancing endeavors—family, social and community obligations, vacations and sleep—in the hope that this crisis will pass. The crisis, however, will only deepen. Peter Vaill, in *Managing as a Performing Art* (1990), calls it living in "permanent white water."

What is needed is a breakthrough, and organizations are experimenting with a variety of solutions. For example, McDonald's is paying starting salaries of $30,000 for many entry-level management positions. Some companies are building Help Wanted signs right into their new buildings. Congress still argues over the minimum wage, but the issue is moot in many businesses; many entry-level people are already demanding higher pay than what is being legislated.

Without a breakthrough to keep the people that today's organizations require, declines in profitability, adaptability, resilience, and innovation await.

Organizations in search of talent are finding that the people they are looking for are, in turn, looking for a workplace that provides a welcoming environment, creates true opportunities for their professional and personal development and advancement, treats them with respect and dignity, and enables them to feel valued as contributors to the organization's success. They are looking for a place where they can affect the success of the organization and, for some, make a difference in the world.

A growing number of people are looking for workplaces that will appreciate and draw on their passions. Given the choice between comparably salaried positions, most people choose the one that offers the greatest opportunity to grow and do their best work (Stum, 1998).

The traditional organization's implied offer of a job for life did not include any promises of respect or consideration, yet demanded loyalty in return. In the emerging scenario, the organization makes no promises of longevity but instead offers respect, consideration, and opportunity in the hope of winning loyalty it can no longer demand.

A New Human Frontier

Many people believe that when diversity efforts are successful and the organization changes, the only difference will be *which* group is in charge. To paraphrase Elizabeth Dodson Gray (1982) in *Patriarchy as a Conceptual Trap*: The belief that inclusion of all people is an impossibility becomes a person's "conceptual trap or limitation." We can imagine going to the moon and creating futuristic products, yet when it comes to the human condition, most people look to the past (discrimination, wars, oppression) and assume that these negative occurrences more accurately predict our future. All too often, when a diverse team is working well together, leveraging its talents and including all its members, we find ways to dismiss the possibility that this way of effectively working together can be the new norm. The creation of cultures that are truly inclusive provides the possibility of a new vision—a *new human frontier*.

Imagining the Possibilities

Imagine an organization that engages people's differences as resources for creating higher performance and greater success.

Imagine an organization in which people striving to improve their ideas, products and decisions seek out collaborators who have differing points of view, backgrounds, experiences, perspectives, and ideas.

Imagine an organization whose members whistle on their way to work because they feel energized, gratified, and acknowledged on the job, they learn something new every day, and they add value through their contributions and thinking.

Imagine an organization whose senior leadership team includes a rotating group of people from all levels of the organization. This new way may seem difficult to imagine, too Pollyanna to be possible, but the fact is that inclusive behaviors and attitudes change virtually every aspect of an organization's operations.

Creating a culture of inclusion requires radical change. But the improvements that result from the change are equally radical. People must learn to work differently—every project team scans the organization to make sure it has the best and most diverse team for the job. Instead of disagreements in meetings that lead to strained compromises or avoidance, disagreements lead to better decisions based on a more complete vision of the problem and possible solutions. Work assignments are made with consideration for outside-of-work responsibilities, so people freely give their whole selves without worrying about their jobs consuming their lives. Members of the organization and customers feel loyalty to the organization because of the quality of its products and services and its social, environmental, and commercial values.

Dealing with the permanent white water in today's business climate underscores the problems organizations face to grow and prosper, and how two similar organizations can take different paths.

Two large regional banks located in urban areas, spurred on by an increasingly competitive marketplace and challenges in the banking industry, felt it crucial to address the issue of diversity. Both launched their diversity efforts with great sincerity and good intentions, each stating in nearly identical terms their commitment to being an "equal opportunity institution both for our customers and our people while maximizing shareholder values."

Bank #1 emphasized its moral imperative to become a good corporate citizen and to help improve conditions in the disadvantaged areas of its community. Bank #2 framed its effort in terms of a business imperative to expand the reach of the bank's services into new and previously underserved market areas. Then each underwent a series of mergers, followed by a period of downsizing, and their approaches took significantly different turns.

Bank #1 put its diversity effort on hold, citing organization-wide pressures that required it to "refocus on core business issues." Staffing and branch location decisions were based on performance history. The lowest-performing people and locations were phased out. Acknowledging its moral imperative, the bank restated its commitment to continue its good corporate citizen campaign as soon as its internal situation was stabilized. Basing personnel-retention decisions on past performance, Bank #1's downsizing program adopted a decidedly last-in, first-out direction. A high percentage of its most recent hires, especially those from underrepresented social identity groups, were let go. Similarly, most branches located in low-income neighborhoods were closed.

The overall results for Bank #1, according to its public communications, were "quite satisfactory, considering the unsettled situation" from the mergers and downsizing. It retained a significant percentage of commercial lending and depositor accounts from the combined pre-merger banks and was able to serve them at reduced cost thanks to closing low-performing branches. And although its penetration into new market areas was low, improvements were expected after more stable times resumed.

Unlike Bank #1, Bank #2 continued to view its diversity effort as a business imperative throughout the merger and downsizing process. Instead of basing personnel and branch-location decisions on past performance, it based them on an assessment of their relevance to the future strategies and changing dynamics in the workforce and the community. Bank #2 strove to eliminate duplication of services and functions, while preserving resources necessary for penetrating new market areas and connecting with previously under-served constituencies.

Bank #2's pre-merger efforts had positioned it well for capitalizing on opportunities in new market areas. With judicious consolidation of branches and services in its core areas, it was able to retain a large percentage of its former business. And with its more diverse staff and advantageous locations, it was able to quickly capture a high percentage of commercial and mortgage lending, as well as private checking and deposit accounts, in previously underserved areas of its marketing region.

More than a year after the merger, Bank #1, still "committed in principle" to its moral imperative, announced another round of layoffs as it sought to achieve "post-merger stability." Bank #2, focused firmly on its business imperative, began planning an inner-city internship and scholarship program to develop future staffing resources for its new core market areas.

The contrasting experience of these two banks is a telling example of a strategy that succeeds when it is tied to a mission-critical imperative versus the losing strategy resulting from a strictly moral imperative for initiating and implementing a diversity strategy. Although Bank #2 was forging into unknown territory with its strategy, it had much more upside potential, whereas Bank #1 used the old tried-and-true strategy common to most organizations in times of trouble.

Bank #2 embarked on an effort that represented a radical change from the way it had always conducted business—and the strategy yielded positive results. Making such a radical approach work, however, required leaders who were willing take risks and deal with resistance. Equally important, Bank #2 was willing to tie the initial, ongoing effects and opportunities related to its leveraging diversity strategy to its current and future business strategy. It integrated the effort into all activities related to its work culture, customers and business plans. It chose a path that led to greater success.

READING 3.2

What is Culture? How Does Culture Affect Communication?

◆

By Alexis Tan

I ntercultural communication is communication in general, with one important distinction: the participants bring with them differing worldviews, values, behavioral norms, and communication styles to the interaction. Let's take a look at culture in more detail and see how culture can affect communication.

In doing the research for this reading, I came across two quotes originally cited in the book *Management Across Cultures* by Steers, Nardon, and Sanchez-Runde (2013) that tell us something about culture:

"We do not see things as they are; we see things as we are."
—Talmud Bavli, Ancient Book of Wisdom, Babylonia

"Water is the last thing a fish notices."
—Lao Tzu

What do these quotes tell us about culture? To me, Bavli says that how we see the world (our realities) is influenced by our cultures; Lao Tzu reminds us that we may not be aware of this influence at all.

Defining Culture

If culture is such a powerful force on how we see and make sense of our environment and other people, then how can we not be aware of its influence? Before we can answer this question, let's define what we mean by culture. This won't be an easy task, considering that there are at least 150 definitions, by one estimate (Kroeber & Kluckhohn, 1952), in anthropology, sociology, social psychology, and communication. Here are some examples:

> Culture … is that complex whole which includes knowledge, belief, art, law, morals, custom, and any other capabilities and habits acquired by man as a member of society. (Taylor, 1871, p. 1)

> Culture may be defined as the totality of the mental and physical reactions and activities that characterize the behavior of individuals composing a social group collectively and individually in relations to their natural environment, to other groups, to members of the group itself and of each individual to himself. It also includes the products of these activities and their role in the life of the groups. The mere enumerations of these various aspects of life, however, does not constitute culture. It is more, for its elements are not independent, they have a structure. (Boas, 1911, p. 149)

> Culture means the whole complex of traditional behavior which has been developed by the human race and is successively learned by each generation. A culture is less precise. It can mean the forms of traditional behavior which are characteristics of a given society, or of a group of societies, or of a certain race, or of a certain area, or of a certain period of time. (Mead, 1937, p. 17)

> Culture has been distinguished from the other elements of action by the fact that it is intrinsically transmissible from one action system to another by learning and diffusion. (Parsons & Shills, 1976, p. 172)

> Man is a biological being as well as a social individual. Among the responses which he gives to external stimuli, some of the full product of his nature, and others to his condition (culture). (Levi-Strauss, 1949, p. 4)

> Culture … is ways of thinking, the ways of acting, and the material objects that together shape a people's way of life. Culture can be nonmaterial or material. (Macionnis & Gerber, 2011, p. 11)

The term culture refers to what is learned ... the things one needs to know in order to meet the standards of others. (Goodenough, 1971, p. 19)

The culture concept denotes an historically transmitted pattern of meanings embodied in symbols, a system of inherited conceptions expressed in symbolic forms by means of which men communicate, perpetuate, and develop their knowledge about and toward life ... (Geertz, 1966, p. 89)

The collective programming of the mind that distinguishes the members of one human group from another. (Hofstede, Hofstede, & Minkov, 2010, p. 3)

An integrated system of learned behavior patterns which are characteristic of the members of a society and which are not the result of biological inheritance. (Hoebel, 1976, p. 2)

The collection of beliefs, values, behaviors, customs, and attitudes that distinguish the people of one society from another. (Kluckhohn, 1949, p. 1)

As you can see, there is no lack of definitions for culture. From these definitions, let's identify the characteristics that stand out and about which there is agreement.

1. Culture is a characteristic of people who identify with a group. This identification may be based on shared geographical boundaries (such as a country); a shared demographic category, such as race or ethnicity, religion, or socioeconomic level; or simply shared interests and goals, such as a corporation or student club (organizational culture).

2. Since culture is dependent on group membership and identification, the individual must be aware of the group's existence and acknowledge his or her membership in the group.

3. Culture includes agreement within the group about how to make sense of or assign meanings to its environment, which behaviors in response to the environment are acceptable, what is important in life, and how to feel about other people and objects in the environment. These components are the *dimensions* of culture: beliefs and worldviews (to make sense), action norms (acceptable behaviors), values (what is important in life), and attitudes (how to feel). Culture is manifested in these nonmaterial human tendencies, but also represented in

material artifacts such as art, language, architecture, laws, rituals, literature, and so on. Our concern in this book is nonmaterial culture.

4. Culture therefore guides an individual's response to and interpretation of the environment. Its influence is distinct from our natural human tendencies, which are hardwired into our genes, such as, according to some scholars, the tendency to be prejudiced or to favor in-groups over out-groups.

5. Culture is a pattern of shared dimensions, each related to and reinforcing the other. For example, beliefs are related to attitudes, attitudes to behavior.

6. Culture is shared by group members using signals, verbal and nonverbal.

7. Culture is transmitted over time from one generation to the next through a process of socialization (discussed later in this reading).

8. Culture can change, as a response to changes in the environment, such as economic growth (Inglehart, 1997), encroachment by other cultures (Inglehart, 1997), proliferation of foreign media (Tunstall, 1977; Scotton & Hatchten, 2008), and migration (Inglehart, 1997).

Incorporating these commonalities, here is my simplified definition that applies to intercultural communication:

> Culture is a pattern of shared beliefs, values, attitudes, behavioral norms, and worldviews shared by members of a group and transmitted over time from one generation to the next. Although generally resistant to change, culture is malleable, as a response to environmental changes. The major form of transmission is communication.

My definition of culture, as well as the other definitions I cited, share a common problem: How do we know that a worldview is shared? One hundred percent agreement? (highly unlikely). By a majority? What about those who don't agree, the outliers?

Scholars have taken different approaches to solving the problem. Some, like Hofstede (1984) and Hofstede et al. (2010) use statistics (i.e., means, standard deviations, factor analysis, and correlations, which I discuss later in this reading) to analyze results of surveys, looking for commonalities within a group, in his case, countries, and then comparing groups. Kluckhohn (1951) also used statistics to compare indigenous groups in the United States on several dimensions of culture. Others have used critical analysis of the artifacts of culture to identify themes representing cultural dimensions, such as in law, literature, the mass media, and observations of everyday behaviors and activities. Still others (Wood & Smith, 2004; Schwartz et al., 2001) have analyzed culture both at the individual and group levels, looking for individual differences in how cultural dimensions are internalized and demonstrated. In this latter approach, outliers, members of a group who deviate from cultural norms, are given special attention by analyzing possible reasons for their deviations. In intercultural communications and other interactions, there is a risk in automatically ascribing to a person a group culture simply because of membership, which is a form of stereotyping. (Perhaps we are interacting with an outlier.) While these generalizations are a useful guide, and in fact they are often accurate in describing a majority, the prudent approach is to use culture as a guide while being cognizant of possible individual differences or deviations.

Dimensions of Culture

Culture is defined by its dimensions—worldviews, beliefs, values, attitudes, and behavioral norms. In this section, I discuss those dimensions that have the most impact on intercultural communication.

Hofstede's National Cultural Dimensions

According to Hofstede (1984) and Hofstede et al. (2010), culture has six dimensions that can differentiate between countries. Here are three of them:

- *Power distance* is the "extent to which the less powerful person accepts inequality in power and considers it as normal" (Hofstede, 2001, p. 139). In a high power distance culture, society is highly stratified into institutionalized hierarchies based on wealth and political authority. People with high power consider people with low power to be different from them; they consider the unequal distribution of power and authority to be "a fact of life," and believe that everybody has a rightful place in society determined by how much power he or she has. In high power distance societies, there is greater centralization of political power, less participation by people with low power, positions of authority are held by people with power, and more importance is placed on status and rank.

- In low power distance cultures, people believe that inequality is undesirable and should be minimized, all people should have access to power, and people in power should be held accountable to the publics they serve. In low power distance cultures, laws, norms, and everyday behaviors minimize power distance.

- According to Hofstede (2001), Malaysia, Guatemala, Panama, and the Philippines are high power distance cultures, whereas Austria, Israel, Denmark, and New Zealand are low power distance cultures. The United States ranks 38 out of 53 countries (53 being the country with the lowest power distance). These rankings were based on a survey of IBM employees in over 50 countries in the late 1960s and early 1970s by Hofstede and his colleagues (Hofstede, 2001).

- *Individualism/collectivism* is a cultural dimension that measures the degree to which members of a culture use the group or the individual as a basis for personal identities (Schwartz, 1994). In collectivist cultures, the group is the most important identity source, meaning that people's identities are anchored on group memberships. Therefore, there is greater emphasis on needs and goals of the in-group; on collaboration, shared interests, and harmony; and on preserving the "face," or positive image, of the group. In contrast, in individualist cultures, personal goals take precedence over group goals, independence of the individual rather than reliance on the group is stressed, and an individual's personal identity and self-image are more important than group identity in guiding behaviors and interpersonal relations. Hofstede et al. (2010) identified the United States as the most individualist culture among more than 50 countries in the IBM surveys, followed by Australia, Great Britain, Canada, the Netherlands, and New Zealand. The most collectivist cultures were Guatemala, Ecuador, Panama, and Venezuela.

- *Uncertainty avoidance* refers to the degree that people in a culture are uncomfortable (or comfortable) with situations that are unstructured, unpredictable, unknown, unfamiliar, or unclear, and the extent to which they are willing to cope with and tolerate these situations. In high uncertainty avoidance cultures, members try to avoid uncertainty and ambiguity because these situations are uncomfortable. To prevent high uncertainty situations from occurring, and to cope with them when they do occur, high anxiety avoidance cultures establish formal rules, seek consensus, rely on authority figures, and are less tolerant of deviant ideas and behaviors. Members of low uncertainty avoidance cultures are more comfortable with unfamiliar, new, and unstructured situations. They are more tolerant of unusual and nonconforming behavior, have fewer rules governing social behavior, dislike hierarchies and rigid social structures, and are more willing to take risks. Hofstede et al. (2010) identified Greece, Portugal, Guatemala, and Uruguay as high uncertainty avoidance countries (do not like uncertainty), and Singapore, Jamaica, Denmark, and Sweden as low uncertainty avoidance countries (do not feel uncomfortable with uncertainty). The United States ranked 43 out of 53 countries (the higher the rank, the lower anxiety avoidance).

These cultural dimensions were identified by Hofstede and his colleagues in a series of studies beginning in 1967, the most recent in 2010.

Hall's High- And Low-Context Cultures

According to Hall (1981), intercultural communication can be analyzed by considering how much emphasis is placed on the context of information and how much emphasis is placed on the explicit message. The context of communication is the physical environment in which communication takes place, including its setting (e.g., formal board room or informal wine bar); the status and social positions of the participants; and nonverbal signs, such as gestures and facial expressions. In high-context cultures, most of the meanings exchanged among participants depend more on context and less on the explicit verbal message. High-context participants often come from homogeneous cultures in which tradition and past experience have taught them what behaviors are expected in social relationships and how to respond to messages from others. Much of the exchange of explicit verbal messages is ritualistic and formal. The real meaning of the interaction is in its context—roles, nonverbal signs, and other situational cues. Communication is often indirect to promote harmony and to avoid public expressions of discord.

In contrast, members of low-context cultures place more emphasis on the explicit verbal message. "Tell me what you think, and put it in writing" is a common expectation. Low-context people have difficulty reading meanings from the context of communication. They expect that meanings will be expressed in explicit verbal messages. Communication is direct, and people are expected to express themselves.

Some high-context cultures, according to Hall (1981) are Japanese, Chinese, and Korean. Examples of low-context cultures are German, Scandinavian, and North American [...].

Kluckhohn and Strodtbeck's Cultural Dimensions

According to Kluckohn and Strodtbeck (1961), culture is best understood by analyzing how people respond to human problems. The solutions to these problems, which could be caused by environmental stresses like drought and earthquakes or by human conflicts like war, depend on values held by members of a group or community. They define a value as "a conception, explicit or implicit, ... of the desirable which influences the selection from available modes, means and ends of action," a definition they borrowed from Kluckhohn (1951, p. 395). Therefore, values are deeply held beliefs about what is important in life (goals), what are the best means to achieving these goals, and what are the important results (ends). In a group, community, or society (an aggregate of many communities), members will share a few values that guide the selection of solutions to problems and which are manifestations of the group's, community's, or society's culture. Kluckhohn and Strodtbeck (1961) identified five problems confronted by human societies with different possible strategies for finding solutions. The preferred strategies are based on cultural values. Here are the societal problems, posed as questions, and possible strategies for solving them (Hills, 2002):

- *Time*: Should we focus on the past, present, or future?

- *Humans and the natural environment*: Should we master the environment? Live in harmony with it? Submit to it?

- *Relations with other people*: Should we relate to others hierarchically (*lineal*)? As equals (*collateral*)? According to individual merit?

- *Motivation for human behavior*: Is the prime motivation to express one's self, to grow, or to achieve?

- *Human nature*: Are humans naturally good, bad, or a mixture?

The possible answers to these questions indicate a society's values, which, in turn, reflect that society's culture. The preferred solutions help us understand how people in the culture respond to common problems. Here is a summary adapted from Hills (2002, p. 5):

- Time
    - Past: Focus on the time before now—or the past—and on preserving and maintaining traditional teachings and beliefs.
    - Present: Focus on what is now—the present—and on accommodating changes in beliefs and traditions.
    - Future: Focus on the time to come—the future—and on planning ahead and seeking new ways to replace the old.

- Natural environment
    - Mastery: Can and should exercise total control over nature.
    - Harmonious: Can and should exercise partial, but not total, control by living in balance with nature.
    - Submissive: Cannot and should not exercise control over nature; subject to the "higher power" of these forces.

- Relating to other people
    - Hierarchical (lineal): Deferring to higher authorities within the group.
    - As equals (collateral): Seeking consensus within the group as equal members.
    - Individualistic: Making decisions independently from others in the group.

- Motive for individual actions
    - To express oneself: Emphasizes activity valued by the individual but not necessarily by others in the group.
    - To grow: Emphasizes growth in abilities that are valued by the individual, but not necessarily by others.

o   To achieve: Emphasizes activity valued by the individual and approved by others.

As you can see, each of these values leads to a particular response that might be used in solving a problem. According to Kluckhohn and Strodtbeck (1961), these values are indicative of a group's culture, and agreement on which values are important can be found within many groups. They began their research to determine how much agreement can be found within cultural groups by interviewing Navahos, Mexican Americans, Texan homesteaders, Mormon villagers, and Zuni pueblo dwellers in the American Southwest. They developed scenarios to describe real-life situations that all five cultural groups would find realistic and relevant. They then asked their participants how they would respond to the situations, and assigned the participants, based on responses, to a value orientation category (e.g., past, present, or future time orientation). They drew value orientation profiles of each group, showing how much agreement there was within the groups, and how similar or different the groups were from each other. These profiles described the cultures of each group based on their value orientations.

Other researchers have used Kluckhohn and Strodtbeck's value orientation model to describe and compare cultures in different contexts and geographical regions. Russo (2000) and Russo, Hills et al. (1984) analyzed the value orientations of the Lumni, an indigenous community in Washington state. Hills (1977) and Hills & Goneyali 1980) studied generational changes in values between young people and their parents as a result of migration. They looked at samples of migrants to New Zealand from Samoa, Fiji, and the Cook Islands. Using Kluckhohn and Strodtbeck's value orientations, they interviewed young people ages 16 to 18 and their parents, using tape-recorded questions in the respondent's native language. Here are some examples of the interview questions (from Hills, 2002, p. 8):

I will ask you 25 questions. There are three possible answers to each question. Please listen carefully to each question and then each of the three suggested answers to that question. I can play them again if you would like to listen to them again. We do not want your name. There are no right or wrong answers to these questions—we want to know how you feel about them. Take as much time as you need to answer them.
Here is the first one.

When our group sends a delegate to a meeting I think it's best—
Relational

1. To let everyone discuss it until everyone agrees on the person.
      Collateral
2. To let the important leaders decide. They have more experience than us.
      Lineal

3. For a vote to be taken and the one with the most votes goes, even if some people disagree.
   Individualistic

Now please tell me the answer which comes closest to the way you feel. Now tell me the answer which is your second choice.
Thanks. Here's the next one.

When I get sick I believe:
Humanity and Nature

1. Doctors will be able to find a way to cure it.
   Mastery
2. I should live properly so I don't get sick.
   Harmony
3. I cannot do much about it and just have to accept it.
   Subjugation

Here's the third …

When I send money for use overseas, I think it should be spent to:
Time

1. Make a better life for the future.
   Future
2. Make a better life now.
   Present
3. Keep the old ways and customs alive.
   Past

Using this interview protocol, Hills (1977) and Hills and Goneyali 1980) showed changes in value orientations between young immigrants and their parents, which he attributed to migration. Young people showed more agreement with the predominant values of the new environment (New Zealand) than did their parents.

Kluckhohn and Strodtbeck (1961) provide us with a useful tool for differentiating between cultures. However, we should be aware of two possible weaknesses in their theory. First, the definitions of values are heavily influenced by the researchers' perceptions of how cultures might differ from each other. The starting point is their theory, which they then test in different cultures. An alternative strategy is to first ask people to describe their cultures and then build a theory based on the responses. Thus, theory is developed from the ground up, respondents to researcher, rather than from the top, researcher to respondents. Second, the theory does not adequately provide for the possibility that respondents may use different values as a basis for solving a problem, depending on context. These values are not necessarily mutually exclusive. For example, on the relational value orientation, I may be individualistic at work but lineal in my family.

Nonetheless, Kluckhohn and Strodtbeck's values orientation theory has provided researchers with a useful tool for differentiating between cultures. These weaknesses are not unique to their theory, but are weaknesses of most of the other cultural dimension theories as well. The common problem is how do we generalize from individual data or information obtained from the individual through interviews and questionnaires to the entire group, and how do we account for individual differences within the group? Researchers continue to grapple with this problem with varying degrees of success.

Trompenaars and Hampden-Turner's Seven Dimensions of Culture

According to Trompenaars and Hampden-Turner (1997), culture has seven dimensions, which they identified from surveys of 40,000 teenagers in 40 countries. These dimensions are as follows:

1. *Universalism (rules) versus particularism (relationships)*: People with a universalism point of view place a high value on laws, rules, and obligations; rules come before relationships. People who are particularistic place relationships above rules; their actions are determined by the situation and who is involved, rather than by rules and laws.

2. *Individualism (the individual) versus communitarianism (the group)*: Individualistic people value personal freedom and achievement, and believe that the individual should make his or her own decisions. People who value communitarianism believe that the group is more important than the individual, the group provides help and safety in exchange for loyalty, and the group always comes before the individual.

3. *Specific versus diffuse relationships at work*: People with a specific perspective believe that personal relationships are separate from work and that people can work together without having a good relationship. People with a diffuse relationship believe that good relationships are important at work and are necessary for success at work.

4. *Neutral versus emotional*: Neutral people control their emotions. They believe more in reason than in emotions. They keep their emotions to themselves. Emotional people express how they feel more openly; their behaviors are influenced by emotions.

5. *Achievement versus ascription*: People who value ascription believe that a person's worth should be based on performance, what a person does. People who subscribe to ascription believe that a person's worth is based on status, power, title, and position.

6. *Sequential time versus synchronous time*: People who value sequential time believe that time is valuable and that events should happen in order, in a linear fashion. They value punctuality, planning, and sticking to a schedule. To people who value synchronous time, the past, present and future are interchangeable and related. Therefore, time is not linear, but circular. It's more important to complete many tasks and projects rather than sticking to a schedule to finish one task.

7. *Internal direction (internal locus of control) versus outer direction (external locus of control)*: People who are internally directed believe that they can control their environment to achieve goals. People who are externally directed believe that their environment controls them; therefore, they must work within the constraints of what is around them, including other people.

The dimensions of culture defined above give the end points of a scale, meaning that they are bipolar extremes. A culture could be assigned to any point between these extreme anchors based on responses to a questionnaire by individuals within the culture. Again, we are faced with the problem of generalizing from individuals to the group and accounting for individual differences.

The cultural dimensions I have discussed are a convenient way of describing and categorizing cultures based on their worldviews and values. And, as you can see, there is quite a bit of commonality among these dimensions. [...] I discuss how the cultures of several countries have been placed along several of these dimensions. I also suggest communication strategies that might be appropriate and effective in several cultures based on their placement on the continuum. A word of caution, though: these dimensions are generalizations, so we should take care to first know whether the individual we are interacting with fits into the cultural mode we have assigned to him or her. There is no substitute to treating people as individuals first before we consider their culture.

How Do We Learn Culture?

So far, we have looked at several dimensions on which culture can be described. These dimensions do not exhaust all the possible manifestations of culture, but they are the ones that are most relevant to intercultural communication. Remember that culture is learned and transmitted from one generation to the next. Further, culture is patterned, meaning that the dimensions are all related to and consistent with each other and they, taken together, provide a general guide for making sense of and acting within a person's environment in the context of membership in a group. How then is such a complex pattern of accepted norms for action and believing learned within a group?

A number of theories from anthropology, sociology, education, and social psychology explain how culture is learned. In this section, I focus on those theories that assign an important role to communication.

Motivation to Learn a Culture: Social Identity Theory

Why should a person be motivated to learn a culture? Tajfel and Turner's (1986) social identity theory gives us a clue. First, group membership provides us with a source of identity, a sense of who we are. Research has shown that, indeed, our sense of who we are is determined by groups we strongly identify with—for example, student organizations, work organizations, ethnic and racial groups, religious groups, countries, or nationalities. Not all of these groups will be salient or will influence our actions, perceptions, and beliefs at all times; group influence on the individual is situational rather than general. For example, organizational culture may influence my behavior at work (e.g., I work 12-hour days because everybody else seems to do so) while national or country culture (e.g., "American") may influence my behavior when travelling abroad. In intercultural communication, much of the emphasis has been on national cultures. We ask, how does culture at this level affect communication interactions? We are also interested in how co-cultures, defined as smaller group cultures within a nation, such as the cultures of racial and ethnic groups, interact with each other. The basic premises of social identity theory hold regardless of the level of analysis from small to large groups for two reasons. First, group membership is a source of self-identity. Second, the stronger the individual's identification with the group, the greater the motivation to learn its culture.

Another motivation for learning a group's culture is self-preservation, meaning that the individual needs the group to survive and thrive in the natural and social environment. The group provides the resources needed by the individual to function effectively in interactions with other groups and with nature. At the national level, consider social security, laws, disaster relief, health insurance, and the military. These resources are available to us because we identify as "Americans" and are members of this national group.

The Process of Learning Culture: Enculturation and Socialization

Learning a culture continues over time from childhood to adulthood. Although most of the research emphasis has been on children and adolescents, attention has also been given to how immigrants, sojourners (temporary visitors to a country), and adults in new environments learn cultures.

Two general and related theories explain the process of learning culture. *Enculturation* is defined by Kottak (2011) as:

> the process where the culture that is currently established teaches an individual the accepted norms and values of the culture or society where the individual lives. The individual can become an accepted member and fulfill the needed functions and roles of the group. Most importantly the individual knows and establishes a context of boundaries and accepted behavior that dictates what is acceptable and not acceptable within the framework of that society. It teaches the individual their role within society as well as what is accepted behavior within that society and lifestyle.

Socialization is a similar concept, defined as:

1. A lifelong process of learning the norms, customs and ideologies of a society that are needed for participation, functioning, and continued membership (Macionis, 2010);

2. A learning process influenced by agents such as the family (Macionis & Gerber, 2011); peers (other members of the group who are important to the learner, sometimes referred to as "significant others") (Macionis & Gerber, 2011); teachers and schools (Macionis & Gerber, 2011); and the media, new and traditional (McQuail, 2005).

These definitions help us understand what is learned and who the teachers might be, but gives little information on how culture is learned. The next two theories tell us about the learning process.

Social Cognitive Theory

Most theories of how behaviors, beliefs, values, and other dimensions of culture are learned include two processes: learning by direct experience and by purposive teaching. Traditional learning theories, for example, explain that learning occurs by actually performing the behavior and then experiencing its consequences. Learning is facilitated by reinforcement, or the extent to which the behavior is rewarded or punished. People will learn culture by acting out its components and then repeating the actions if they are rewarded. They learn these behaviors from information and instruction given to them by parents, peers, and teachers. For example, how does a child learn that in American culture he or she is supposed to act independently and not depend too much on a group? The child may be instructed to do so by parents or teachers; then he or she does a class assignment independently of a group; parents or teachers show approval; and consequently, this behavior, acting independently, becomes part of the child's pattern of responses to the environment.

Unlike traditional learning theories, *social cognitive theory* (SCT) explains how behaviors are learned from observation. The opportunity to learn and practice or enact behaviors from direct instruction is present in most cultures, particularly in classrooms and the home. However, there is also a great deal of opportunity to learn indirectly from observation without direct instruction—for example, children observing their parents' interaction with people in the mall; actions of their favorite characters in television and the movies, and the consequences of these actions; and the behavior of classmates in the playground. Developed by Albert Bandura (1986, 2002), SCT explains how we learn by observation. This theory is particularly relevant to intercultural communication because many of the behaviors we can learn, such as those included in cultural dimensions, are presented in new and traditional media, including television and the movies.

According to SCT (Bandura 1985, 2002), learning by observation occurs in sequential steps:

1. The learner, such as a child being socialized into a culture, is motivated to acquire knowledge about a behavior. Motivation will depend on the child' sense of self-efficacy, the ability to learn and repeat the observed behavior, and on perceived rewards from performing the behavior, such as parental approval: the higher the sense of self-efficacy, the greater the motivation; also, the greater the expectation that the behavior will be rewarded, the greater the motivation to learn it.

2. The behavior to be learned is presented in a medium that reaches the learner. Children watch television. They play video games on their electronic devices. Behaviors and values demonstrated or implied in these media can be observed by children and potentially learned.

3. The learner pays attention to the behavior presented in a medium. Attention is facilitated by repetition; portrayals of characters that the observer identifies with because they have similar characteristics ("They are just like me"); portrayals of situations that the learner identifies with because of experience (e.g., "I have been there") or relevance (e.g., "This applies to me"); distinctiveness (portrayals that stand out); simple (easy to understand and follow); and positive emotional arousal ("This makes me feel good," "This is funny," "The good people won").

4. The learner remembers the behavior learned, stores it using symbolic codes (language and visually), and rehearses it mentally. Retention is facilitated by simplicity of the act and its prevalence or repetition in the environment.

5. When the occasion arises, the remembered behavior is enacted or produced, such as child preferring to work alone rather than in a group. Enactment will be consistent and repeated when the behavior is rewarded, as when a child is praised by parents and teachers.

SCT, as you can see, is a powerful model for explaining how *deliberate* learning occurs by observation. The learner actively processes information from observed events and re-enactment occurs consciously and with purpose. Because much of a culture's values and behavioral norms are indeed reenacted by socialized members repeatedly in everyday life and in the media, the opportunity for deliberate observational learning is not only present, but inviting to the novice learner. But what about unconscious learning?

Cultivation Theory

Not all learning is deliberate and conscious. We also learn cultural beliefs and behaviors unconsciously. That is, we are learning them but we do not actively exert effort to learn them. And we are not consciously aware of having learned these behaviors until we enact them. Bias and prejudice are examples of cultural behaviors that many of us learn unconsciously.

So how do we learn culture unconsciously? *Cultivation theory* (CT) provides an explanation of unconscious learning from the mass media. Developed by George Gerbner and Larry Gross more than 30 years ago, CT continues to be an influential theory about how we learn from television (e.g., Morgan & Shanahan, 2010). The basic premise of CT is that heavy viewers of television learn to believe the social realities portrayed in television. And most of us, especially children, are heavy viewers. This learning is cumulative, happens over time after repeated exposure, and is unconscious and not deliberate. We learn from constant exposure; we do not deliberately seek out behaviors and norms that will help us adapt and function in a culture.

Gerbner and his colleagues propose the following propositions about television's effects on culture:

1. Television is "the source of the most broadly shared images and messages in history. Television cultivates from infancy the very predispositions that used to be acquired from other primary sources. The repetitive pattern of television's mass produced messages and images forms the mainstream of a common symbolic environment" (Gerbner, Gross & Signorielli, 1986). Further, Gerbner et al. (1986) propose that "the substance of consciousness cultivated by television is not so much specific attitudes and opinions as more basic assumptions about the facts of life and standards of judgment on which conclusions are based."

   In other words, television has supplanted parents, peers, and the school as the primary agents of cultural socialization because of its ubiquity (especially today, with availability in a variety of platforms); the effects of television are not on specific attitudes, but on a person's worldview (dimensions of culture in our previous discussion); and these effects are cumulative and happen over time.

2. Television presents a reality that supports existing institutions, power structures, and cultural norms. Television's reality does not always (one might say rarely) coincide with realities in our natural environment. For example, more violence is portrayed in television than actually happens in the real world. Although Gerbner's cultural indicators project, which maps out television realities through content analysis, does not address most of the cultural dimensions I discussed earlier, several themes related to culture have been identified. These include gender roles; racial and ethnic representation and status; fear of crime; police presence and effectiveness; mistrust of people; and, the television reality that has attracted the most attention from researchers, violence in the real world.

3. Heavy viewers of television have accepted television realities as their own and natural realities. For example, research has found that heavy viewers in comparison to light viewers:

   a. Are more afraid of being victims of crime;

   b. Believe that there are more police officers in the real world and that police are more effective in solving crimes than they are in the real world;

   c. Have a greater mistrust of people.

There is, therefore, evidence that television "cultivates" in heavy viewers some indicators of a culture and that this cultivation can be found across co-cultures, such as racial groups within a society, thereby resulting in a common outlook, at least on some cultural indicators, a process Gerbner calls "mainstreaming." Further research can confirm our expectation that television might be able to similarly influence viewer adaptations of other cultural dimensions discussed earlier in this reading.

Does Culture Change?

The short answer is "yes." Learned patterns of behavior and beliefs can be unlearned and replaced with new ones when human needs change or when external pressures support change (Rochon, 1998). Although resistant to change, considering that its many dimensions are imbedded in group members over a long period of time, culture can change in response to the following forces (Rochon, 1998):

1. *Discovery and invention.* Discovery is "addition to knowledge" and invention is "new application of knowledge" (Linton, 1955). To lead to cultural change, an invention or discovery would first have to be understood and accepted and then used regularly. Acceptance comes after the invention or discovery is shown to be beneficial to the individual and society. Examples in the United States are technological inventions such as the automobile, new energy sources, and new digital technologies, all of which have affected how Americans view the world and related behaviors.

2. *Internal changes within a society, such as changes in political and economic structures.* Much has been written in the media about changes in some values and related behaviors, particularly among young people, in some Middle Eastern countries and China because of changes in political and economic conditions. Whether and to what extent the cultural dimensions discussed earlier in this reading have changed in these countries is a matter for empirical research.

3. *Influence from foreign countries.* Powerful countries and cultures such as the United States have the potential to change cultures in less powerful countries. This process is called *acculturation*, the replacement of native cultures with foreign cultures. This process can take many forms: conquest through war; economic domination; and, most relevant to intercultural communication, influence through the media. Many scholars have expanded on the original notion that "the media are American" (Tunstall, 1977; Scotton and Hatchen, 2008), showing that American media, particularly movies and television, have indeed influenced young people around the world to adopt the American cultural realities portrayed (accurately or not), from the more superficial manifestations in dress, music, and food to values emphasizing consumption and hedonism.

4. *Influence of a new culture.* To be accepted, an immigrant is expected to adapt the values and behavioral norms of the new culture. When this change occurs, the process is called *transculturation*. The extent to which total transculturation is functional for the immigrant and the new culture continues to be subject of debate, especially as migration increases around the world, significantly changing the demographics in host societies, including the United States. One view says that complete transculturation is necessary to preserve the culture of the

host country. Another view says that the diversity in cultures brought by immigrants adds to the richness of the host culture. Others say that diverse values, worldviews, and behavioral norms indeed add to the host culture and should be accepted and respected, but that certain fundamental values, such as those identified in the host country's constitution, should be upheld. (In the United States these values include freedom and equality.)

REFERENCES

Bandura, A. (1985). *Social foundations of thought and action.* Englewood Cliffs, NJ: Prentice Hall.

Bandura, A. (2002). Social cognitive theory in cultural context. *Applied Psychology, 51*(2), 269–290.

Boas, F. (1911). *The mind of primitive man.* New York, NY: Macmillan Publishing.

Geertz, C. (1966). Religion as a cultural system. In M. Banton (Ed.), *Anthropological approaches to the study of religion.* New York, NY: Routledge.

Gerbner, G., Gross, L., Morgan, M., & Signorielli, N. (1986). Living with television: The dynamics of the cultivation process. In J. Bryant and D. Zillman (Eds.), *Perspectives on media effects* (pp. 17–40). Hillsdale, NJ: Lawrence Erlbaum Associates.

Goodenough, W. (1971). *Culture, language, and society.* Reading, MA: Addison-Wesley.

Hall, E. (1981). *Beyond culture.* New York, NY: Anchor Books.

Hills, M. D. (2002). Kluckhohn and Strodtbeck's values orientation theory. *Online Readings in Psychology and Culture, 4*(4). Retrieved from http://dx.doi.org/10.9707/2307-0919.1040.

Hills, M.D. (1977). *Values in the South Pacific.* Paper presented at the Annual Conference of the New Zealand Psychological Society, Auckland, New Zealand.

Hills, M. D., & Goneyali, E. (1980). *Values in Fijian families* (Monograph). Hamilton, New Zealand: University of Waikato, Dept. of Psychology.

Hoebel, E. A. (1976). *Cultural and social anthropology.* New York, NY: McGraw-Hill.

Inglehart, R. (1997). *Modernization and postmodernization: Cultural, economic, and political change in 43 societies.* Princeton, NJ: Princeton University Press.

Hofstede, G. (1984). *Culture's consequences: International differences in work-related values.* Beverly Hills, CA: Sage.

Hofstede, G. (2001). *Culture's consequences: Comparing, values, behaviors, institutions, and organizations across nations.* Beverly Hills, CA: Sage.

Hofstede, G., Hofstede, G. J., & Minkov, M. (2010). *Cultures and organizations: Software of the mind.* New York, NY: McGraw-Hill.

Kluckhohn, C. K. (1949). *Mirror for man: The relation of anthropology to modern life.* Berkeley, CA: Whittlesey House.

Kluckhohn, C. K. (1951). Values and value orientations in the theory of action. In T. Parsons and E. A. Shils (Eds.), *Toward a general theory of action.* Cambridge, MA: Harvard University Press.

Kluckhohn, F. R., & Strodtbeck, F. L. (1961). *Variations in value orientations.* Evanston, IL: Row, Peterson.

Kottak, C. P. (2011). *Window on humanity: A concise introduction to Anthropology.* New York: McGraw-Hill. Kroeber, A. L., & Kluckhohn, C. K. (1952). *Culture: A critical review of concepts and definitions.* Cambridge, MA: Peabody Museum.

Levi-Strauss, C. (1949). *Myth and meaning.* New York, NY: Schocken Books. Linton, R. (1955). *The tree of culture.* New York, NY: Alfred Knopf. Macionis, J. (2010). *Sociology.* New York, NY: Pearson Education.

Macionis, J., & Gerber, L. (2011) *Sociology.* New York, NY: Pearson Education.

McQuail, D. (2005). *McQuail's mass communication theory.* Beverly Hills, CA: Sage.

Mead, M. (1937). *Cooperation and competition among primitive peoples.* New York, NY: McGraw-Hill.

Morgan, M., & Shanahan, J. (2010). The state of cultivation research. *Journal of Broadcasting & Electronic Media, 54*(2), 337–355.

Parsons, T., & Shils, A. (Eds.). (1976). *Toward a general theory of action.* Cambridge, MA: Harvard University Press.

Rochon, T. (1998). *Culture moves: Ideas, activism, and changing values*. Princeton, NJ: Princeton University Press.

Russo, K. W. (Ed.). (2000). *Finding the middle ground: Insights and applications of the value orientations method*. Yarmouth, ME: Intercultural Press.

Russo, K., Hills, M.D. et al. (1984). *Value orientations in the Lumni Indian community and their commercial associates*. Report to the Lumni Indian Council. Bellingham, WA.

Schwartz, S. (Ed.). (1994). *Beyond individualism/collectivism: New cultural dimension of values*. Thousand Oaks, CA: Sage.

Schwartz, S., Melech, G., Lehmann, A., Burgess, S., Harris, M., & Owens, V. (2001). Extending the cross-validity of the theory of basic human values with a different method of measurement. *Journal of Cross-Cultural Psychology*, *32*(5), 519–542.

Scotton, J., & Hachten, W. (2008). *New media for a new China*. New York, NY: Wiley.

Steers, R., Nardon, L., & Sanchez-Runde, C. (2013). *Management across cultures: Developing global competencies*. Cambridge: Cambridge University Press.

Tajfel H., & Turner, J.C. (1986). The social identity theory of intergroup behavior. In S. Worchel & W.G. Austin (Eds.). *Psychology of intergroup relations* (pp. 7–24). Chicago, IL: Nelson-Hall.

Taylor, E. (1871). *Primitive culture*. London: John Murray.

Trompenaars, F., & Hampden-Turner, C. (1997). *Riding the waves of culture: Understanding diversity in global business*. (3rd ed.). New York, NY: McGraw-Hill.

Tunstall, J. (1977). *The media are American*. New York, NY: Columbia University Press.

Wood, A., & Smith, M. (2004). *Technology, identity, & culture*. New York, NY: Psychology Press.

READING 3.3

The Pressure to Cover

◆

From The *New York Times Magazine* By Kenji Yoshino

When I began teaching at Yale Law School in 1998, a friend spoke to me frankly. "You'll have a better chance at tenure," he said, "if you're a homosexual professional than if you're a professional homosexual." Out of the closet for six years at the time, I knew what he meant. To be a "homosexual professional" was to be a professor of constitutional law who "happened" to be gay. To be a "professional homosexual" was to be a gay professor who made gay rights his work. Others echoed the sentiment in less elegant formulations. Be gay, my world seemed to say. Be openly gay, if you want. But don't flaunt.

I didn't experience the advice as antigay. The law school is a vigorously tolerant place, embedded in a university famous for its gay student population. (As the undergraduate jingle goes: "One in four, maybe more/One in three, maybe me/One in two, maybe you.") I took my colleague's words as generic counsel to leave my personal life at home. I could see that research related to one's identity—referred to in the academy as "mesearch"— could raise legitimate questions about scholarly objectivity.

I also saw others playing down their outsider identities to blend into the mainstream. Female colleagues confided that they would avoid references to their children at work, lest they be seen as mothers first and scholars second. Conservative students asked for advice about how open they could be about their politics without suffering repercussions at some imagined future confirmation his intellect would be placed on a 25 percent discount. Many of us, it seemed, had to work our identities as well as our jobs.

It wasn't long before I found myself resisting the demand to conform. What bothered me was not that I had to engage in straight-acting behavior, much of which felt natural to me. What bothered me was the felt need to mute my passion for gay subjects, people, culture. At a time when the law was transforming gay rights, it seemed ludicrous not to suit up and get in the game.

"Mesearch" being what it is, I soon turned my scholarly attention to the pressure to conform. What puzzled me was that I felt that pressure so long after my emergence from the closet. When I stopped passing, I exulted that I could stop thinking about my sexuality. This proved naïve. Long after I came out, I still experienced the need to assimilate to straight norms. But I didn't have a word for this demand to tone down my known gayness.

Then I found my word, in the sociologist Erving Goffman's book "Stigma." Written in 1963, the book describes how various groups—including the disabled, the elderly and the obese—manage their "spoiled" identities. After discussing passing, Goffman observes that "persons who are ready to admit possession of a stigma … may nonetheless make a great effort to keep the stigma from looming large." He calls this behavior covering. He distinguishes passing from covering by noting that passing pertains to the visibility of a characteristic, while covering pertains to its obtrusiveness. He relates how F.D.R. stationed himself behind a desk before his advisers came in for meetings. Roosevelt was not passing, since everyone knew he used a wheelchair. He was covering, playing down his disability so people would focus on his more conventionally presidential qualities.

As is often the case when you learn a new idea, I began to perceive covering every-where. Leafing through a magazine, I read that Helen Keller replaced her natural eyes (one of which protruded) with brilliant blue glass ones. On the radio, I heard that Margaret Thatcher went to a voice coach to lower the pitch of her voice. Friends began to send me e-mail. Did I know that Martin Sheen was Ramon Estevez on his birth certificate, that Ben Kingsley was Krishna Bhanji, that Kirk Douglas was Issur Danielovitch Demsky and that Jon Stewart was Jonathan Leibowitz?

In those days, spotting instances of covering felt like a parlor game. It's hard to get worked up about how celebrities and politicians have to manage their public images. Jon Stewart joked that he changed his name because Leibowitz was "too Hollywood," and that seemed to get it exactly right. My own experience with covering was also not particularly difficult—once I had the courage to write from my passions, I was immediately embraced.

It was only when I looked for instances of covering in the law that I saw how lucky I had been. Civil rights case law is peopled with plaintiffs who were severely punished for daring to be openly different. Workers were fired for lapsing into Spanish in English-only workplaces, women were fired for behaving in stereotypically "feminine" ways and gay parents lost custody of their children for engaging in displays of same-sex affection. These cases revealed that far from being a parlor game, covering was the civil rights issue of our time.

The New Discrimination

In recent decades, discrimination in America has undergone a generational shift. Discrimination was once aimed at entire groups, resulting in the exclusion of all racial minorities, women, gays, religious minorities and people with disabilities. A battery of civil rights laws—like the Civil Rights Act of 1964 and the Americans with Disabilities Act of 1990—sought to combat these forms of discrimination. The triumph of American civil rights is that such categorical exclusions by the state or employers are now relatively rare.

Now a subtler form of discrimination has risen to take its place. This discrimination does not aim at groups as a whole. Rather, it aims at the subset of the group that refuses to cover, that is, to assimilate to dominant norms. And for the most part, existing civil rights laws do not protect individuals against such covering demands. The question of our time is whether we should understand this new discrimination to be a harm and, if so, whether the remedy is legal or social in nature.

Consider the following cases:

Renee Rogers, an African-American employee at American Airlines, wore cornrows to work. American had a grooming policy that prevented employees from wearing an all-braided hairstyle. When American sought to enforce this policy against Rogers, she filed suit, alleging race discrimination. In 1981, a federal district court rejected her argument. It first observed that cornrows were not distinctively associated with African-Americans, noting that Rogers had only adopted the hairstyle after it "had been popularized by a white actress in the film '10.'" As if recognizing the unpersuasiveness of what we might call the Bo Derek defense, the court further alleged that because hairstyle, unlike skin color, was a mutable characteristic, discrimination on the basis of grooming was not discrimination on the basis of race. Renee Rogers lost her case.

Lydia Mikus and Ismael Gonzalez were called for jury service in a case involving a defendant who was Latino. When the prosecutor asked them whether they could speak Spanish, they answered in the affirmative. The prosecutor struck them, and the defense attorney then brought suit on their behalf, claiming national-origin discrimination. The prosecutor responded that he had not removed the potential jurors for their ethnicity but for their ability to speak Spanish. His stated concern was that they would not defer to the court translator in listening to Spanish-language testimony. In 1991, the Supreme Court credited this argument. Lydia Mikus and Ismael Gonzalez lost their case.

Diana Piantanida had a child and took a maternity leave from her job at the Wyman Center, a charitable organization in Missouri. During her leave, she was demoted, supposedly for previously having handed in work late. The man who was then the Wyman Center's executive director, however, justified her demotion by saying the new position would be easier "for a new mom to handle." As it turned out, the new position had less responsibility and half the pay of the original one. But when Piantanida turned this position down, her successor was paid Piantanida's old salary. Piantanida brought suit, claiming she had been discharged as a "new mom." In 1997, a federal appellate court refused to analyze her claim as a sex-discrimination case, which would have led to comparing the treatment she received to the treatment of "new dads." Instead, it found that Piantanida's (admittedly vague) pleadings raised claims only under the Pregnancy Discrimination Act, which it correctly interpreted to protect women only while they are pregnant. Diana Piantanida lost her case.

Robin Shahar was a lesbian attorney who received a job offer from the Georgia Department of Law, where she had worked as a law student. The summer before she started her new job, Shahar had a religious same-sex commitment ceremony with her partner. She asked a supervisor for a late starting date because she was getting married and wanted to go on a celebratory trip to Greece. Believing Shahar was marrying a man, the supervisor offered his congratulations. Senior officials in the office soon learned, however, that Shahar's partner was a woman. This news caused a stir, reports of which reached Michael Bowers, the attorney general of Georgia who had successfully defended his state's prohibition of sodomy before the United States Supreme Court. After deliberating with his lawyers, Bowers rescinded her job offer. The staff member who informed her read from a script, concluding, "Thanks again for coming in, and have a nice day." Shahar brought suit, claiming discrimination on the basis of sexual orientation. In court, Bowers testified that he knew Shahar was gay when he hired her, and would never have terminated her for that reason. In 1997, a federal appellate court accepted that defense, maintaining that Bowers had terminated Shahar on the basis of her conduct, not her status. Robin Shahar lost her case.

Simcha Goldman, an Air Force officer who was also an ordained rabbi, wore a yarmulke at all times. Wearing a yarmulke is part of the Orthodox tradition of covering one's head out of deference to an omnipresent god. Goldman's religious observance ran afoul of an Air Force regulation that prohibited wearing headgear while indoors. When he refused his commanding officer's order to remove his yarmulke, Goldman was threatened with a court martial. He brought a First Amendment claim, alleging discrimination on the basis of religion. In 1986, the Supreme Court rejected his claim. It stated that the Air Force had drawn a reasonable line between "religious apparel that is visible and that which is not." Simcha Goldman lost his case.

These five cases represent only a fraction of those in which courts have refused to protect plaintiffs from covering demands. In such cases, the courts routinely distinguish between immutable and mutable traits, between being a member of a legally protected group and behavior associated with that group. Under this rule, African-Americans cannot be fired for their skin color, but they could be fired for wearing cornrows. Potential jurors cannot be struck for their ethnicity but can be struck for speaking (or even for admitting proficiency in) a foreign language. Women cannot be discharged for having two X chromosomes but can be penalized (in some jurisdictions) for becoming mothers. Although the weaker protections for sexual orientation mean gays can sometimes be fired for their status alone, they will be much more vulnerable if they are perceived to "flaunt" their sexuality. Jews cannot be separated from the military for being Jewish but can be discharged for wearing yarmulkes.

This distinction between being and doing reflects a bias toward assimilation. Courts will protect traits like skin color or chromosomes because such traits cannot be changed. In contrast, the courts will not protect mutable traits, because individuals can alter them to fade into the mainstream, thereby escaping discrimination. If individuals choose not to engage in that form of self-help, they must suffer the consequences.

The judicial bias toward assimilation will seem correct and just to many Americans. Assimilation, after all, is a precondition of civilization—wearing clothes, having manners and obeying the law are all acts of assimilation. Moreover, the tie between assimilation and American civilization may be particularly strong. At least since Hector St. John de Crèvecoeur's 1782 "Letters from an American Farmer," this country has promoted assimilation as the way Americans of different backgrounds would be "melted into a new race of men." By the time Israel Zangwill's play "The Melting Pot" made its debut in 1908, the term had acquired the burnish of an American ideal. Theodore Roosevelt, who believed hyphenations like "Polish-American" were a "moral treason," is reputed to have yelled, "That's a great play!" from his box when it was performed in Washington. (He was wrong—it's no accident the title has had a longer run than the play.) And notwithstanding challenges beginning in the 1960's to move "beyond the melting pot" and to "celebrate diversity," assimilation has never lost its grip on the American imagination.

If anything, recent years have seen a revival of the melting-pot ideal. We are currently experiencing a pluralism explosion in the United States. Patterns of immigration since the late 1960's have made the United States the most religiously various country in the history of the world. Even when the demographics of a group—like the number of individuals with disabilities—are presumably constant, the number of individuals claiming membership in that group may grow exponentially. In 1970, there were 9 disability-related associations listed in the Encyclopedia of Associations; in 1980, there were 16; in 1990, there were 211; and in 2000, there were 799. The boom in identity politics has led many thoughtful commentators to worry that we are losing our common culture as Americans. Fearful that we are breaking apart into balkanized fiefs, even liberal lions like Arthur Schlesinger have called for a recommitment to the ethic of assimilation.

Beyond keeping pace with the culture, the judiciary has institutional reasons for encouraging assimilation. In the yarmulke case, the government argued that ruling in favor of the rabbi's yarmulke would immediately invite suits concerning the Sikh's turban, the yogi's saffron robes and the Rastafarian's dreadlocks. Because the courts must articulate principled grounds for their decisions, they are particularly ill equipped to protect some groups but not others in an increasingly diverse society. Seeking to avoid judgments about the relative worth of groups, the judiciary has decided instead to rely on the relatively uncontroversial principle of protecting immutable traits.

Viewed in this light, the judiciary's failure to protect individuals against covering demands seems eminently reasonable. Unfortunately, it also represents an abdication of its responsibility to protect civil rights.

The Case Against Assimilation

The flaw in the judiciary's analysis is that it casts assimilation as an unadulterated good. Assimilation is implicitly characterized as the way in which groups can evade discrimination by fading into the mainstream—after all, the logic goes, if a bigot cannot discriminate between two individuals, he cannot discriminate against one of them. But sometimes assimilation is not an escape from discrimination, but precisely its effect. When a Jew is forced to convert to Protestantism, for instance, we do not celebrate that as an evasion of anti-Semitism. We should not blind ourselves to the dark underbelly of the American melting pot.

Take the cornrows case. Initially, this case appears to be an easy one for the employer, as hairstyle seems like such a trivial thing. But if hair is so trivial, we might ask why American Airlines made it a condition of Renee Rogers's employment. What's frustrating about the employment discrimination jurisprudence is that courts often don't force employers to answer the critical question of why they are requiring employees to cover. If we look to other sources, the answers can be troubling.

John T. Molloy's perennially popular self-help manual "New Dress for Success" also tells racial minorities to cover. Molloy advises African-Americans to avoid "Afro hairstyles" and to wear "conservative pinstripe suits, preferably with vests, accompanied by all the establishment symbols, including the Ivy League tie." He urges Latinos to "avoid pencil-line mustaches," "any hair tonic that tends to give a greasy or shiny look to the hair," "any articles of clothing that have Hispanic associations" and "anything that is very sharp or precise."

Molloy is equally frank about why covering is required. The "model of success," he says, is "white, Anglo-Saxon and Protestant." Those who do not possess these traits "will elicit a negative response to some degree, regardless of whether that response is conscious or subconscious." Indeed, Molloy says racial minorities must go "somewhat overboard" to compensate for immutable differences from the white mainstream. After conducting research on African-American corporate grooming, Molloy reports that "blacks had not only to dress more conservatively but also more expensively than their white counterparts if they wanted to have an equal impact."

Molloy's basic point is supported by social-science research. The economists Marianne Bertrand and Sendhil Mullainathan recently conducted a study in which they sent out résumés that were essentially identical except for the names at the top. They discovered that résumés with white-sounding names like Emily Walsh or Greg Baker drew 50 percent more callbacks than those with African-American-sounding names like Lakisha Washington or Jamal Jones. So it seems that even when Americans have collectively set our faces against racism, we still react negatively to cultural traits—like hairstyles, clothes or names—that we associate with historically disfavored races.

We can see a similar dynamic in the termination of Robin Shahar. Michael Bowers, the state attorney general, disavowed engaging in first-generation discrimination when he said he had no problem with gay employees. This raises the question of why he fired Shahar for having a religious same-sex commitment ceremony. Unlike American Airlines, Bowers provided some answers. He argued that retaining Shahar would compromise the department's ability to deny same-sex couples marriage licenses and to enforce sodomy statutes.

Neither argument survives scrutiny. At no point did Shahar seek to marry her partner legally, nor did she agitate for the legalization of same-sex marriage. The Georgia citizenry could not fairly have assumed that Shahar's religious ceremony would entitle the couple to a civil license. Bowers's claim that Shahar's wedding would compromise her ability to enforce sodomy statutes is also off the mark. Georgia's sodomy statute (which has since been struck down) punished cross-sex as well as same-sex sodomy, meaning that any heterosexual in the department who had ever had oral sex was as compromised as Shahar.

Stripped of these rationales, Bowers's termination of Shahar looks more sinister. When she told a supervisor she was getting married, he congratulated her. When he discovered she was marrying a woman, it wasn't long before she no longer had a job. Shahar's religious ceremony was not in itself indiscreet; cross-sex couples engage in such ceremonies all the time. If Shahar was flaunting anything, it was her belief in her own equality: her belief that she, and not the state, should determine what personal bonds are worthy of celebration.

The demand to cover is anything but trivial. It is the symbolic heartland of inequality—what reassures one group of its superiority to another. When dominant groups ask subordinated groups to cover, they are asking them to be small in the world, to forgo prerogatives that the dominant group has and therefore to forgo equality. If courts make critical goods like employment dependent on covering, they are legitimizing second-class citizenship for the subordinated group. In doing so, they are failing to vindicate the promise of civil rights.

So the covering demand presents a conundrum. The courts are right to be leery of intervening in too brusque a manner here, as they cannot risk playing favorites among groups. Yet they also cannot ignore the fact that the covering demand is where many forms of inequality continue to have life. We need a paradigm that gives both these concerns their due, adapting the aspirations of the civil rights movement to an increasingly pluralistic society.

The New Civil Rights

The new civil rights begins with the observation that everyone covers. When I lecture on covering, I often encounter what I think of as the "angry straight white man" reaction. A member of the audience, almost invariably a white man, almost invariably angry, denies that covering is a civil rights issue. Why shouldn't racial minorities or women or gays have to cover? These groups should receive legal protection against discrimination for things they cannot help. But why should they receive protection for behaviors within their control—wearing cornrows, acting "feminine" or flaunting their sexuality? After all, the questioner says, I have to cover all the time. I have to mute my depression, or my obesity, or my alcoholism, or my shyness, or my working-class background or my nameless anomie. I, too, am one of the mass of men leading lives of quiet desperation. Why should legally protected groups have a right to self-expression I do not? Why should my struggle for an authentic self matter less?

I surprise these individuals when I agree. Contemporary civil rights has erred in focusing solely on traditional civil rights groups—racial minorities, women, gays, religious minorities and people with disabilities. This assumes those in the so-called mainstream—those straight white men—do not also cover. They are understood only as obstacles, as people who prevent others from expressing themselves, rather than as individuals who are themselves struggling for self-definition. No wonder they often respond to civil rights advocates with hostility. They experience us as asking for an entitlement they themselves have been refused—an expression of their full humanity.

Civil rights must rise into a new, more inclusive register. That ascent makes use of the recognition that the mainstream is a myth. With respect to any particular identity, the word "mainstream" makes sense, as in the statement that straights are more mainstream than gays. Used generically, however, the word loses meaning. Because human beings hold many identities, the mainstream is a shifting coalition, and none of us are entirely within it. It is not normal to be completely normal.

This does not mean discrimination against racial minorities is the same as discrimination against poets. American civil rights law has correctly directed its concern toward certain groups and not others. But the aspiration of civil rights—the aspiration that we be free to develop our human capacities without the impediment of witless conformity—is an aspiration that extends beyond traditional civil rights groups.

To fulfill that aspiration, we must think differently both within the law and outside it. With respect to legal remedies, we must shift away from claims that demand equality for particular groups toward claims that demand liberty for us all. This is not an exhortation that we strip protections from currently recognized groups. Rather, it is a prediction that future courts will be unable to sustain a group-based vision of civil rights when faced with the broad and irreversible trend toward demographic pluralism. In an increasingly diverse society, the courts must look to what draws us together as citizens rather than to what drives us apart.

As if in recognition of that fact, the Supreme Court has moved in recent years away from extending protections on the basis of group membership and toward doing so on the basis of liberties we all possess. In 2003, the court struck down a Texas statute that prohibited same-sex sodomy. It did not, however, frame the case as one concerning the equality rights of gays. Instead, it cast the case as one concerning the interest we all—straight, gay or otherwise—have in controlling our intimate lives. Similarly, in 2004, the court held that a state could be required by a Congressional statute to make its courthouses wheelchair accessible. Again, the court ruled in favor of the minority group without framing its analysis in group-based equality rhetoric. Rather, it held that all people—disabled or otherwise—have a "right of access to the courts," which had been denied in that instance.

In these cases, the court implicitly acknowledged the national exhaustion with group-based identity politics and quieted the anxiety about pluralism that is driving us back toward the assimilative ideal. By emphasizing the interest all individuals have in our own liberty, the court focused on what unites us rather than on what divides us. While preserving the distinction between being and doing, the court decided to protect doing in its own right.

If the Supreme Court protects individuals against covering demands in the future, I believe it will do so by invoking the universal rights of people. I predict that if the court ever recognizes the right to speak a native language, it will protect that right as a liberty to which we are all entitled, rather than as a remedial concession granted to a particular national-origin group. If the court recognizes rights to grooming, like the right to wear cornrows, I believe it will do so under something akin to the German Constitution's right to personality rather than as a right attached to racial minorities. And I hope that if the court protects the right of gays to marry, it will do so by framing it as the right we all have to marry the person we love, rather than defending "gay marriage" as if it were a separate institution.

A liberty-based approach to civil rights, of course, brings its own complications, beginning with the question of where my liberty ends and yours begins. But the ability of liberty analysis to illuminate our common humanity should not be underestimated. This virtue persuaded both Martin Luther King Jr. and Malcolm X to argue for the transition from civil rights to human rights at the ends of their lives. It is time for American law to follow suit.

While I have great hopes for this new legal paradigm, I also believe law will play a relatively small part in the new civil rights. A doctor friend told me that in his first year of medical school, his dean described how doctors were powerless to cure the vast majority of human ills. People would get better, or they would not, but it would not be doctors who would cure them. Part of becoming a doctor, the dean said, was to surrender a layperson's awe for medical authority. I wished then that someone would give an analogous lecture to law students and to Americans at large. My education in law has been in no small part an education in its limitations.

As an initial matter, many covering demands are made by actors the law does not—and in my view should not—hold accountable, like friends, family, neighbors, the "culture" or individuals themselves. When I think of the covering demands I have experienced, I can trace many of them only to my own censorious consciousness. And while I am often tempted to sue myself, I recognize this is not my healthiest impulse.

Law is also an incomplete solution to coerced assimilation because it has yet to recognize the myriad groups that are subjected to covering demands even though these groups cannot be defined by traditional classifications like race, sex, orientation, religion and disability. Whenever I speak about covering, I receive new instances of identities that can be covered. The law may someday move to protect some of these identities. But it will never protect them all.

For these and other reasons, I am troubled that Americans seem increasingly inclined to turn toward the law to do the work of civil rights precisely when they should be turning away from it. The primary solution lies in all of us as citizens, not in the tiny subset of us who are lawyers. People confronted with demands to cover should feel emboldened to seek a reason for that demand, even if the law does not reach the actors making the demand or recognize the group burdened by it. These reason-forcing conversations should happen outside courtrooms—in public squares and prayer circles, in workplaces and on playgrounds. They should occur informally and intimately, in the everyday places where tolerance is made and unmade.

What will constitute a good-enough reason to justify assimilation will obviously be controversial. We have come to some consensus that certain reasons are illegitimate—like racism, sexism or religious intolerance. Beyond that, we should expect conversations rather than foreordained results—what reasons count, and for what purposes, will be for us all to decide by facing one another as citizens. My personal inclination is always to privilege the claims of the individual against countervailing interests like "neatness" or "workplace harmony." But we should have that conversation.

Such conversations are the best—and perhaps the only—way to give both assimilation and authenticity their due. They will help us alleviate conservative alarmists' fears of a balkanized America and radical multiculturalists' fears of a monocultural America. The aspiration of civil rights has always been to permit people to pursue their human flourishing without limitations based on bias.

Focusing on law prevents us from seeing the revolutionary breadth of that aspiration. It is only when we leave the law that civil rights suddenly stops being about particular agents of oppression and particular victimized groups and starts to become a project of human flourishing in which we all have a stake.

I don't teach classes on gay rights any more. I suspect many of my students now experience me as a homosexual professional rather than as a professional homosexual, if they think of me in such terms at all. But I don't experience myself as covering. I've just moved on to other interests, in the way scholars do. So the same behavior—not teaching gay rights—has changed in meaning over time.

This just brings home to me that the only right I have wanted with any consistency is the freedom to be who I am. I'll be the first to admit that I owe much of that freedom to group-based equality movements, like the gay rights movement. But it is now time for us as a nation to shift the emphasis away from equality and toward liberty in our debates about identity politics. Only through such freedom can we live our lives as works in progress, which is to say, as the complex, changeful and contradictory creatures that we are.

chapter *four*

Introduction

This chapter begins with a reading that reminds us that we have all felt as though there were parts of ourselves that we need to keep hidden from others, that are in some way just "not good enough." Too often, when we talk about diversity, the tension tends to place us in a defensive, "us vs. them" mentality. This is not only unpleasant, it's not productive. We can't learn from someone else, or them from us, if we can't hear each other. It's always important to remember that the purpose of developing our diversity consciousness is so that we can help create a world in which we can each be our best, authentic selves.

The two readings focus on a perennial controversial issue when discussing diversity: race. The readings were selected for a few reasons, and remembering them as you read will help you as you work through your research project as well as when you're working on developing your cultural competency. The readings, though both about race, also provide great examples and explanations of theories that are applicable as you interrogate other aspects of your own identity and, thus, your research project. There has been, and continues to be, much written about race, because it's a conversation we've been trying to have for hundreds of years. Though each facet of your identity, and the sociocultural implications of it, has its own unique aspects, all civil rights movements (those that have advanced the rights of marginalized and/ or oppressed groups) have their roots in the Civil Rights movement (the movement that advanced the rights of African Americans in the 1950s–1960s). Race was the first of many difficult conversations we, as a society, attempted to have, and many of the lessons we learned in that conversation can also be useful in other difficult conversations. As you read the second of the two readings, try to remember that race is not the only important aspect of your identity, nor is it the only important conversation our society is engaged in as we grow into an ever more aware and competent society.

READING 4.1

What is White Privilege?

◆

from *Anti-Racist Teaching* By Richard P. Amico

White privilege is a form of domination, hence it is a *relational* concept.[1] It positions one person or group over another person or group. It is a concept of racial domination that enables us to see this relationship from the perspective of those who benefit from such domination. Traditionally in the United States, racial domination has been portrayed as discrimination against people of color—that is, from the perspective of those who are disadvantaged by such domination. But you can't have one without the other—you can't have racial domination and disadvantage without racial dominators who are advantaged. This is the insight of Peggy McIntosh's seminal paper "White Privilege and Male Privilege: A Personal Account of Coming to See Correspondences through Work in Women's Studies": "As a white person, I realized I had been taught about racism as something which puts others at a disadvantage, but had been taught not to see one of its corollary aspects, white privilege, which puts me at an advantage."[2]

As a white male, I know what Peggy McIntosh is talking about. What we are taught to see and not see shapes our view of the world—of what is real. My education through high school, college, and graduate school never included any discussion of white privilege and only discussed racism as a historical phenomenon, something that happened to people of color centuries ago.

Personal Anecdote

I remember watching television with my family in September 1957. I was ten years old and in the fifth grade. President Dwight D. Eisenhower had ordered the 101st Airborne Division of the US Army to Little Rock, Arkansas, to enforce the integration of Central

High School and protect the nine black students enrolled that fall. My parents, like many whites at that time, thought that these black students were "troublemakers" who were trying to force themselves on people who didn't want to associate with them. They saw these black students as encroachers on "regular" people's freedom of association. I remember seeing the faces of all the angry white parents standing behind the line of troops and shouting racial epithets at these nine black children. I remember my parents making derogatory comments about African Americans that day and for many years after and telling me that people should "stick to their own kind." They made it clear to me that they did not approve of integration and wanted me to keep my distance from blacks. Three years after the *Brown v. Board of Education* decision, "separate but equal" was the prevailing norm in the world I inhabited. I believed my parents and parroted their views throughout my childhood—their view was my view. And white privilege was not even on the radar.

The natural question that arises from the introduction of the concept of white privilege is, What exactly are these advantages that white people enjoy at the expense and to the detriment of people of color? Since we whites have not been taught to see such advantages, we generally do not. Peggy McIntosh came to see some of her advantages as a white person through first understanding some of her disadvantages as a woman and observing men's inability or unwillingness to recognize their advantages as men: "I have often noticed men's unwillingness to grant that they are over-privileged in the curriculum, even though they may grant that women are disadvantaged. Denials, which amount to taboos, surround the subject of advantages, which men gain from women's disadvantages. These denials protect male privilege from being fully recognized, acknowledged, lessened, or ended."[3]

Again, as a male I know what Peggy McIntosh is talking about. For much of my life I believed that "it's a man's world" because we men deserve to be on top. We are simply better at certain things than women. The idea that we men are privileged was, in my view, "sour grapes" from women who couldn't make the grade. This unwillingness to acknowledge any male privilege is deeply connected to the American myth of meritocracy, which maintains that all advantage in society is based on merit. Some have more than others because they have earned it through hard work, perseverance, and right living. And conversely, those who have less have only themselves to blame. The idea that even some of my advantages are unearned and undeserved and are a function of my status as a male was in my mind, for many years, preposterous and unfounded. But the idea that we live in a meritocracy in the United States is a myth because it has proven to be inconsistent with sociological fact. Structured inequality would be impossible in a meritocracy. Those of every "race," ethnicity, and gender who worked hard, persevered, and lived right would excel in a meritocracy. Yet we have serious structured inequalities along racial, ethnic, and gender lines.[4]

White privilege and male privilege have the common feature that, in both cases, those who are advantaged cannot see their own advantage, although they can see that others are disadvantaged, and those who are privileged tend to fault those who are disadvantaged for their disadvantage. Conversely, those who are disadvantaged can see that they are disadvantaged and that some are advantaged, and they can see that both their disadvantage and the advantages of those who are privileged are unearned and undeserved. Ironically, then, those who enjoy privileges are epistemically disadvantaged, while those who are disadvantaged are epistemically advantaged! Hence, listening to someone who is epistemically advantaged due to her social disadvantage makes sense. The following anecdote illustrates my point.

Personal Anecdote

Many years ago I was settling down with my partner to enjoy a TV movie at home. It was an action-adventure film, and I was excited to watch it. As we began to watch, my partner started to get agitated and said to me, "I am so sick and tired of watching television! Every time I turn it on, all I see is women being victimized, women being brutalized, women being assaulted sexually, women portrayed as stupid, helpless bimbos, as sexual objects! I can't watch another minute!" With that, she left the room. A lot of thoughts went through my mind all at once, and they were all dismissive and condescending: What's the matter with her? Is she having her period? Did she have a bad day? Something must have happened because this is a really good movie. I am embarrassed to reveal those thoughts even now. But although I discounted everything she said, I started to click the remote control (of course, I was always the one to hold the remote, to control the TV) to see what was on other channels. To my surprise I found quite a few programs showing women just the way my partner had described! At that point I could not have admitted this to her, but I did let it sink in. I wondered why I had never noticed it before. I am an educated, observant person; yet I was oblivious to what was obvious to her. That is how I understand epistemic disadvantage and advantage now.

Through comparative analysis with male privilege, Peggy McIntosh reached the following explanation of white privilege: "I have come to see white privilege as an invisible package of unearned assets, which I can count on cashing in each day, but about which I was 'meant' to remain oblivious. White privilege is like an invisible weightless backpack of special provisions, maps, passports, codebooks, visas, clothes, tools and blank checks."[5] After months of reflection McIntosh was able to list forty-six such advantages she enjoys as a white person. They include items like the following:

> #13. Whether I use checks, credit cards, or cash, I can count on my skin color not to work against the appearance of financial reliability.

> #15. I do not have to educate my children to be aware of systemic racism for their own daily physical protection.

#21. I am never asked to speak for all the people of my racial group.

#25. If a traffic cop pulls me over or if the IRS audits my tax return,
I can be sure I haven't been singled out because of my race.[6]

For those of us who enjoy one form of privilege or another (e.g., race, gender, sexual orientation, socioeconomic class, ability, age, religion), why don't we feel privileged? As sociologist Allan Johnson explains, privilege attaches itself to social categories, not individuals.[7] So society values whiteness, not a particular person who is white; it values maleness, not a particular person who is male; it values heterosexuality, not any particular person who is heterosexual, and so forth. Hence, the perception that someone is white or male or heterosexual may be sufficient for that person to receive the privilege attached to that social category. And conversely, the perception that someone belongs to a social category that is disvalued in society may cause that person to receive the disadvantages attached to that category. So paradoxically, perception is more important than truth when it comes to who is advantaged and who is disadvantaged in society. How others perceive me may determine whether I am stopped by the police while driving my car, whether I am hired for a job, or whether I am followed in a department store by security. Because privilege does not attach itself to individuals for who they are, I may be privileged without feeling privileged. If I were a king, I would be privileged and feel privileged for who I was. But the kind of privilege we are talking about here is not like that. And the same holds true for disadvantage. Society disvalues certain social categories, and disadvantage attaches to them. Hence, it is possible to be disadvantaged without feeling disadvantaged.

Perception and Truth

Earlier I said that perception is more important than truth, and that may have given the impression that there is a truth to the matter of whether the social category actually applies to a particular individual. Is the individual actually white? Well, the question itself presupposes that there is such a thing as actual whiteness, and there is not. We have learned from biology and history that "race" is a social construction; it is not a biologically real category. There is as much or more genetic variation between any two individuals of the same so-called race as there is between two individuals of two different so-called races.[8] In the late seventeenth century, wealthy, landowning, Christian men who invaded this land created the category of "race" based on superficial differences in skin tone and hair texture for the purpose of exploitation and permanent domination.[9] These men created social systems and institutions (e.g., laws, rules, practices, value systems) to reify "racial" difference and continually empower some and disempower others on the basis of this constructed "difference." Hence "race" is a social rather than a biological reality.

Many of the social categories surrounding privilege and oppression—gender, sexual orientation, socioeconomic class, ability, and disability—are largely social constructions.

To be sure, there are real differences between people, but we define the social categories, and we assign meaning to those differences. For example, on the face of it, it would seem that nothing is more clear-cut than whether a person is male or female, whether a baby is born a boy or a girl. After all, that is the first question most ask when a baby is born: Is it a boy or a girl? But the experiences of many people born intersexed have led us to understand that whether someone is born a boy or a girl is a matter of definition. Some are born neither. Some are born both. Some simply defy such categorization and force us to realize that this scheme of categorization is a human invention. Some cultures recognize that a binary system of categorization is inadequate and have multiple categories within which to understand gender. Both sex and gender are more complicated than our binary categories allow.[10]

Systemic Privilege: What Does It Look Like?

Understanding the relational nature of white privilege helps us see that white racism and white privilege are two sides of the same coin. Whereas some are undeservedly disadvantaged because they are perceived to be of color, others are undeservedly advantaged because they are perceived to be white. Here are a few examples to illustrate the ubiquity and systemic nature of white privilege.[11]

The Job Market

Tim Wise writes that a 2003 Milwaukee study

> had young black and white male job testers who were otherwise equally qualified apply for jobs in the metropolitan area. Some of the whites and some of the blacks claimed to have criminal records and to have served eighteen months in prison for possession of drugs with intent to distribute, while other whites and blacks presented themselves as having no prior criminal convictions. Whites without records received callbacks for interviews thirty-four percent of the time, compared to only fourteen percent for blacks, and whites with criminal records received callbacks seventeen percent of the time, compared to only five percent for blacks with records. So whites without records were 2.4 times more likely than comparable blacks

to receive an interview, and whites with criminal records were 3.4 times more likely to receive a callback than similar blacks. So, at seventeen percent, whites with prior drug convictions were more likely than blacks without records (at fourteen percent) to be called back for an interview, even when all other credentials were equal.[12]

This study reveals the systemic nature of white privilege and white racism. Without the study a person looking for a job would only know that he either did or did not get a callback. From his experience alone, he would have no evidence that he was either privileged or disadvantaged because of his perceived race. The systemic nature of white privilege and white racism explains, in part, why those who receive such privilege are not aware of it and why those who are disadvantaged may not know it. From the outside it simply looks like one person got a callback and another did not. White privilege is embedded in the values, beliefs, and practices of those who are hiring. Even though it is illegal to discriminate in employment on the basis of perceived race, the practice is alive and well, but hidden. Only those explicitly looking for evidence of white privilege will find it.

Housing

In December 2011 Bank of America's Countrywide Financial agreed to pay $335 million to settle a lawsuit claiming it discriminated against black and Latino borrowers. The Justice Department alleged that Countrywide charged a higher interest rate on the mortgages of more than two hundred thousand minority borrowers, despite the fact that their creditworthiness was comparable to whites that received lower rates. The Justice Department called it the "largest residential fair lending settlement in history." According to the Center for Responsible Lending, borrowers of color are twice as likely to receive subprime loans than their white counterparts, and once the housing bubble burst, borrowers of color were more than twice as likely to lose their homes as white households.[13]

Subprime loans are five times more likely in black neighborhoods than in white neighborhoods. In predominantly black neighborhoods, high-cost subprime lending accounted for 51 percent of home loans in 1998—compared with only 9 percent in predominately white areas. Comparable 1993 figures were 8 percent in black neighborhoods and 1 percent in white neighborhoods. Homeowners in high-income black neighborhoods are twice as likely as homeowners in low-income white neighborhoods to have subprime loans. Only 6 percent of homeowners in upper-income white neighborhoods have subprime loans, while 39 percent of homeowners in upper-income black neighborhoods have subprime loans, more than twice the 18 percent rate for homeowners in low-income white neighborhoods.[14]

Again, without the studies, lawsuits, and statistics, we would be unable to see the systemic nature of white privilege and white racism. To the individual person pursuing a home mortgage loan, it either seems easy to obtain a prime lending rate or impossible. The white person who receives a prime mortgage loan will have no reason to think she or he is being privileged, and the person of color who receives the subprime rate may or may not understand that she or he is being discriminated against on the basis of perceived race.

Environment

A 1992 study by staff writers for the *National Law Journal* examined the Environmental Protection Agency's response to 1,177 toxic-waste cases and found that polluters of sites near the greatest white population received penalties 500 percent higher than polluters in minority areas—fines averaged $335,566 for white areas contrasted with $55,318 for minority areas. Income did not account for these differences. The penalties for violating all federal environmental laws regulating air, water, and waste pollution were 46 percent lower in minority communities than in white communities.[15]

Race has been found to be an independent factor, not reducible to class, in predicting exposure to a broad range of environmental hazards, including polluted air, contaminated fish, lead poisoning, municipal landfills, incinerators, and toxic-waste dumps.[16]

What white person would feel privileged not to live near toxic-waste dumps, breathe polluted air, or ingest chemicals that make people sick? Who would take the time and energy to investigate where toxic-waste dumps and incinerators are located if those facilities are not near one's neighborhood? As a white person, the first time I heard the term "environmental racism" I had no idea what it meant.

Health

On average white Americans live 5.5 years longer than black Americans do. Blacks die from stroke 41 percent more often than whites, from heart disease 30 percent more often, and from cancer

25 percent more often. Asians, Pacific Islanders, and Hispanics all have lower heart disease rates than whites.

During the 1980s federal government researchers came up with a new way to measure "excess deaths" (i.e., deaths that would not have occurred if a minority population's mortality rate had been the same as the white population's). By that standard there were sixty-six thousand "excess deaths" of African Americans in 1940 and roughly one hundred thousand in 1999. That is the equivalent of one plane crash—with no survivors—occurring every day of the year.[17]

One can begin to see how multiple disadvantages compound the effects of each disadvantage and multiple privileges have a synergistic positive effect on those who receive them. It can begin to look like the "natural order" of things, but it is not. It is the result of interlocking systems of privilege and disadvantage in every aspect of life that maintain white supremacy and domination.

Law Enforcement and Crime

In New York City, from 1997 to 1998, the Street Crimes Unit of the New York Police Department (NYPD) stopped and frisked 135,000 people, 85 percent of whom were people of color. Only 4,500 persons were ultimately arrested and prosecuted, meaning that over 95 percent of those harassed were innocent. Interestingly, whites who were stopped were significantly more likely to be found with drugs or other contraband, indicating not only that this policy of racial stops and searches was biased but that it failed the test as valid crime control on its own merits as well.[18]

A federal judge ruled on August 12, 2013, that the NYPD had violated the civil rights of New Yorkers with its broad "stop-and-frisk" policy. US District Court Judge Shira Scheindlin called for an independent monitor to oversee major changes to the policy. She did not end the policy, however, instead saying that an independent monitor would develop an initial set of reforms, as well as provide training, supervision, monitoring, and discipline. "The city's highest officials have turned a blind eye to the evidence that officers are conducting stops in a racially discriminatory manner," she wrote in a lengthy opinion. "In their zeal to defend a policy that they believe to be effective, they have willfully ignored overwhelming proof that the policy of targeting 'the right people' is racially discriminatory." Police brass had received warnings since at least 1999 that officers were violating rights, she said. "Despite this notice, they deliberately maintained and even escalated policies and practices that predictably resulted in even more widespread Fourth Amendment violations."[19]

Criminal Procedure Law § 140.50 (the stop-and-frisk law) became effective on September 1, 1971. That means that for more than forty years, it has been the law in New York City. According to the statistic cited above, in one year (1997–1998) NYPD officers stopped 135,000 people, 85 percent of whom were people of color—that is approximately 115,000 people of color stopped in one year. If we multiply that number by forty-three years (as of the time of this writing in 2014) we get just under 5 million people of color! I cannot verify the total number of people of color affected by this policy, but the *New York Times* reported in 2014, "At the height of the program, in the first quarter of 2012, the police stopped people—mostly black and Latino men—on more than 200,000 occasions. A vast majority of those stopped were found to have done nothing wrong."[20] That is at least two hundred thousand people stopped in three months! These policies and practices are known to be ineffective as law enforcement tools to fight crime. What white person living in New York City thinks that not being stopped and frisked on her or his way to work is a privilege? Yet it is.

Government Policies

Beginning in the 1930s the federal government began offering low-interest, taxpayer-guaranteed, underwritten loans through the Federal Housing Administration (FHA). Between the 1930s and the 1960s, more than $100 billion in home equity was loaned through these housing initiatives, boosting the overall rate of home ownership from 44 percent in 1934 to 66 percent in 1969. But loans went almost exclusively to white families. The Home Ownership Lending Corporation made it clear that these preferential loans were off-limits to people who lived in "declining" neighborhoods (every black neighborhood was rated as declining) and that loans were also to be denied to anyone whose receipt of the loan would result in a reduction in a neighborhood's racial homogeneity. The FHA underwriting manual stated to lenders, "If a neighborhood is to retain stability, it is necessary that properties shall continue to be occupied by the same social and racial classes." As a result of these policies, 27 million of the 28 million Americans who moved into suburban areas from 1950 until 1966 were white.[21]

The government, through the FHA, set up a national neighborhood appraisal system, explicitly tying mortgage eligibility to race.

Integrated communities were deemed a financial risk ipso facto and made ineligible for home loans, a policy known today as "redlining." Between 1934 and 1962, the federal government backed $120 billion in home loans. More than 98 percent went to whites. Of the 350,000 new homes built with federal support in northern California between 1946 and 1960, fewer than 100 went to African Americans.[22]

These governmental policies and practices continue to affect the relative wealth of whites compared to African Americans and Latinos. The privileges of parents and grandparents get passed down to children, grandchildren, and great-grandchildren in the form of inherited wealth, giving each generation an ever-increasing advantage. How many whites today think of the FHA loans their grandparents received as an example of white privilege? Yet they are.

Education

The average black student attends a school with twice as many low-income students as the typical white youth, and schools that are mostly attended by black and Latino students are more than ten times as likely as mostly white schools to have concentrated levels of student poverty. Even black kids with family incomes higher than those of whites are more likely to attend schools with concentrated poverty levels.[23]

High-poverty schools (disproportionately serving a large number of students of color) have, on average, three times as many uncertified teachers or teachers who are teaching outside their field of study as teachers serving low-poverty and mostly white schools.[24]

Even when their prior performance would justify higher placement, students of color are still significantly less likely to be given honors or advanced-placement opportunities than whites, even when white students have lower grades or test scores. While this may be partly due to teacher bias, it is also the result of systematic inequity: schools serving mostly white students offer about three times as many advanced-level courses as schools serving mostly students of color. Thus, even in the total absence of racial bias on the part of school officials, the lack of certain course offerings deprives capable and hardworking students of color of opportunities available to their white counterparts.[25]

Because it is a policy and practice to fund public schools through property taxes, and because white students generally live in more affluent communities due in part to the practice of "redlining" cited above (which is responsible for much of the residential segregation in the United States), white students are again privileged from preschool and kindergarten all the way through their higher education. The educational, legal, housing, health-care, law enforcement, employment, and environmental policy systems all interlock to create a white hegemony in which we live and breathe, without noticing it so long as we are its beneficiaries—so long as we whites are breathing the clean air, drinking the clear water, attending the "good" schools, landing the best jobs, getting the prime loans, not being harassed by police, and living longer with fewer diseases—as long as we are on top! This is what white privilege looks like.

Personal Anecdote

I graduated from the University of Massachusetts, Amherst, in 1970 with a bachelor's degree in philosophy. After graduation I traveled to Los Angeles, California, and took a job in a Danish restaurant as a sandwich preparer. I didn't yet know what I wanted to do as a career, so cooking was a useful way to make money while I figured that out. While I had experience working in restaurants, I'd never worked in a Danish restaurant, and I had a lot to learn about that. I worked alongside two Mexican guys who had been at the restaurant for a couple of years and knew the routine backward and forward. They were incredibly fast and skilled at their job and taught me how to prepare for and keep pace with a very busy luncheon service. I knew nothing about the lived experiences of Mexican people in Los Angeles. I was naive. After a month or two, I sensed that they resented me, and I didn't know why. Had I done something to offend them? There was a clear tension and hostility in our working environment, and I felt that hostility directed at me. The hostility finally came to a head with an argument between them and me. Management stepped in to quell the tempers. Why were they being so critical of my work? Why were they so belligerent? I had improved my speed since I started. Many of their verbal assaults were in Spanish, and I did not understand what they were saying. I only felt their anger. The manager, who was the daughter of the Danish couple who owned the restaurant, asked me if I had told my two coworkers how much I was being paid. I said yes; they had asked me one day, and I had told them. I still didn't get it. She told me not to discuss my salary with anyone. I wasn't being paid a lot, given the experience I had going into the restaurant, but my two Mexican coworkers, I found out, were being paid a lot less than I, even though they were more experienced and more skilled and had been on that job much longer than I had. I was surprised. My first thought was, Why would they work for so little? I wouldn't. And then I thought, Well, that's their problem, not mine! I've got my fair salary! That is white privilege.

Summary

White privilege is a form of domination—it positions one group of people over another group. It is a relational concept that enables us to see clearly that some benefit and others suffer from racial oppression (racism). Both racial oppression and white privilege are two sides of the same coin; you cannot have one without the other. And both racial oppression and white privilege attach to social categories, not individuals. They describe how systems operate to benefit some and disadvantage others on the basis of perceived group membership (white or of color).

This reading provides but a few examples of how our American social system manifests systemic white privilege and racial oppression of people of color. Once we begin to look at the extent of this system-wide domination, more and more features appear. As Joe Feagin explains, "Systemic racism encompasses a broad range of white-racist dimensions: racist ideology, attitudes, emotions, habits, actions, and institutions of whites in this society. Systemic racism is far more than a matter of racial prejudice and individual bigotry. It is a material, social and ideological reality that is well-imbedded in major U.S. institutions."[26] [...]

ENDNOTES

1. Gary R. Howard, *We Can't Teach What We Don't Know: White Teachers, Multiracial Schools*, 2nd ed. (New York: Teachers College Press, 2006), 67.

2. Peggy McIntosh, "White Privilege and Male Privilege: A Personal Account of Coming to See Correspondences through Work in Women's Studies" (Working Paper 189, Wellesley College, 1988).

3. Ibid., 1.

4. See Adalberto Aguirre Jr. and David V. Baker, *Structured Inequality in the United States: Critical Discussions on the Continuing Significance of Race, Ethnicity, and Gender*, 2nd ed. (Upper Saddle River, NJ: Pearson Prentice Hall, 2008).

5. Peggy McIntosh, "White Privilege: Unpacking the Invisible Backpack," *Peace and Freedom* (July/August 1989).

6. McIntosh, "White Privilege and Male Privilege."

7. Allan G. Johnson, *Privilege, Power, and Difference*, 2nd ed. (New York: McGraw-Hill, 2006), 34–37.

8. See Christine Herbes-Sommers, dir., *Race: The Power of an Illusion*, Part 1 (San Francisco: California Newsreel, 2003), for an explanation of the work of evolutionary biologist Richard Lewontin, or see R. C. Lewontin, "The Apportionment of Human Diversity," *Evolutionary Biology* 6 (1972): 381–398.

9. See Ronald Takaki, *A Different Mirror: A History of Multicultural America*, rev. ed. (New York: Little, Brown and Co., 2008); Theodore W. Allen, *The Invention of the White Race*, Vol. 2: *The Origin of Racial Oppression in Anglo-America* (New York: Verso, 1997); Richard Delgado and Jean Stefancic, eds., *Critical White Studies* (Philadelphia: Temple University Press, 1997).

10. See Anne Fausto-Sterling, "The Five Sexes: Why Male and Female Are Not Enough," *Sciences* (March/April 1993): 20–24; Anne Fausto-Sterling, "The Five Sexes Revisited," in *Women's Voices, Feminist Visions*, ed. Susan Shaw and Janet Lee, 5th ed. (New York: McGraw-Hill, 2012), 121–125.

11. In fact I provide my students with a twenty-three-page, single-spaced, documented handout listing hundreds of such examples.

12. Tim Wise, *Affirmative Action: Racial Preference in Black and White* (New York: Routledge, 2005), 21, cited in Devah Pager, "The Mark of a Criminal Record," *American Journal of Sociology* 108, no. 5 (March 2003): 937–975.

13. Eyder Peralta, "BofA's Countrywide to Pay $335 Million, Settling Lending Discrimination Case," *The Two-Way*, December 21, 2011, www.npr.org/blogs /thetwo-way/2011/12/21/144083080/ bofas-countrywide-will-pay-335-million-in-lending-discrimination-case.

14. US Department of Housing and Urban Development, "Unequal Burden: Income and Racial Disparities in Subprime Lending in America," HUD User, http:// www.huduser.org/Publications/pdf/unequal_full.pdf.

15. George Lipsitz, *The Possessive Investment in Whiteness* (Philadelphia: Temple University Press, 1998), 8. Also see John R. Logan and Harvey Molotch, *Urban Fortunes: The Political Economy of Place* (Berkeley: University of California Press, 1987), 113.

16. Lipsitz, *The Possessive Investment*, 9. See also Robert D. Bullard, "Anatomy of Environmental Racism and the Environmental Justice Movement," in *Confronting Environmental Racism: Voices from the Grassroots*, ed. Robert D. Bullard (Boston: South End Press, 1993), 15–39.

17. David R. Williams and James Lardner, "Cold Truths about Class, Race and Health," in *Inequality Matters*, ed. James Lardner and David A. Smith (New York: The New Press, 2005), 105.

18. Tim Wise, "See No Evil," Tim Wise, August 2, 2001, http://www.timwise .org/2001/08/see-no-evil-perception-and-reality-in-black-and-white, originally published as a ZNet Commentary.

19. "Judge Rules NYPD's 'Stop-and-Frisk' Policy Violates Rights," Fox News, August 12, 2013, http://www. foxnews.com/politics/2013/08/12/judge-rules-nypd-stop-and-frisk-policy-violates-rights.

20. Benjamin Weiser and Joseph Goldstein, "Mayor Says New York City Will Settle Suits on Stop-and-Frisk Tactics," *New York Times*, January 30, 2014, http://www.nytimes.com/2014/01/31/nyregion/de-blasio-stop-and-frisk.html.

21. Wise, *Affirmative Action*, 31–32. For a detailed analysis of the FHA and Veterans Administration loan programs and how they discriminated racially, see Douglas Massey and Nancy Denton, *American Apartheid: Segregation and the Making of the Underclass* (Cambridge, MA: Harvard University Press, 1993); Melvin L. Oliver and Thomas Shapiro, *Black Wealth, White Wealth: A New Perspective on Racial Inequality* (New York: Routledge, 1997); Michael K. Brown et al., *Whitewashing Race: The Myth of a Color-Blind Society* (Berkeley: University of California Press, 2003); Leonard Steinhorn and Barbara Diggs-Brown, *By the Color of Our Skin: The Illusion of Integration and the Reality of Race* (New York: Dutton, 1999), 95–96.

22. Herbes-Sommers, *Race*.

23. Judith R. Blau, *Race in the Schools: Perpetuating White Dominance?* (Boulder, CO: Lynne Rienner, 2003), 48; Gary Orfield et al., "Deepening Segregation in American Public Schools: A Special Report from the Harvard Project on School Desegregation," *Equity and Excellence in Education* 30 (1997): 5–24; Gary Orfield and John T. Yun, "Resegregation in American Schools," eScholarship, June 6, 1999, http://escholarship.org/ uc/item/6d01084d; Massey and Denton, *American Apartheid*, 153.

24. Deborah L. McKoy and Jeffrey M. Vincent, "Housing and Education: The Inextricable Link," in *Segregation: The Rising Costs for America*, ed. James H. Carr and Nandinee K. Kutty (New York: Routledge, 2008), 128.

25. Rebecca Gordon, *Education and Race* (Oakland, CA: Applied Research Center, 1998), 48–49; Claude S. Fischer et al., *Inequality by Design: Cracking the Bell Curve Myth* (Princeton, NJ: Princeton University Press, 1996), 164–165; Steinhorn and Diggs-Brown, *By the Color of Our Skin*, 47; Gary Orfield and Susan Eaton, *Dismantling Desegregation: The Quiet Reversal of Brown v. Board of Education* (New York: The New Press, 1996), 68.

26. Joe R. Feagin, *Systemic Racism: A Theory of Oppression* (New York: Routledge, 2006), 2.

READING 4.2

White Privilege: The Other Side of Racism

◆

from *Recognizing Race and Ethnicity: Power, Privilege,
and Inequality* By Kathleen Fitzgerald

Part of white privilege involves the treatment of white people as individuals, without all of their actions' being attributed to their membership in a racial group or reflecting on other members of a racial group. An example of white privilege involves media treatment of terrorists or mass murderers. When a white Norwegian man, Anders Behring Breivik, murdered seventy-seven people on July 22, 2011, the media immediately declared him a "lone wolf." The lone-wolf theory implies that this heinous act was committed by a deranged or evil individual, but was not the result of the radical ideologies of some larger group he may be connected to. While we may never fully understand why Breivik committed this horrendous act, the important point for our discussion is that all white people were not implicated by his actions. On the contrary, terrorist acts committed by Muslims result in the extension of collective guilt to the entire Muslim community (Chen 2011). Muslim community leaders are forced to denounce such radical actions and to defend their community and their religion. Similarly, African Americans experience a collective shaming when a mass murderer is found to be black, such as the case of the DC sniper in October 2002. When the news reported the arrest of the DC sniper and it turned out he was a black man, all black people were shamed by his individual actions (Harris Perry 2011). His actions were at least partially interpreted as if they were connected to his blackness.

How are these examples of white privilege? White people have the privilege of being treated as individuals, whose actions are not a reflection of their whiteness. Most mass murderers, for instance, have been white. Yet white Americans do not feel a collective guilt or shaming when the racial identity of a white serial killer is discovered. Even in the case of lynching, which is, at its core, a race-related phenomenon, there is no evidence that whites felt a sense of collective guilt when a person of color was lynched by a white mob. In the late 1990s, there were a number of disturbing mass shootings at US high schools and the FBI insisted there was no profile for the perpetrators. Frustrated by this denial, antiracist activist Tim Wise writes, "White boy after white boy after white boy, with very few exceptions to that rule ... decide to use their classmates for target practice, and yet there is no profile?" (Wise 2001). More recently, the Boston Marathon bombing in April 2013 elicited similar conversations about white privilege and terrorism. As Tim Wise (2013) stated the day after the incident, "White privilege is knowing that even if the bomber turns out to be white, no one calls for whites to be profiled as terrorists as a result, subjected to special screening, or threatened with deportation." The ethnicity of the Boston Marathon bombers and some of their friends were scrutinized, leading to them being "othered" along ethnic lines rather than racial lines. However, their whiteness did not result in the labeling of other whites as terrorists.

In this reading, the focus is on race privilege, the idea that if some racial/ethnic groups experience disadvantages, there is a group that is advantaged by this very same system. Studying whiteness forces us to acknowledge that all of us have a place in the relations of race. As obvious as this may seem, this is a concept many people are unfamiliar with and it is also a relatively new focus in the social sciences. Prior to the late twentieth century, sociologists were guilty of either ignoring race or focusing on racial/ethnic "others" in their analysis of the "race problem." Scientists avoided analyzing and interrogating the role of whites in American race relations as did the average white American. For people of color, the advantages whites receive due to their racial group membership are more than obvious. Such differences in perspective are at least partially the result of people's standpoint; where one exists in the social structure influences how one views the world. Examples of whiteness as a social construction and white privilege follow:

- Hispanics are being described as the "new Italians," emphasizing their assimilation into whiteness (Leonhardt 2013).

- A Delavan-Darien, Wisconsin, high school "American Diversity" class came under fire for teaching white privilege. A parent's complaint that the subject matter was indoctrinating students into white guilt received national attention ("'White Privilege' lesson ..." 2013).

- White privilege plays out in the restaurant industry, as front-of-the-house, tipped employees are overwhelmingly white, while back-of-the-house, hourly wage employees are overwhelmingly black or Latino.

- White privilege provides its recipients with protection from suspicion; thus, whites are unlikely to face the kind of situation Trayvon Martin faced in February 2012, when a neighborhood watchman decided he looked suspicious and eventually shot the unarmed seventeen-year-old to death.

- European soccer is seen by some fans as the privileged domain of whites, as black players are taunted with racist chants from fans, causing at least one of the black players and his teammates on AC Milan to walk off the field during a match ("AC Milan Players ..." 2013).

The Social Construction of Whiteness

We introduced the idea of the social construction of race [...]; to say race is socially constructed is to recognize that racial groups are socially designated categories rather than biological ones; thus, racial categories change across time and place. Whiteness is also a social construction, although recognizing this requires that we first acknowledge that "white" is a race rather than simply the norm. Thus, to say that whiteness is socially constructed is to emphasize which groups have been defined as white has changed across time and place (see Box 4.2.1 Global Perspectives).

BOX 4.2.1
Global Perspectives: *Constructing Whiteness in Brazil*

Racial categories change across time and place. Someone that is defined as white in Brazil may not be defined as white in the United States, whereas an African American may be defined as white in Brazil. Much like the United States, Brazil has a multiracial history, with people of indigenous, African, and European ancestry making up its population. Brazil has had a much more pronounced history of interracial relationships, however, that has resulted in an amalgamation of races to a greater extent than in the United States. Due to such amalgamation, Brazil used to be referred to as a racial democracy, a notion that is today considered to be a misrepresentation of Brazilian race relations.

While Brazil never established a system of racial segregation like that in the United States, other strategies were used to privilege whiteness. During the period of massive immigration into Brazil, 1882 to 1934, the Brazilian government openly expressed a preference for white migrants (Pinho 2009). During other periods in Brazilian history, whitening was promoted through encouraging miscegenation, where they were encouraged to marry white to better the race (Telles 2009). During the 1930s, there was an emphasis on "behavioral whitening," which involved rejecting cultural practices associated with African or indigenous cultures and instilling new habits of education, health, hygiene, and diet that were considered to be closer to white (Pinho 2009).

While Brazilians are less likely to use the term *race* and instead refer to color, due to the discrimination associated with blackness, many Brazilians seek to avoid that designation (Telles 2009). On the 2000 census, 54 percent of Brazilians declared themselves to be *branco* (white) (Bailey 2008). However, racial census categories are rarely used. Instead, Brazilians tend to use terms referring to skin color, of which there are over one hundred, albeit only about six of those terms are used with any consistency: (*branco* (white), *moreno* (brown, although not the census term for brown), *pardo* (the census term for brown), *Moreno claro* (light brown), *preto* (the census term for black) and *negro* (a common term for black not found on the census)) (Telles 2004). To be defined as white in Brazil is about more than skin color. It involves concerns with gradations of skin colors and hair types, as well as social class affiliation (Pinho 2009). While in the United States, gradations of color within racial groups are noted (for instance, the light skin preference found within Latino and African American communities), in Brazil, color differences within the entire population are significant. Being white in Brazil, as in the United States, imparts economic advantages, social prestige, and political power to its recipients.

Instead of white being about skin color or one's genetic makeup as we have been socialized to understand it, being designated as white is a social and political process. Many racial/ethnic groups that are considered white today have not always been defined as white. Irish Americans, Italian Americans, Greek Americans, and Jewish Americans have, instead, become white over time. "Becoming white" is a process whereby a formerly racially subordinate group is granted access to whiteness and white privilege, with all the benefits this entails. **White privilege** refers to the rights, benefits, and advantages enjoyed by white persons or the immunity granted to whites that is not granted to nonwhites; white privilege exempts white people from certain liabilities others are burdened with.

Racial Categorization and Power

The privileges associated with being designated white may make it seem like the option of becoming white is in the best interest of racial/ethnic minority groups. However, while racial categorization is fluid and does change over time, racial/ethnic minority groups do not have complete agency in determining whether they become white. During some eras in US history, Mexican Americans demanded they be recognized as white, while at other times they have actively worked to maintain their Mexican heritage (Foley 2008; Rodriguez 2005). This has resulted in Latinos' having a somewhat ambiguous racial status even to this day. Another reason for a group's ambiguous racial status is the power given to official documentation, such as who has been defined as white in legal decisions (Lopez 1996). The US Census, for instance, uses such racial and ethnic categories as "non-Hispanic white" and "Hispanic," which are intended to emphasize the ethnic status of Latinos, but are also about race. Thus, there are **structural** constraints, such as government racial categorizations and legal decisions, to defining a group's racial/ethnic status.

However, there is also **agency**, the extent to which a group of people have the ability to define their own status. People are not simply pawns existing within larger social structures. Individuals and groups act within these structures and, through such actions, can change them.

Figure 4.1 Native American students at the Carlisle Indian School, a government-run boarding school. The primary objective of Native American boarding schools was the forced assimilation of Native American children, as this photo exemplifies by the children's appearance, specifically, their short haircuts and mainstream clothing.

Since the 1960s, many Mexican Americans have embraced pluralism rather than assimilation. **Pluralism** is when a group embraces and adapts to the mainstream society without giving up their native culture. For instance, Mexican Americans' choosing to keep their language alive by speaking Spanish in their homes while learning English so as to participate in the dominant culture, is an example of pluralism. **Assimilation**, long the preferred model for race relations among the dominant group in American society, is the push toward acceptance of the dominant, Anglo culture, at the expense of one's native culture. Groups are expected to become American by dropping any connection to their native culture, such as language, customs, or even a particular spelling of their name.

Historically, immigrants were encouraged to assimilate into "American" society. What this really meant was that they were expected to assimilate to the white norm, known as Anglo-conformity. Thus, "American" culture was synonymous with "white culture." Previous generations of immigrants were pressured to become American by dropping their accents or native language and cultural practices associated with their native country. Today, the assimilationist thrust remains, as the English-Only movement emphasizes. This is a movement that attempts to make English the national language, to get states to pass laws eliminating bilingual education in schools, and to make government materials, such as signs in Social Security offices or Medicaid brochures, for instance, available only in English.

There are both push and pull factors at work, when it comes to whitening: the dominant group may embrace the assimilation of the subordinate group for political reasons and the subordinate group may seek assimilation, and thus embrace whitening, for access to the privileges it accords. This is accomplished by embracing, or at least acquiescing to, the racial hierarchy. As mentioned previously, racial/ethnic groups do have agency, yet they are not always operating under conditions that allow them to exercise their agency. While some groups challenge the assimilationist push, as did many Chicanos (a term Mexican activists embraced during the 1960s), most succumb. They succumb because access to white privilege makes life easier; such as by offering certain children advantages that every parent hopes for. White privilege is a difficult offer to resist—acceptance versus exclusion; benefits versus obstacles.

BECOMING WHITE

Many groups of people that are today unquestionably seen as white have not always been so. Irish, Greek, Jewish, and Italian Americans have all experienced a "whitening process" in different historical eras, when their group shifted from being perceived as nonwhite to being seen as white. The process of becoming white varied for each group, but each group becomes white in response to larger social and cultural changes. There are three specific eras in the history of whiteness in the United States (Jacobson 1998). The first is the passage of the first naturalization law in 1790 that declared "free white persons" to be eligible for citizenship. The second era (from the 1840s to 1924) emerged as significant numbers of less desirable European immigrants, such as the Irish, challenged this notion of citizenship and required a redefinition of whiteness and, ultimately, the implementation of a white racial hierarchy. Whiteness was redefined again in 1920 at least partially in response to the rural to urban migration of African Americans, which solidified the previously fractured white racial grouping. Groups such as the Irish and Jews, who had held a "probationary" white statuses in previous generations, were now "granted the scientific stamp of authenticity as the unitary Caucasian race" (Jacobson 1998:8).

Irish Americans

Historian Noel Ignatiev (1995) explored how an oppressed group in their home country, the Catholic Irish, became part of the oppressing racial group in the United States. The whitening process for Irish Americans involved the denigration of blacks. This transformation was even more shocking because Irish Americans were not considered white during the early periods of Irish immigration. In fact, early Irish immigrants lived in the black community, worked with black people, and even intermarried with blacks.

The Irish becoming white, thus increasing their status in the racial hierarchy, has essentially been attributed to a larger political agenda. In this case, the Democratic Party sought the support of the Irish during the antebellum and immediate postbellum eras and was able to attract them primarily due to the party's proimmigrant position at the time. This was a very successful strategy, as Irish voters became the most solid voting bloc in the country by 1844, throwing their support overwhelmingly behind the Democratic Party (Ignatiev 1995).

Although the Democratic Party is recognized today as the party that passed civil rights legislation and generally is supported by the black community, at the time, racial politics looked very different. By the end of the Civil War, southern whites ruled the Democratic Party, and President Lincoln, a Republican, was held responsible for the emancipation of slaves. African American men that could vote during Reconstruction and in the North during Jim Crow tended to support the Republican Party. Most southern whites, on the other hand, overwhelmingly supported the Democratic Party, including their explicitly racist ideologies. Thus, in the mid-nineteenth century, Irish Americans were assimilated into American society through a politics of race: their acceptance as whites hinged on their acceptance and perpetuation of a racist system, particularly, antiblack sentiment (Ignatiev 1995).

Irish Americans intentionally distanced themselves from blacks and even supported Jim Crow and other racist policies that were designed to oppress blacks. An essential truth emerged: in the United States, to be considered white, a person must not be associated with blackness and subordination. Black and white are relational concepts, meaning they only have meaning in relation to each other. We learn to understand who we are partially through an understanding of who we are not. For many groups that are now considered white, distancing themselves from blacks involved accepting the American racial hierarchy and participating in the racism directed at people of color.

Mexican Americans

Racial categorization is not a straightforward process. Some racial/ethnic groups maintain a more fluid racial status. As mentioned previously, Hispanics represent this kind of ambiguity. The term "Hispanic" refers to US residents whose ancestry is Latin American or Spanish, including Mexican Americans, Cuban Americans, Central Americans, and so on. The term "Hispanic" was first used by the US government in the 1970s and first appeared on the US Census in 1980. Thus, all Mexican Americans are considered to be Hispanic, but not all Hispanics are Mexican Americans.

The racial status of Mexican Americans has shifted throughout the nineteenth and twentieth centuries. Mexicans in the newly conquered Southwest at the close of the Mexican-American War in 1848, for instance, were accorded an intermediate racial status: they were not considered to be completely uncivilized, as the indigenous Indians of the region were, due to their European (Spanish) ancestry (Almaguer 1994). They were treated as an ethnic group, similar to European white ethnic immigrants. However, by the 1890s, as whites began to outnumber Mexicans throughout the Southwest, Mexicans became racialized subjects (Rodriguez 2005).

Mexican Americans have been legally defined as white, despite the fact that their social, political, and economic status has been equivalent to that of nonwhites (Foley 2008). According to the 2010 US Census, "Hispanic" is an ethnic group, not a racial group. This was not always how the census categorized Mexicans, however. In 1930, the Census Bureau had created a separate racial category for Mexicans, which for the first time, declared Mexican Americans to be nonwhite. This designation did not end the ambiguity surrounding the racial categorization of Mexicans, however. Census takers at the time were instructed to designate people's racial status as Mexican if they were born in Mexico or if they were "definitely not white," with no real instruction for differentiating how anyone would know which Mexican was "definitely not white." Consequently, due to such ambiguity, the US Census discontinued this designation in subsequent censuses. In 1980, the bureau created two new ethnic categories of whites: "Hispanics" and "non-Hispanic" (Foley 2008). This resulted in many Latinos' choosing "other" for their race, which motivated the Census Bureau to add a question concerning ethnic group membership after the question concerning racial group membership, to try to determine who is Hispanic. The Census Bureau is considering adding "Hispanic" as a racial category on the 2020 census.

While such official maneuverings provided structural constraints on the racial/ethnic identification choices of Latinos, Latinos also exercised their agency. Many Mexican Americans during the 1930s through 1950s, for instance, demanded to be recognized as white as a way to avoid Jim Crow segregation. Much like the whitening process for Irish Americans, for Mexican Americans, distancing themselves from blacks became the objective rather than challenging the racial hierarchy through an embrace of a nonwhite racial status. Mexican Americans, particularly those in the middle class, often supported the racial segregation of schools and the notion of white supremacy. Today, while some Latinos enjoy a status as white ethnics, many others, primarily Mexicans and recent Latino immigrants, remain excluded from the privileges of whiteness. Often this exclusion has been linked to their social class or skin color, as "a dark-skinned non-English-speaking Mexican immigrant doing lawn and garden work does not share the same class and ethnoracial status as acculturated, educated Hispanics … Hispanicized Mexican Americans themselves often construct a 'racial' gulf between themselves and 'illegal aliens' and 'wetbacks'" (Foley 2008:62–3).

REFLECT AND CONNECT

Do you belong to a racial/ethnic group that has experienced a changing racial status, such as those discussed here, that became white? If so, were you aware of this? If not, why do you think you were unaware of this? Reflect on the significance of this for your life today.

Social Class, Mobility, and "Whitening"

The process of becoming white has often been directly linked to **collective social mobility**, a group's changing class status over time in the United States. For instance, whitening often occurs simultaneously with a group's entrance into the American middle class, making becoming white and becoming middle class an interconnected phenomenon (Brodkin 2008). Whiteness has also been closely connected to the formation of the American working class (Roediger 1991). Finally, class has been used to divide whites, as in the case of the derogatory notion of "white trash."

Because race is socially constructed, it is always changing, always open to challenge, which means there is always potential for destabilization. Yet, despite this potential, the societal racial hierarchy endures. One of the reasons is that some groups have been provided with membership into the dominant group and have obtained access to white privilege. Thus, the hierarchy remains, with whites at the top and nonwhites at the bottom. For instance, when Irish immigrants were relatively limited in number, their association with the black community and marginalization from the white community was tolerated and even encouraged by many whites. Yet, as their numbers grew and they became a potentially powerful political force, their assimilation into the white mainstream was encouraged and embraced.

Jewish Americans

The process through which Jewish Americans became white involved their simultaneous entrance into the middle class. Today, much like the situation for Irish Americans, most US citizens see Jewish Americans as white ethnics. However, Jewish Americans have not always been considered white in the United States. Prior to World War II, there was considerable anti-Semitism in the United States that manifested in immigration restrictions for Jews and limiting Jewish admission to elite universities, among other forms of discrimination (Karabel 2005; Tichenor 2002). Their whitening process involved access to the GI Bill, which was overwhelmingly denied to black soldiers in the post-World War II era. Access to this basic government program enabled Jewish Americans, along with thousands of white Americans, to obtain college educations and enter middle-class professions. In this example, class and race are intertwined, as entering the middle class is part of the whitening process for this previously defined nonwhite group. It is unclear whether becoming white paved the way to their middle-class status or whether their middle-class status contributed to their whitening (Brodkin 2008).

Psychological Wage

One of the most significant ways white privilege has manifested itself has been in the economic sphere, so it is not surprising that there is also a significant link between the emergence of the American working class and whiteness. In 1935, African American sociologist W. E. B. Du Bois argued that white workers, despite their extremely low wages, received an intangible benefit, which he called a **psychological wage**, because they were white. What he meant was that, while all workers were exploited, a racially divided labor force meant that white workers received a psychological boost from simply not being black. This psychological wage manifested in public deference, titles of courtesy, such as being referred to as "Mr." or "Mrs.," and inclusion at public functions, parks, and countless places that excluded blacks. Later, labor unions continued this practice of offering white workers access to good jobs through the exclusion of black workers from many unionized occupations.

Historian David Roediger (1991) argues that the formation of the US working class is intimately linked to the development of a sense of whiteness because the United States is the only nation where the working class emerged within a slaveholding republic. Thus, the working class defined itself in opposition to slavery, with race attached to each concept; whiteness was connected to the working class, while blackness was linked to slavery. As Roediger argues, "In a society in which Blackness and servility were so thoroughly intertwined—North and South—assertions of white freedom could not be raceless" (1991:49). Part of the whitening process for Irish Americans involved avoiding the stigma of blackness, and one way they did this was through their access to what was known as "white man's work," which simply referred to employment that excluded African Americans (Ignatiev 1995). Irish Americans, for instance, were unwilling to work in the same occupations as free blacks in the North, thus solidifying their whiteness through an insistence on racially differentiated employment.

Race is a fluid category, rather than fixed; the boundaries of whiteness are continually in flux. Inequality exists even within the white racial/ethnic group. We can see this through an exploration of the ways whiteness is related to social class in the notion of "poor white trash" or "white trash." This clearly derogatory notion emerged in the mid-1800s and was created by higher status whites to not just describe poor whites, but to imply their moral inferiority (Wray 2006). The term *cracker*, emerging in the late 1700s, has similar origins. While today *cracker* is a term often used as a generalized racial slur against whites by people of color, it originated as a term higher-status whites used to describe poor whites who were viewed as dangerous, lawless, shiftless, lazy, and people who often associated with other stigmatized groups (Wray 2006). This intersection of class and race is evidence of the power of higher status whites to define who is included in the category of white. Such derogatory terms are used to describe poor whites not just to emphasize their poverty, but to make their racial status questionable as well.

Race Matters

While sociologists speak of race as socially constructed rather than biologically based, it is not meant to imply that race is insignificant and can thus be disregarded. Race still matters. We live in a society that attaches meaning to race and individuals attach meaning to their race. It informs who we are, is an aspect of one's identity if, for no other reason, than it has been externally ascribed to us our entire lives. We learn to see ourselves as white, black, Asian, or Latino, through our interactions with others. Thus, the fact that people racially identify does not negate the idea of the social construction of race. Instead it emphasizes the power of socially defined ideals.

White Privilege

While the privileges associated with whiteness are not new, the academic exploration and understanding of white privilege is relatively new. Sociologists that study race have shifted the analysis from a focus solely on people of color to one that includes whites and their role in race relations. This necessary shift focuses on what Paula Rothenberg (2008) refers to as "the other side of racism," white privilege. In the United States, individuals identified and defined as white make up the group with the unearned advantages known as white privilege. Whiteness refers to the multiple ways white people benefit from institutional arrangements that appear to have nothing to do with race (Bush 2011). This analytical shift to an analysis of and an understanding of white privilege requires that we recognize "white" as not only a race but as a social construction.

Racial hierarchies, status hierarchies based upon physical appearance and the assumption of membership in particular categories based upon these physical features, exist in the United States and throughout the world, albeit with much variation. Hierarchies imply that a group exists at the top while others exist somewhere in the middle, and still others on the bottom rungs of the hierarchy. The group at the top is the group that benefits from the racial hierarchy in the form of race privilege. The seminal work on white privilege is the self-reflexive essay by Peggy McIntosh (2008), "White Privilege: Unpacking the Invisible Knapsack." McIntosh defines *white privilege* as "an invisible package of unearned assets which I can count on cashing in each day, but about which I was 'meant' to remain oblivious. White privilege is like an invisible weightless knapsack of special provisions, maps, passports, codebooks, visas, clothes, tools, and blank checks" (2008:123). There are several aspects to this definition that warrant attention: the claims that white privilege is invisible, it is unearned, and that white people are socialized to count on this, while simultaneously not recognizing it as privilege.

Race affects every aspect of our lives: it informs how all of us view the world, our daily experiences, and whether or not opportunities are available due to our membership in particular racial/ethnic groups. While the importance of race has long been recognized for racial/ethnic minorities, until recently, even social scientists have overlooked the significance of race in the daily lives of whites. Part of this problem emerges from a lack of recognition that "white" is a race, rather than merely the norm, the human standard against which all other groups are measured (a perspective which is itself part of white privilege). Some have called for the development of a **new white consciousness**, "an awareness of our whiteness and its role in race problems" (Terry 1970:17). Social scientists have finally heeded this call and white people are now being asked to recognize how race and privilege operate in their world.

White Privilege as Taboo

The discussion of white privilege will undoubtedly make many students uncomfortable. Recently, a high school in Wisconsin has come under fire for teaching white privilege in an "American Diversity" class. Some parents complained that the subject matter was akin to indoctrination and meant to divide the students and provoke white guilt (*The Huffington Post* 2013).

This is the invisible side of racism—the advantages offered to the dominant group by an unjust system. Why has it taken so long for social scientists to focus on something as seemingly obvious as the "other side of racism"? A racial bias embedded not only in the discipline of sociology but in our culture is part of the explanation. Additionally, whiteness has been normalized to the point of invisibility in both our culture and in science. In addition, privilege is meant to remain invisible. Those benefiting from such societal arrangements, even if these are people that actively oppose racism, have difficulty seeing the advantages they reap from these arrangements.

Interrogating white privilege is not meant to alienate white people or exclude people of color from conversations concerning race. Instead, it is meant to bring everyone to the table to discuss race, racism, racial inequality, and race privilege. Professor Helen Fox provides a strong argument for why it is so essential to engage white people in discussions of race and privilege:

> I am convinced that learning how to reach resistant white students is central to our teaching about race. These are the future power brokers of America, the ones who by virtue of their class, their contacts, and their perceived "race" will have a disproportionate share of political and economic clout (2001:83).

For people of color, conversations surrounding race are not new; such conversations have likely been quite common for them. People of color experience explicit **racial socialization**, meaning they are taught in their families, in schools, and through the media that their race matters. White people, on the other hand, may have difficulties with the topic of race and privilege for the simple fact that such conversations have likely been uncommon in their lives.

White people experience racial socialization as well, it is just more subtle. White racial socialization comes in the form of an unspoken entitlement. Whites are socialized to protect their privilege, partially through denial of such privilege. White privilege allows whites the privilege of not having to think about race—not having to think about how race might affect them that day.

Whiteness is understood by whites as a culture void, as lacking culture, as an unmarked category in direct opposition to the view that minorities have rich and distinct cultures (Frankenberg 1993). People of color are seen to have a recognizable culture (for instance, the presence of BET (Black Entertainment Television), Latin music, Asian food, etc.) that whites are perceived to lack. For example, Frankenberg (1993) found that white women in interracial relationships often viewed themselves as having no culture, often citing envy of racial/ethnic minorities because of their obvious culture and accompanying identity.

REFLECT AND CONNECT

Take a moment and think about your childhood, specifically reflecting on when you discovered your race. When did you discover you were white, African American, or Latino, or whatever? For people of color, this is generally not a difficult task. For whites, this might be more difficult.

There are some problems with viewing white culture as actually cultureless. The first is that it reinforces whiteness as the cultural norm. Whites are everywhere in cultural representations—advertising, film, television, books, museums, public history monuments—yet the claim is made that this is just culture, not white culture. Additionally, by claiming to be cultureless, whites can ignore white history. Thus, the political, economic, and social advantages whites have accumulated historically are easier to overlook when claiming there is no such thing as white culture (Frankenberg 1993).

WITNESS

"And here I am, just another alienated middle-class white girl with no culture to inform my daily life, no people to call my own" (interviewee quoted in Frankenberg 1993).

Seeing Privilege

White privilege—"an elusive and fugitive subject" as Peggy McIntosh described it in 1998—has gone unexamined primarily because it is the societal **norm**. For sociologists, social norms are a significant aspect of culture and they refer to the shared expectations about behavior in a society, whether implicit or explicit. There are several reasons why white privilege is hard for white people to see. The first problem is the intentional invisibility of white privilege. Privilege is maintained through ignoring whiteness. According to McIntosh, "in facing [white privilege], I must give up the myth of meritocracy ... [M]y moral condition is not what I had been led to believe. The appearance of being a good citizen rather than a troublemaker comes in large part from having all sorts of doors open automatically because of my color" (McIntosh 1988). Part of privilege is the assumption that your experience is normal; it does not feel like a privileged existence.

While inequality is easy to see, privilege is more obscure. White people can easily see how racism "makes people of color angry, tired, and upset, but they have little insight into the ways that not having to worry about racism affects their own lives" (Parker and Chambers 2007:17). For people of color, white privilege is not a difficult concept to grasp—it is clear from their standpoint that racial disadvantage has a flip side that amounts to advantages for the dominant group. Despite this, for white people, seeing race is difficult and is the "natural consequence of being in the driver's seat" (Dalton 2008:17).

It is difficult for most white people to discuss ways they benefit from white privilege, and many get offended when asked to think about some advantage they have accrued due to being white. Many students can recognize whether they attended a well-funded public school that adequately prepared them for college. Recognition of privilege does not negate hard work, but it is an acknowledgment that not everyone had the same educational opportunities, particularly individuals that attended poor schools predominantly populated with racial/ethnic minority students.

White privilege is problematic for many white people because it can feel insulting. Americans are taught that we live in a **meritocracy**, where individuals get what they work for, where rewards are based upon effort and talent. This ideology helps us understand poverty along individualized "blame the victim" lines rather than thinking of it as a social problem. In other words, if people are poor, it is presumed to be due to some inadequacy on their part. The opposite of the "blame the victim" ideology is also true. When people succeed in American society their success is often attributed to hard work, motivation, intelligence, or other individualized characteristics that are meant to set the person apart from less successful individuals. The idea of white privilege challenges this. It forces us to recognize that some people, due to their membership in particular racial/ethnic groups, are systematically disadvantaged and face more obstacles in their lives while members of other racial/ethnic groups are systematically advantaged, with more doors opened and more opportunities available to them. It may take their individual talents, motivation and intelligence to take advantage of the open door, but it must be acknowledged that not everyone had the door opened for them in the first place. This is often how privilege manifests itself.

White privilege is uncomfortable for many white students to grasp because the word *privilege* does not appear to describe their life. Poor and working-class white people are often offended by such a notion because they do not see themselves as beneficiaries of the system in any way. They work hard and have very little, relatively speaking. Indeed, many white people are members of the **working poor**, people who work full-time and still fall below the poverty line in the United States. How can they be considered privileged? To be able to understand this, we have to recognize the complexities involved in the multiple status hierarchies that exist in American society. One can lack class privilege, but still have race privilege, for instance.

The idea of white privilege is that all people identified and treated as white benefit from that status, even if they face disadvantages in other arenas, such as social class. To truly understand how race operates in the United States, it is essential that we recognize this. White privilege offers poor whites something: the satisfaction that at least they do not exist on the bottom rungs of the societal hierarchy—that, despite their poverty, they are at least not black. Additionally, despite any other disadvantages a white person may have, when they walk into a job interview, or restaurant, or any situation, the primary characteristic noted is that they are white, which is their passport for entry, as Peggy McIntosh (2008) describes. Race and gender are what sociologists call **master statuses** in our society, statuses that are considered so significant they overshadow all others and influence our lives more than our other statuses.

The combination of the invisibility of white privilege and the fact that all white people are implicated in the racial hierarchy through their privilege also makes it a disturbing concept for many white people. Interrogating white privilege is a particularly difficult task because it is both structural and personal. It forces those who are white to ask questions that concern not only structural advantage (such as, how are schools structured in ways that benefit white people?) but individual privilege as well (in what ways was my educational attainment at least partially a result of racial privilege?). Again, while it is uncomfortable to acknowledge being unfairly advantaged, this is exactly what white privilege is.

Additionally, it is important to recognize in what arenas we may be advantaged (oppressors) and in what arenas we may be disadvantaged (oppressed). As a white person,

I have race privilege (see Box 4.2.2 Race in the Workplace). As a woman, I have disadvantages within a **patriarchy**, a male-dominated society. On a global scale, there are certain advantages, from my odds of survival to the educational and economic opportunities I have had access to, to having been born in a wealthy, First World country versus in an impoverished nation.

BOX 4.2.2
Race in the Workplace: *White Teachers Making Meaning of Whiteness*

Alice McIntyre, teacher and author of *Making Meaning of Whiteness: Exploring Racial Identity with White Teachers* (1997), explains that entering the teaching profession offered her "numerous occasions to 'see' my whiteness and to experience the ways in which race and racism shaped my life, my teaching, my politics, and my understanding of privilege and oppression, especially as they relate to the educational system in the United States" (1997:2). Upon returning to graduate school after twelve years of classroom teaching, she became interested in how white student teachers embrace the cultural understandings of children and how those understandings reinforced white privilege. One of the primary questions motivating her research was, what impact does one's white racial identity have on one's notion of what it means to be a teacher?

McIntyre believes that for white teachers to be more effective in the classroom, they must interrogate their own racial socialization, specifically how they are socialized into a position of privilege and a sense of entitlement. She argues that white teachers have an obligation to reflect on their race and its influence on their teaching. "White student teachers need to be intentional about being self-reformers … *purposefully thinking through their racial identities as salient aspects of their identities*" (italics in original, 1997:5). This cannot be achieved without linking identities to the larger social structure and institutions.

Her goal is to help white student teachers "develop teaching strategies and research methodologies aimed at disrupting and eliminating the oppressive nature of whiteness in education" (1997:7). She is aware of the difficulties surrounding such a task. As she explains, "There is no comfort zone for white people when it comes to discussing white racism" (1997:43).

White Privilege Versus White Racism

Discussing white privilege makes many whites feel uncomfortable because it implicates them in a racist social structure. Thus, doesn't that make them racist? Is there a difference between white privilege and **white racism**? Feagin and Vera (1995) define white racism as "the socially organized set of attitudes, ideas, and practices that deny African Americans and other people of color the dignity, opportunities, freedoms and rewards that this nation offers white Americans" (p. 7). That is clearly a broad definition of white racism—it certainly goes above and beyond the idea that many whites take comfort in, which is that a racist is someone that is actively involved in a white supremacist organization, participates in hate crimes, or believes in the innate inferiority of nonwhites. However, it is not that clear-cut. As the definition implies, as long as people of color are denied opportunities, it is white racism, and what goes unspoken is that the flip side of this racism is that those become opportunities for white people. In other words, these are two sides of the same coin—without white racism, there is no white privilege. To work actively against racism, whites also have to work against privilege. For instance, if a white employee of a restaurant recognizes racialized patterns, such as people of color working in the kitchen and white staff working the dining room, they can point these out to management. Additionally, there are those who argue that simply living in American society makes one racist—it is the norm in our society, found in the subtle messages we all receive every day. Thus, neutrality is not equated with being nonracist. The only way to be nonracist in American society is to actively work against racism, such as by joining a racial justice organization. Many racial justice organizations are affiliated with religious institutions, for instance, or can be found on university campuses. They can also easily be found online by searching "antiracist activism" or "racial justice activism." Beyond actually joining a racial justice organization, one can simply work to be an ally to people of color in the struggle to end racism. Being an ally involves speaking up when you see racial injustice occurring, assuming racism is everywhere, everyday, and understanding the history of whiteness and racism (Kivel 2011).

Ideologies, Identities, and Institutions

[...] We explored the ways race operates in the form of racial ideologies, racial identities, and institutional racism. We expand on that discussion to show the ways race privilege informs racial ideologies and racial identities, as well as fostering institutional privileges.

Racial Ideologies of Color-blindness

Ideologies are not just powerful; they operate in the "service of power" through providing a frame for interpreting the world (Bonilla-Silva 2010; Thompson 1984). It is through cultural belief systems that so many nonwhite groups embrace the racial hierarchy, embrace racism, as a way to obtain white privilege. The current reigning racial ideology is that of color-blindness.

Color-blindness supports white privilege because it encourages a mentality that allows us to say we don't see race, that essentially we are color-blind. Paradoxically, this ideology persists within a society literally obsessed with race. The elections of President Barack Obama and the ongoing racial discourse surrounding both elections are good examples. In 2007, discussions of race surrounded Super Bowl XLI because it was the first time an African American head coach had led their team to the Super Bowl, much less the fact that both teams, the Chicago Bears and the Indianapolis Colts, had black head coaches. People of mixed-race ancestry continually report being asked, "What are you?," which is evidence of the ongoing significance of race rather than a commitment to color-blindness.

Clearly, Americans see color, we see race, and we attach significance to it. The power of the color-blind ideology is threefold:

1. **We ignore racism.** We have a racist society without acknowledging any actual racists (Bonilla-Silva 2006). Racism is alive and well, yet individuals cling to color-blindness, thus, eliminating their personal responsibility for it. Sociologist Eduardo Bonilla-Silva (2010) argues that the color-blind ideology "barricades whites from the United States' racial reality" (p. 47).

2. **We ignore white privilege.** Haney-Lopez (2006) refers to this as "color-blind white dominance." By claiming color-blindness white people can ignore the ways white privilege benefits them and can ignore ongoing racism.

3. **We perceive whiteness as the norm.** Color-blindness fuels perceptions of whiteness as the norm and as synonymous with racial neutrality.

A glaring example of the preceding third item, perceiving whiteness as the norm, was found in media coverage of Hurricane Katrina in 2005. For days, media coverage showed thousands of displaced and desperate people, overwhelmingly black, seeking shelter from the rising flood waters, yet race was never mentioned. When it finally was mentioned, many white people were angered by what they saw as the media "racializing" what they perceived as a race-neutral tragedy; clinging to color-blind ideologies, they insisted that those left behind to face the devastation were simply people, not black people. The fact that they were black was somehow deemed irrelevant or mere coincidence. Yet, this tragedy was clearly "raced" and "classed" as well. It was not simply coincidence that it was predominantly poor black people that were left behind to drown as the levees broke and the city of New Orleans experienced devastating flooding.

Figure 4.2 A home damaged by the flooding of New Orleans due to the levee breaches after Hurricane Katrina in 2005. These homes are in New Orleans' Ninth Ward, an overwhelmingly poor and African American community that suffered some of the worst flooding.

New Orleans is an overwhelmingly black city and a very poor city. When the mayor announced a mandatory evacuation due to the impending hurricane, transportation should have been provided because so many poor, black New Orleanians did not own an automobile. As a matter of public policy, when considering a mandatory evacuation, one has to consider not just transportation but where people are going to go. Poor people are not able to simply get a hotel room in another city to wait out the storm as a middle-class person could.

Racial ideologies change over time as culture changes. What is essential is that we recognize how the racial ideologies manifest themselves in different eras, that we gauge the influence of such ideologies, and perhaps most important, recognize how the dominant group benefits from such ideologies.

White Racial Identity

Social scientists have only recently begun studying white racial identity development (Helms 1990; McDermott and Samson 2005). Much effort has been put into the study of white ethnic identity development (Alba 1990; Rubin 1994; Stein and Hill 1977; Waters 1990), black racial identity development (Burlew and Smith 1991; Helms 1990; Resnicow and Ross-Gaddy 1997), and shifting racial identities (Fitzgerald 2007; Korgen 1998; Rockquemore and Brunsma 2002), while white racial identities went unexamined. When sociologists have focused on white racial identity development, it has generally been in conjunction with white supremacist movements, but of course, all whites have a racial identity not just those belonging to such organizations (Dees and Corcoran 1996; Gallagher 2003). Some research finds that white racial identity development is surprisingly similar for white supremacists as well as for white racial justice activists (Hughey 2010, 2012).

For the most part, people of color have been forced to think about race, not just in the abstract, but as something fundamental to who they are, how they are perceived, and thus, how they see themselves. Whites, however, develop a white racial identity without much conscious thought or discussion. As James Baldwin has said, being white means never having to think about it. Janet Helms (1990) identifies stages of white racial identity development beginning with whites who have had no contact with other races, moving to those who learn about race and privilege, to those who see inequalities as the fault of the other races. For white people progressing through these first three of six stages of racial identity development, the question becomes, how do they get to see themselves as white in a raced world rather than as neutral, nonraced, or the norm?

In the first stage of white racial identity development, whites have had little contact with people of color and thus, have developed a sense of superiority over them based upon social stereotypes and media representations. Whites in stage one have difficulty seeing white privilege and may even resist the idea. Some of these folks are outright racists, while others are not blatant racists but may perceive people of color in stereotypical ways, such as lazy or dangerous. There is nothing inevitable about identity development—most whites are in stage one and many never move beyond the first stage (Helms 1990).

For those whites who progress in their identity development, according to Helms (1990), stage two is characterized by fear and guilt that stems from seeing themselves, perhaps for the first time, as holding racial prejudices. As they learn more about race in American society, it challenges what they thought they knew about the world. They are seeing racism and privilege for the first time. Often, whites respond to this guilt and fear through retrenchment, which is the third stage.

In the retrenchment stage, whites deal with their guilt by blaming the victim, declaring that racial inequality is the fault of minorities. Not all white people move backward at this stage. Instead, some progress through the next stages, eventually developing a healthy white identity that is not based on guilt or a sense of superiority.

Many whites struggle with seeing themselves as white. As mentioned previously, whiteness is viewed by many whites as bland, cultureless, thus, white people are more likely to lack an overt racial identity. In fact, this lack of a sense of white identity is due to the fact that whiteness is generally seen as the norm. By bemoaning their lack of a racial identity, whites help maintain the separate status of racial/ethnic minorities, who are perceived as different, as "other" in American society. What is in operation is white privilege: the privilege to *not* think about race, the privilege to *not* recognize the dominant culture as white culture rather than as racially neutral, and the privilege to overlook the fact that whiteness, rather than being absent, is ever present as the unnamed norm.

Identities are more than personal. They are products of particular sociohistorical eras. Thus white identities, like all racial identities, are social, historical, and political constructions.

The fact that white as a racial identity is rarely visible is evidence of the operation of white privilege in our lives today. Identities are political and they are a response to changing social and political contexts. Native American activism during the 1970s resulted in more individuals officially identifying as Native American (Nagel 1996). The racial identity of white Americans often goes unacknowledged, with the exception of historical eras that challenge the taken-for-grantedness of whiteness and white privilege. For instance, during the civil rights movement, white Americans began to explicitly claim their whiteness if for no other reason than they viewed the privileges associated with their whiteness as being challenged. The racial socialization of whites, their sense of entitlement, was being challenged every day. As black civil rights activists demanded equal rights, whites coun-terattacked with rhetoric concerning the perceived loss of their own rights (Sokol 2006). Today, in a less racially charged atmosphere, most whites are unlikely to see themselves in racial terms. However, white people working toward racial justice do view white as a race and their life experiences as racialized (see Box 4.2.3 Racial Justice Activism).

Figure 4.3 Antiracist activist, author, and speaker Tim Wise.

BOX 4.2.3
Racial Justice Activism: *Tim Wise on White Identity and Becoming a Racial Justice Activist*

Tim Wise has been working as an antiracist activist since he was twenty-one years old. He details his path to antiracist work in his book *White Like Me:*

Reflections on Race from a Privileged Son (2005). During his college years at Tulane University in New Orleans, he immersed himself in activist work, primarily working as an anti-apartheid activist and a Central American peace activist.

Wise explains that he was not aware that, even as he worked to eradicate racism across the globe, he was doing absolutely nothing about racism in his own community, thus he was reinforcing his own white privilege despite his activism. This contradiction was pointed out to him by an African American woman and New Orleans native during a question-and-answer period concerning the university's decision to divest in South Africa. She pointedly asked him, in his four years of living in New Orleans, "What one thing have you done to address apartheid in this city, since, after all, you benefit from that apartheid" (2005:114). After his inability to adequately respond to that question and much self-reflection, he explained "I had been blind to the way in which my own privilege and the privilege of whites generally had obscured our understanding of such issues as accountability, the need to link up struggles (like the connection between racism in New Orleans and that in South Africa), and the need to always have leadership of color in any antiracist struggle, however much that requires whites to step back, keep our mouths shut and just listen for a while" (2005:117).

After graduating from college, Wise took that lesson seriously and began his career as an antiracist activist, working as a youth coordinator for the Louisiana Coalition Against Racism and Nazism, which opposed the political candidacy of neo-Nazi Senate candidate David Duke. He moved up the ranks of the organization and eventually became one of the most visible faces associated with the anti-Duke effort (2005:11). Wise now earns a living lecturing and writing about white privilege and antiracist activism.

Wise acknowledges that there is significant resistance to whites' engaging in antiracist activist work because they lack antiracist role models to whom they can look for guidance, they fear alienating family and friends with their views, and "because resistance is difficult ... many whites who care deeply about issues of racism and inequality will find ourselves paralyzed either by uncertainty, fear or both" (2005:62). He emphasizes that despite these obstacles to resistance, "experiences taught me that to be white in this country doesn't have to be a story of accepting unjust social systems. There is not only one way to be in this skin. There are choices we can make, paths we can travel, and when we travel them, we will not be alone" (p. 63).

While engaging in this kind of work has resulted in some death threats, hate mail, and being followed by skinheads on at least one occasion, Wise argues that "I put up with whatever cost I have to put up with, because the cost of not doing the work is greater ... People of color have to do this work as a matter of everyday survival. And so long as they have to, who am I to act as if I have a choice in the matter? Especially when my future and that of my children in large part depends on the eradication of racism? There is no choice" (2005:6).

Institutional Privilege

Just as sociologists have identified racial discrimination within all of our major social institutions, white privilege can be found in these arenas as well: in banks/lending institutions, educational systems, media, religious institutions, and government, just to name a few. This is the most difficult arena to make race privilege visible. Institutional racism refers to everyday business practices and policies that result in disadvantage for some racial groups, intentionally or not. **Institutional privilege** is even more difficult to identify since privilege is designed to remain invisible, in its institutionalized form it becomes even more obscure. In addition to the advantages individuals accumulate through white privilege; it also takes the form of customs, norms, traditions, laws, and public policies that benefit whites (Williams 2003). Throughout this text, various societal institutions will be explored exposing not only the racial inequality embedded in them but also the ways white privilege is built into the specific business practices and policies within each institution. In exploring institutional privilege, it is useful to ask, what group benefits from a particular arrangement, policy, or practice?

To help understand what is meant by institutional privilege, we explore several policies and practices that have allowed whites to accumulate wealth and inhibited people of color from wealth accumulation. This includes the policies and practices of banking and lending institutions as well as government policies and practices.

Racial minorities have been systematically excluded from wealth creation with very real, concrete consequences. Slavery is the most obvious example. In addition to the cruelty and inhumanity of this institution, it was also a system that deterred wealth accumulation by the great majority of blacks and supported the massive accumulation of wealth by some whites. For over 240 years, blacks labored in America without being compensated. Clearly that places them in a disadvantaged position in terms of wealth accumulation. While only a small portion of the population owned slaves, it is estimated that about 15 million white Americans today have slave-owning ancestors (Millman 2008). Of our first eighteen presidents, thirteen owned slaves. Two recent presidents, father and son George H. W. and George W. Bush, are descendants of slave owners, contributing, of course, to their great wealth and political power to this day.

Upon emancipation, reparations for former slaves were promised, most in the form of land. The promised "forty acres and a mule," however, never materialized. During the Reconstruction era, the federal government established the Freedmen's Bureau to provide food, education, medical care, and in some cases, land, to newly freed slaves as well as to needy whites. Although this agency only lasted one year and was unable to meet the needs of the great majority of newly freed slaves, it is significant that more whites benefited from this government agency than blacks.

Native American Land Loss

The exploitation of Native Americans often involved the taking of land; an estimated 2 billion acres of land was transferred to the United States government from American Indian Tribes through treaties in exchange for tribal sovereignty (Newton 1999). European Americans confiscated land that Native peoples populated, forced their removal, and sometimes engaged in acts of genocide so as to acquire land. This theme of Native land loss at the hands of whites is hardly new; most of us learned of this in grade school. However, we need to reflect more on the significance. Native land loss is always presented as a collective problem, which it was, as tribes lost their lands and livelihoods as they were repeatedly relocated to less valuable lands. What we tend not to realize is that this is a significant loss at the individual level as well. Land is equivalent to wealth in the white mainstream culture (Native peoples, however, generally did not believe people could own the land and they instead saw themselves as stewards of the land). Who benefited when all those Native people were forced off of the lands on which they lived? White people took the land as their own, thus acquiring wealth. Native land loss at the hands of whites goes beyond giant land swindles involving treaties between the federal government and tribal governments. Throughout the country there were smaller, everyday, localized swindles. Additionally, many states established laws that did not allow Native people to own land, thus, limiting their ability to accumulate wealth and simultaneously contributing to the ability of white people to accumulate wealth.

Issues of Wealth Accumulation

These historical examples of the exploitation of racial minorities in terms of wealth accumulation have a flip side: white advantage. Whites historically and currently benefit from the exclusion of other racial/ethnic groups. For instance, laws supported the rights of white Americans to own homes and businesses while banks and lending institutions provided them the necessary capital to do so. This was not a given for people of color. Until the 1960s, laws explicitly excluded people of color from obtaining business loans in many places. White people were subsidized in acquiring their own homes, and thus establishing equity, which eventually became wealth that was passed on to the next generation (Oliver and Shapiro 1995). This is significant if for no other reason than wealth accumulates. Federal Reserve studies confirm that even today, minorities get fewer home loans, even when their economic situations are comparable to whites. "The poorest white applicant, according to this [the Federal Reserve] report, was more likely to get a mortgage loan approved than a black in the highest income bracket" (Oliver and Shapiro 1995:20). The consequences of this are profound since for most Americans home ownership represents their primary and often only source of wealth.

Ideologies of white supremacy fuel white identities of entitlement and, thus, the creation of institutions that deny access to anyone but whites are deemed acceptable. Ideologies of color-blindness in our current era fuel a "raceless" identity in whites that allows them to deny ongoing racism, while still enjoying race privilege.

REFLECT AND CONNECT

Think about how much white privilege you may have. If you are white, did your ancestors own slaves? Ask your parents the following questions: Did your parents or grandparents have access to home and/or business loans? Did they own their own homes or land? Did your parents or grandparents own a business? Did your parents or grandparents attend college? Have you received or do you expect to receive an inheritance? Are your parents paying for your college, thus making significant student loan borrowing unnecessary? If you can answer yes to any of these, you have more than likely benefited from white privilege in a very material, concrete way.

Challenging White Privilege

What can or should be done about white privilege? Is it necessary to challenge white privilege? Is it possible? It is easier to condemn racism than to challenge one's own privilege. Understanding white privilege is essential, yet incomplete, because, as McIntosh notes, "describing white privilege makes one newly accountable" (2008:109). In other words, if we see privilege, do we not have an obligation to work to eradicate it? While white privilege allows whites to ignore their race and avoid confronting the advantages associated with it, many white Americans actively challenge white privilege as part of their commitment to racial justice and as a way to challenge their own sense of entitlement (e.g., Warren 2010; Wise 2005). White civil rights activists were rejecting their own race privilege through their activism on behalf of full civil rights for people of color, for instance (e.g., Murray 2004; Zellner 2008).

Racial justice activists argue that white privilege is the proverbial "elephant in the room" that white people agree to ignore (Parker and Chambers 2007). White theologians have called for an end to the silence surrounding white privilege within religious institutions (Cassidy and Mikulich 2007). Stories of racial justice activism are featured in "Racial Justice Activism" boxes. Now, we are going to explore why challenging white privilege is not only necessary, but is actually in the interests of white people.

For many white people, being introduced to the concept of white privilege invokes intense feelings of guilt. They often respond by saying they should not be made to feel guilty for being white, as it was hardly their choice. Or they feel that by focusing on privilege, it takes away from their achievements or the achievements of their parents. This is not the intent. White guilt is a normal reaction to learning about historical and current atrocities inflicted upon racial minorities by whites. When it comes to race, our country has an ugly history that cannot be ignored. Guilt is uncomfortable psychologically, so people tend to work to alleviate the feeling. Thus, such guilt has the potential to motivate change, to get white people to understand how they are racist, how they contribute to racial oppression, and what they can do to end it. It is important to recognize white privilege. It is necessary for a complete understanding of the role race plays in all of our lives, both at the individual and societal levels. Additionally, opposing the racial inequities associated with whiteness is not the same thing as opposing white people (Williams 2003).

It is important to critically investigate white privilege because while privilege offers advantages, whites are also losers under this system of structural inequality. There are many unrecognized ways whites lose under this system: it is expensive, financially and morally, to ignore white privilege in the workplace because it remains an uncomfortable environment for people of color and thus, their retention is less likely. The only way white people can remain part of this racial hierarchy is to compartmentalize—separate their head from their heart. There are long-term consequences of such compartmentalization, primarily in terms of failing to recognize our common humanity (Kendall 2006). Helms's stages of racial identity development are helpful in understanding our common humanity. Through this model, we can see that racial identity is not fixed. We can change; we can progress in terms of understanding ourselves along racial lines as well as understanding the operation of our societal racial hierarchy.

Tim Wise (2008) argues that white people pay a tremendous price for maintaining white privilege and that it is actually in the interest of whites to dismantle the racial hierarchy. Wise offers the following bit of advice to whites interested in working for racial justice: "The first thing a white person must do to effectively fight racism is to learn to listen, and more than that, to believe what people of color say about their lives ... One of the biggest problems with white America is its collective unwillingness to believe that racism is still a real problem for nonwhite peoples, despite their repeated protestations that it is" (2005:67).

WITNESS

"I think it's the price of the soul. You're internally diminished when you dominate other people or when you're trying to convince yourself you're not dominating others" (Warren 2010:88).

One of the reasons offered by whites fighting for racial justice is the moral one: that this is an unjust system and, thus, it should be dismantled. Ignoring both inequality and privilege dehumanizes all of us. Racial justice activists find that they engage in this work because it is personally fulfilling and because they believe that working for racial justice will produce a better society for all. For racial justice activists, having healthier communities, more empowered citizens, and more humane culture that focuses on compassion and community will provide a better society for all (Warren 2010).

WITNESS

One of the racial justice activists interviewed by Warren (2010) explains why she believes this work is part of her civil and political responsibility: "We have got to do something about that for the good of democracy. It's just not healthy for a democracy to have that kind of racism at its core" (Warren 2010:85).

Another reason it is in the interest of whites to dismantle white privilege is economic. It is costly to maintain inequality. Whiteness privileges some whites more than others. It is estimated that an affluent 20 percent of whites reap the benefits of whiteness (Hobgood 2007). Having a labor force that is divided along racial lines deflates all workers' wages. The prison industrial complex disproportionately incarcerates racial minority males. The mass incarceration of minority males becomes self-perpetuating in that they become the face of crime, leaving white criminals privileged in that they are not immediately suspect. However, whites are disadvantaged by the mass incarceration of minorities simply because more and more tax dollars go toward incarcerating citizens rather than toward supporting schools, for instance.

Summary

This reading focuses on the social construction of whiteness, including how some groups have become white over time. For many groups, such as Jewish Americans, becoming white is intimately connected to social class and social mobility. The desire to assimilate into whiteness is a result of benefits associated with white privilege. White privilege can be thought of as the other side of racism. White privilege tends to be invisible. Part of the benefits associated with our racial hierarchy involves establishing cultural belief systems that contribute to the invisibility of privilege. White racial identities emerge out of the intersection of these cultural belief systems and institutionalized privilege. Ultimately, many whites working for racial justice argue that white privilege actually hurts whites as well as people of color. They maintain that it is necessary to dismantle the racial hierarchy by ending both racism and white privilege so as to create a more compassionate society.

As we work to bring white people into discussions of race, we must be careful not to render racial/ethnic "others" invisible. To address this, the goal should be to work at understanding the racial hierarchy—what groups are designated as dominant, what groups are subordinate, and how this system inequitably distributes power, privilege, and oppression. Understanding the totality of the system is essential to adequately take account of race, racism, and privilege.

Key Terms and Concepts

Agency
Assimilation
Collective social mobility
Institutional privilege
Master status
Meritocracy
New white consciousness
Norm
Patriarchy

Pluralism
Psychological wage
Racial hierarchies
Racial socialization
Structure
White privilege
White racism
Working poor

Personal Reflections

1. If you are white, describe at least five ways you have benefited from white privilege. Discuss whether it was difficult to think of five examples and, if so, speculate on why that was. Discuss whether you had considered yourself privileged in any way, but specifically along racial lines, before. In other words, was white privilege visible to you? If so, why do you think that was so? If not, explore why that was not the case.

    If you are a nonwhite student, reverse the questions. For instance, list five ways you have been discriminated against due to your race. Were these examples difficult to come up with? Speculate on why or why not that was so. Additionally, speculate on a few ways you think your life might have been different had you been born white in American society.

2. If possible, describe white privilege to two white people you know—friends, coworkers, or family members. What is the general reaction to this notion? Why do you think this is so? Is it possible for you to not see white privilege after reading this [selection]? If so, why do you think that is? If not, why not? Describe white privilege to two people of color that you know—friends, co-workers, or family members. Describe the general reaction to this notion [...]

Critical Thinking Questions

1. Thinking about Tim Wise's story (Racial Justice Activism), to what extent do you think this kind of transformation (his development of a white racial identity and eventually becoming an anti-racist activist) is likely for most whites? What do you base your speculation on? Explain how white racism and white privilege are two sides of the same coin. In other words, without one, the other does not exist. Provide examples that go beyond the examples provided in the text to show how white racism and white privilege are interconnected.

2. Think about some arena in which you hold privilege (race, gender, sexual orientation, disability, nationality). Identify five ways you see privilege operating in your life.

Essential Reading

Ignatiev, Noel. 1995. *How the Irish Became White*. New York: Routledge.

Kimmel, Michael S. and Abby L. Ferber, eds. 2014. *Privilege: A Reader*. Boulder, CO: Westview Press.

McIntosh, Peggy. 1988. "White Privilege and Male Privilege: A Personal Account of Coming to See Correspondences through Work in Women's Studies." Working Paper 189, Wellesley College. Center for Research on Women, Wellesley, MA 02481.

Rothenberg, Paula, ed. 2011. *White Privilege: Essential Readings on the Other Side of Racism*, 4th ed. New York: Worth Publishers.

Warren, Mark R. 2010. *Fire in the Heart: How White Activists Embrace Racial Justice*. Oxford, UK: Oxford University Press.

Wise, Tim. 2005. *White Like Me: Reflections on Race from a Privileged Son*. New York: Soft Skull Press.

Recommended Films

Mirrors of Privilege: Making Whiteness Visible (2006). Produced by Shakti Butler. This film features stories of antiracist activists, how and why they choose to fight not only racism, but also white privilege. These stories of racial justice activism emphasize the stages of white racial identity development.

Tim Wise On White Privilege: Racism, White Denial, and the Costs of Inequality (2008). Produced and edited by Sut Jhally. This video is an engaging lecture by one of the most prominent antiracist activists today, Tim Wise. Emphasis is placed not only on the damage white privilege does to people of color, but also on its costs to white people and, thus, why it is in all of our interests to challenge white privilege.

Recommended Multimedia

Check out the WPC (White Privilege Conference) website, particularly the WPC University, which offers online courses (some for credit) exploring issues of diversity, white privilege, and social justice. http://www.whiteprivilegeconference.com/university.html.

On a lighter note, to have fun with the idea of white identity, check out "Stuff White People Like," a humorous book and website by Christian Lander. http://stuffwhitepeoplelike.com/stuff-white-people-like-the-book/

Check out the website for the National Collegiate Dialogue on Race. If you find this interesting, ask your professor to sign your class up for the dialogue so that you can participate in it. http://www.usaonrace.com/category/department/national-collegiate-dialogue.

FIGURE CREDITS

Appendix 1: Cultural Autobiography Rubric

	4	3	2	1
Class	Explains how group's dominant/nondominant positioning has influenced identity	Explains how group positioning has influenced identity & explains dominant/nondominant positioning	Explains how group positioning has influenced identity	Identifies group positioning
Race	Explains how group's dominant/nondominant positioning has influenced identity	Explains how group positioning has influenced identity & explains dominant/nondominant positioning	Explains how group positioning has influenced identity	Identifies group positioning
Ethnicity	Explains how group's dominant/nondominant positioning has influenced identity	Explains how group positioning has influenced identity & explains dominant/nondominant positioning	Explains how group positioning has influenced identity	Identifies group positioning
Sex, Gender, & Sexuality	Explains how group's dominant/nondominant positioning has influenced identity	Explains how group positioning has influenced identity & explains dominant/nondominant positioning	Explains how group positioning has influenced identity	Identifies group positioning
Language	Explains how group's dominant/nondominant positioning has influenced identity	Explains how group positioning has influenced identity & explains dominant/nondominant positioning	Explains how group positioning has influenced identity	Identifies group positioning
Religion	Explains how group's dominant/nondominant positioning has influenced identity	Explains how group positioning has influenced identity & explains dominant/nondominant positioning	Explains how group positioning has influenced identity	Identifies group positioning

	4	3	2	1
Exceptionality	Explains how group's dominant/nondominant positioning has influenced identity	Explains how group positioning has influenced identity & explains dominant/nondominant positioning	Explains how group positioning has influenced identity	Identifies group positioning
Age	Explains how group's dominant/nondominant positioning has influenced identity	Explains how group positioning has influenced identity & explains dominant/nondominant positioning	Explains how group positioning has influenced identity	Identifies group positioning
Geography	Explains how group's dominant/nondominant positioning has influenced identity	Explains how group positioning has influenced identity & explains dominant/nondominant positioning	Explains how group positioning has influenced identity	Identifies group positioning
Structure, Mechanics, & Grammar	Intro & conclusion that insightfully introduce & conclude topics, university-level grammar & mechanics, transitions & flow that enhance readability	Intro & conclusion that insightfully introduce & conclude topics, university-level grammar & mechanics	Intro & conclusion that introduce & conclude topics, university-level grammar & mechanics	Intro & conclusion, university-level grammar & mechanics

Appendix 2: Cultural Autobiography

Cultural Autobiography

My growth as a person has been rapid in recent years. Many contributing factors have made me, my morals, and my ideals very different from even one year ago. However, there are factors with which I have lived since birth that are still affecting the way I perceive others and the way I am perceived. These factors may affect me negatively in some ways, but they are also what drives me to be successful.

Growing up, I never realized the difficulties my family had with money. Neither of my parents were raised with a lot of money in their households, so the fact that they had issues with spending money is not surprising. My parents struggled from the moment they were married, but when I, their last child, was born, they seemed to be at their peak financially. Recently, I have been able to experience the lives of middle-class families simply from friendships, so I would not go as far as to say that my family has ever been middle class. However, when I was growing up, both of my parents had jobs and were able to support us. My older siblings would tell me stories of how much harder they had it before I was born, so I figured we were pretty well off. I would say now that we were **lower class**, even though I never thought we were. I do remember being denied a lot of luxuries, and that has affected the way I spend my money now. I tend to treat myself a lot, even if it's out of my budget, as if to make up for what I couldn't have when I was a kid. I have always felt the desire to look as though I have more money than I actually do for fear of being judged by the people around me.

The desire to avoid judgement has sort of followed me my entire life. With a Black mother and a White father, I had difficulty fitting in immediately into my schools. I am mixed, with very light skin, but I **racially identify more as Black**. Although people like to pretend the racial prejudice in public schools has mostly been resolved, I and a lot of my peers have firsthand experience that says otherwise. I think it is a learned behavior to group with people that look like you, especially in social settings such as public schools where people are desperate to make friends. Because of this, I found it difficult to make friends with the White students in my school; it was easier with the Black students but easiest with the students who were also mixed or were of a different race. I found it difficult to make friends in high school as well. I had a lot of White friends the first couple of years, but when my race was mentioned, it seemed as though I had to make fun of myself for being Black to get their acceptance. As I got older, my friend group changed and became more diverse, and I realized that I didn't have to put up with casual racism to have friends and in fact felt entitled to dispute it. I still feel this drive in my life now and feel it is only getting stronger in recent years.

Ethnically, I would describe myself as "other." My father, although he is a White American, had a grandmother who was full American Indian. My mother, although she is an African American, has a father who is half Irish. Although "other" is not an actual ethnicity, it is the bubble I circle, it is the blank line I fill, it is the ambiguous identity with which I find solemn comfort. By identifying myself as "other," I do not really identify my ethnicity at all, and in this way, I feel a slight superiority. I feel that I am unable to be immediately judged by my ethnicity in some situations.

I find sexuality confusing and usually default to **heterosexual**, but I have not felt comfortable enough with myself to open up that can of worms. I identify my gender as **female**, and as a female person, I feel that the oppression forced upon the American women before us and most women in the world today is absolutely ridiculous and disgusting. I feel very passionately about equality in every sense of the word, and seeing a nation divided by gender has given me some prejudice against men. I like to avoid generalizations, so I tend to shy away from saying "all men," but it is, in my opinion, extremely ignorant not to realize the inequalities between genders we are facing in our country right now as well as all over this planet. What I believe is being dealt with here is the difference between empathy and sympathy. The most understanding man in the world can sympathize his heart out with an oppressed woman, but he will never be treated as less for his gender; he will never be paid less because of it, and therefore he will never be able to truly empathize with her. And with that lack of empathy comes a lack of true desire to change a system that has wronged others.

I have spoken **English** all of my life. I have taken Spanish classes but have never really grasped onto anything. I lived in Honduras for two years of my life, but because of my circumstances, I was not mentally or emotionally available enough to grasp much of the language. I think this is a huge disadvantage in many ways. I know that now I probably won't be willing to learn the language, and not only will that eventually hold me back in the job market, it will also affect my interaction with other people. I have a large interest in other cultures but have sabotaged myself in a sense by not learning Spanish. I have limited my interactions and conversations to be with people who speak English, and I find this to be extremely unfortunate, and yet I am still, as a spoiled American, crossing my fingers in hopes that everyone else in the world with whom I interact will learn English.

Just as we are divided by most identifiers, I think **religion** stands as one of the most "touchy" ones. I grew up in a Baha'i community, consisting of my immediate family and two other families. Growing up, I do recall finding myself blindly following some of the Baha'i teachings, such as unbiased kindness and oneness of mankind. As a child, although I felt slightly uncomfortable, I would try to befriend everyone I could. This stuck with me through high school as well. Recently, however, I have been finding it extremely difficult to follow the Baha'i faith's laws, and I have been trying to figure out what I truly believe. My desire for the unity of mankind has never diminished, but my blind faith has. I want to figure out what I believe for myself, and the only thing that has been preventing me from doing so is the fear of disappointing my parents. I feel stunted in this way.

I was placed in a **"gifted and talented"** program in elementary school, but being honest with myself, I never truly felt smart enough for that program and honestly felt discouraged attending those classes, even with the bragging rights. I have recently been attending therapy sessions, and my suspicions about having **anxiety** and **depression** were correct. I have spent a lot of time avoiding counseling for fear of being judged, but my counsellor is very unbiased and kind, and just having someone with whom I can discuss my issues has really helped me emotionally. I feel like I am gaining control over emotional issues that have the power to control me, and in this way, I am becoming stronger.

As a **young adult**, I find myself disagreeing with a lot of the baby boomer generation. I feel that a lot of the issues being discussed today are not new: they were simply swept under the rug, and I feel a lot of people would be happy if it were still that way. I think being as young as I am, I have been given the opportunity to grow up in an environment where I am allowed to support people who are different from what a lot of the older generations consider to be "normal." I cannot and never will agree with laws that prevent human beings from expressing themselves in the ways they desire, and I am firm in my belief that any behavior that is not harmful to another person and allows an individual to live happily should not be denied. There are so few joys in this world, especially right now, so I believe the denial of those that are harmless is cruel.

I was born and raised in **Wichita Falls**, and I believe this town leaves a lot to be desired. I tell myself every day that graduation is the key to leaving this town, and that is my main motivator to keep going. I think attending college here was, for me, taking the easy way out. I was offered tempting financial aid, which also influenced my decision. Every time I have visited any other place, be it in the U.S. or otherwise, I have been shocked by the cultural differences. Although there are worse places than Wichita, it is baffling to see how advanced humanity has become in bigger cities. It truly upsets me when I sit down and think about all the art and diversity that I am not currently experiencing by living in Wichita Falls, Texas. But, if nothing else, it motivates me to get out and see the world.

I identify myself, totally and completely, as "other," and I think it is entirely possible for every human being on the planet to do that as well. This exercise has made it possible for me to understand where the ideas I have come from, what sort of hand I have been dealt, and in which situations I find myself feeling unequal to others. I think it is important to understand why a person thinks like they do and that the human mind is soft and malleable, that it can be nourished and it can be broken, and these identifiers that make some human beings have just as easily broken others. It feels enlightening to understand how my mind was molded, and I now feel that I can easily identify if and when it will begin to take a new shape.

Appendix 3: Ethnographic Field Notes

Step 1: Head notes (see chapter 2)

Make mental notes of important observations, specifically as they relate to developing patterns or your research topic.

Step 2: Jottings (see chapter 2)

Before you leave the field site, jot down words and phrases to jog your memory when you do the field notes.

Step 3: Narrative (see chapter 2)

Without concerning yourself with grammar, get everything from your memory onto a page; do this before you sleep or discuss it with classmates. Save this draft for review when you're writing your final paper.

Step 4: Weekly submission

Answer the following four questions each week about the most significant aspect of your field observations that week. Significance should usually be related to emerging patterns or your research topic.

1. Data: Only that which you observed—no interpretation, just what you saw and heard.
2. Interpretation: What you think the data means.

3. Rationale: What is it about your positionality that makes you interpret the data in this way? This answer will be about you and your life experiences, not about the data.

4. Alternative: In what other way could the data be interpreted? This interpretation should be different from the initial interpretation.

Appendix 4: Final Synthesis Paper Rubric

Human Diversity
Core Assessment—Research Portfolio Assessment
Rubric

Civic Engagement Rubric	Capstone 4	Milestones 3	Milestones 2	Benchmark 1
Diversity of Communities and Cultures	Demonstrates evidence of adjustment in own attitudes and beliefs because of working within and learning from diversity of communities and cultures. Promotes others' engagement with diversity.	Reflects on how own attitudes and beliefs are different from those of other cultures and communities. Exhibits curiosity about what can be learned from diversity of communities and cultures.	Has awareness that own attitudes and beliefs are different from those of other cultures and communities. Exhibits little curiosity about what can be learned from diversity of communities and cultures.	Expresses attitudes and beliefs as an individual, from a one-sided view. Is indifferent or resistant to what can be learned from diversity of communities and cultures.
Analysis of Knowledge	Connects and extends knowledge from one's own academic study/field/discipline to civic engagement.	Analyzes knowledge from one's own academic study/field/discipline making relevant connections to civic engagement.	Begins to connect knowledge from one's own academic study/field/discipline to civic engagement.	Begins to identify knowledge from one's own academic study/field/discipline that is relevant to civic engagement.
Civic Identity and Commitment	Provides evidence of experience in civic-engagement activities and describes what she/he has learned about her or himself as it relates to a reinforced and clarified sense of civic identity and continued commitment to public action.	Provides evidence of experience in civic-engagement activities and describes what she/he has learned about her or himself as it relates to a growing sense of civic identity and commitment.	Evidence suggests involvement in civic-engagement activities is generated from expectations or course requirements rather than from a sense of civic identity.	Provides little evidence of her/his experience in civic-engagement activities and does not connect experiences to civic identity.

Intercultural Knowledge and Competence Rubric	Capstone 4	Milestones 3	Milestones 2	Benchmark 1
Knowledge *Cultural self-awareness*	Articulates insights into own cultural rules and biases (e.g. seeking complexity; aware of how her/his experiences have shaped these rules, and how to recognize and respond to cultural biases, resulting in a shift in self-description).	Recognizes new perspectives about own cultural rules and biases (e.g. not looking for sameness; comfortable with the complexities that new perspectives offer).	Identifies own cultural rules and biases (e.g. with a strong preference for those rules shared with own cultural group and seeks the same in others).	Shows minimal awareness of own cultural rules and biases (even those shared with own cultural group(s)) (e.g. uncomfortable with identifying possible cultural differences with others).
Knowledge *Knowledge of cultural worldview frameworks*	Demonstrates sophisticated understanding of the complexity of elements important to members of another culture in relation to its history, values, politics, communication styles, economy, or beliefs and practices.	Demonstrates adequate understanding of the complexity of elements important to members of another culture in relation to its history, values, politics, communication styles, economy, or beliefs and practices.	Demonstrates partial understanding of the complexity of elements important to members of another culture in relation to its history, values, politics, communication styles, economy, or beliefs and practices.	Demonstrates surface understanding of the complexity of elements important to members of another culture in relation to its history, values, politics, communication styles, economy, or beliefs and practices.

Written Communication Rubric	Capstone 4	Milestones 3	Milestones 2	Benchmark 1
Context of and Purpose for Writing *Includes considerations of audience, purpose, and the circumstances surrounding the writing task(s).*	Demonstrates a thorough understanding of context, audience, and purpose that is responsive to the assigned task(s) and focuses all elements of the work.	Demonstrates adequate consideration of context, audience, and purpose and a clear focus on the assigned task(s) (e.g., the task aligns with audience, purpose, and context).	Demonstrates awareness of context, audience, purpose, and to the assigned tasks(s) (e.g., begins to show awareness of audience's perceptions and assumptions).	Demonstrates minimal attention to context, audience, purpose, and to the assigned tasks(s) (e.g., expectation of instructor or self as audience).
Content Development	Uses appropriate, relevant, and compelling content to illustrate mastery of the subject, conveying the writer's understanding, and shaping the whole work.	Uses appropriate, relevant, and compelling content to explore ideas within the context of the discipline and shape the whole work.	Uses appropriate and relevant content to develop and explore ideas through most of the work.	Uses appropriate and relevant content to develop simple ideas in some parts of the work.

Control of Syntax and Mechanics	Uses graceful language that skillfully communicates meaning to readers with clarity and fluency, and is virtually error-free.	Uses straightforward language that generally conveys meaning to readers. The language in the portfolio has few errors.	Uses language that generally conveys meaning to readers with clarity, although writing may include some errors.	Uses language that sometimes impedes meaning because of errors in usage.
Ethical Reasoning Rubric	**Capstone** 4	**Milestones** 3	2	**Benchmark** 1
Ethical Self-Awareness	Student discusses in detail/analyzes both core beliefs and the origins of the core beliefs and discussion has greater depth and clarity.	Student discusses in detail/analyzes both core beliefs and the origins of the core beliefs.	Student states both core beliefs and the origins of the core beliefs.	Student states either their core beliefs or articulates the origins of the core beliefs but not both.
Ethical Issue Recognition	Student can recognize ethical issues when presented in a complex, multilayered (gray) context AND can recognize cross-relationships among the issues.	Student can recognize ethical issues when issues are presented in a complex, multilayered (gray) context OR can grasp cross-relationships among the issues.	Student can recognize basic and obvious ethical issues and grasp (incompletely) the complexities or interrelationships among the issues.	Student can recognize basic and obvious ethical issues but fails to grasp complexity or interrelationships.
Critical Thinking Rubric	**Capstone** 4	**Milestones** 3	2	**Benchmark** 1
Explanation of Issues	Issue/problem to be considered critically is stated clearly and described comprehensively, delivering all relevant information necessary for full understanding.	Issue/problem to be considered critically is stated, described, and clarified so that understanding is not seriously impeded by omissions.	Issue/problem to be considered critically is stated but description leaves some terms undefined, ambiguities unexplored, boundaries undetermined, and/or backgrounds unknown.	Issue/problem to be considered critically is stated without clarification or description.
Student's Position *(perspective, thesis/hypothesis)*	Specific position is imaginative, taking into account the complexities of an issue. Limits of position are acknowledged. Others' points of view are synthesized within position.	Specific position takes into account the complexities of an issue. Others' points of view are acknowledged within position.	Specific position acknowledges different sides of an issue.	Specific position is stated, but is simplistic and obvious.

Critical Thinking Rubric	Capstone 4	Milestones 3	Milestones 2	Benchmark 1
Influence of Context and Assumptions	Thoroughly (systematically and methodically) analyzes own and others' assumptions and carefully evaluates the relevance of contexts when presenting a position.	Identifies own and others' assumptions and several relevant contexts when presenting a position.	Questions some assumptions. Identifies several relevant contexts when presenting a position. May be more aware of others' assumptions than one's own (or vice versa).	Shows an emerging awareness of present assumptions (sometimes labels assertions as assumptions). Begins to identify some contexts when presenting a position.

Appendix 5: Synthesis Paper Outline

Demonstrate a thorough understanding of context, audience, & purpose that is responsive to the assigned task & focuses all elements of the work.
Uses appropriate, relevant, & compelling content to illustrate mastery of the subject, conveying the writer's understanding, & shaping the whole work.
Uses graceful language that skillfully communicates meaning to readers with clarity & fluency, & is virtually error-free.

Intro: How you perceived your diversity issue before this class and what you thought should be done about the issue (specifically as it relates to my career field)

Academic Analysis: Summarize both perspectives, address why each is appealing, utilize analysis questions

> Student can recognize ethical issues when presented in a complex, multilayered (gray) context AND can recognize cross-relationships among the issues.

> Issue/problem to be considered critically is stated clearly and described comprehensively, delivering all relevant information necessary for full understanding.

> Specific position is imaginative, taking into account the complexities of an issue. Limits of position are acknowledged. Others' points of view are synthesized within position.

Cultural Autobiography: What in your cultural identity makes you more inclined to perceive your diversity issue as you do

> Articulates insights into own cultural rules and biases (e.g. seeking complexity; aware of how her/his experiences have shaped these rules, and how to recognize and respond to cultural biases, resulting in a shift in self-description.)

> Student discusses in detail/analyzes both core beliefs and the origins of the core beliefs and discussion has greater depth and clarity.

Thoroughly (systematically and methodically) analyzes own and others' assumptions and carefully evaluates the relevance of contexts when presenting a position.

Ethnographic Field Notes: What did you see in your community partnership that supported/refuted your opinion on your diversity issue

Provides evidence of experience in civic-engagement activities and describes what she/he has learned about her or himself as it relates to a reinforced and clarified sense of civic identity and continued commitment to public action.

Demonstrates sophisticated understanding of the complexity of elements important to members of another culture in relation to its history, values, politics, communication styles, economy, or beliefs and practices.

Conclusion: How you perceive your diversity issue now and what I think should be done about the issue (specifically as it relates to my career field)

Appendix 6: Final Synthesis Paper Example

Final Paper

Poverty

As a White, middle-class, middle-aged woman and an educator raising a multi-racial family, many of whom have disabilities, I believed our educational system was doing its best for our children. I knew that there were problems, but I just had no idea of the lasting problems and the scope of the issues that were facing our educational system today. While raising our children, questions arose about whether we always treat everyone the same and ignore differences. We questioned whether we treat others differently based upon circumstances. We had come across several different instances when we thought something was done because of race or poverty, but we put it out of our minds and brushed it aside, thinking "not in this day and age." These situations were shadowy, almost minute, in that it was hard to put our fingers on them.

Socially, people are held back by society and by how society as a whole sees them. Society can be prejudiced against a person in how they look physically (skin tone, disability), how society sees a person, and how they treat them, and sometimes it also depends on how the person is acting or even how society responds to a person or culture. Society has even been known to be discriminatory towards each other based on personal biases and stereotypes. All of these play a part in how we are or are not successful individuals. All of these are pieces of a puzzle that are put together to assemble our self-esteem and our interrelationships with others. If we have only known prejudices and discrimination, then this will cause us to expect this on all levels and to treat all people the same and, in turn, cause the same reactions mirroring our own.

There needs to be a change in how we approach children in our education system. We need our system to be revamped, and the Ruby Payne study looked at it as a cultural issue, not a race or poverty one. There needs to be a study done across the nation of schools using a growth-mindset foundation, proving that evidence-based practices work instead.

When looking at *A Framework for Understanding Poverty*, written by Ruby Payne (2013), and *Miseducating Teachers about the Poor: A Critical Analysis of Ruby Payne's Claims about Poverty* (by the writers Bomer, Dworin, May, and Semingson [2008]), one is written by an individual, and the other is a peer review that has substantial evidence proving that Ruby Payne's book is based on circumstantial evidence only. It is based on her ideas and the ideas of others whom she has chosen that meet with hers. If Payne had asked others to come alongside her and cowrite the book, her allegations then would have been proven, and there might have been more substance to her book. There could have been a possibility of a peer review and a greater understanding of where her information came from. Her cowriters then would have been able to point out to her the problems in her book and where her wrongful thinking came from and how to fix it. Payne's biggest problem is that she relied solely upon limited information and chose not to have evidence-based documentation. Therefore, the writers of *Miseducating Teachers about the Poor: A Critical Analysis of Ruby Payne's Claims about Poverty* (2008) were able to tear her book completely apart as a piece of fiction that had no merit.

Payne's book is appealing because it falls into the old adage where class and race are bound together, and she uses smoke and mirrors to prove her points (Payne, 2013). Even though Payne has charts and graphs, Bomer et al. are able, through true research, to prove Payne's book is nothing except words in a book. When Bomer et al. point out that when they entered Payne's information into an evidence-based database program called the Tinderbox and presented the information, her information was misleading, if not completely wrong (Bomer et al., 2008).

Payne wants educators to educate those whom they come in contact with based upon their race and their poverty level (Payne, 2013). Our educators have had the wool pulled over their eyes. I believe it was because of the NCLB Act (No Child Left Behind). This study of Payne's book was given as a district-accepted policy nationwide. Many times, the study was paid for by districts. Teachers accepted it as truth because districts told them that they would be teaching using this study. Now it has become a blind-leading-the-blind scenario. It seems that possibly no one truly read this book or thought to do some evidence checking on their own. Our whole country is going to be doing a whiplash of a "second look" at our NCLB program. There will be many professionals who will be upset when they realize that this has been taught across our nation and just accepted as truth when, in fact, this study is anything but truth.

Society treats people who have darker skin tone differently, and laws are not going to change this. Laws will not change people's hearts; only education, love, and acceptance will do it. Bomer et al. did their homework. They have been able to open the eyes of this educator. Starting with my own district, I am going to be opening the eyes of every district I come in contact with about this study. After reading this book and this study, I was able to see that this study has been done in our own school district. My children have been affected by this teaching, and this disturbed me greatly. I have to say, though, that it took going through this class to completely understand what it was that I could not put my finger on.

The problem is Payne's study has no evidence to support her ideas except those based on race and poverty. As Bomer et al. explained so well in their evidence-based and peer-reviewed journal, research-based analysis has proven that Payne's teaching is based on dysfunctional thinking (Bomer et al., 2008). Payne had some good ideas based on cultural teachings. However, when those ideas are turned around and used against the student based on the color of their skin and their class distinction, then we as a society need to make a change and wise up to what has been taught to our educators. We need to bring about an honest conversation as to how our children are being educated. Otherwise, nothing is going to change because we are not expecting it to change.

As a fifty-year-old Caucasian middle-class woman, I identify with African Americans, Hispanics, American Indians, Italians, and Jewish people. I have been married to my husband for almost thirty-one years. I have a good sense about people most of the time. We have raised eight children: some who are adopted, some who have special needs, and several who are multiracial.

My eyes have been opened to prejudice while viewing the world through the eyes of young women of color trying to find a job. I have witnessed the trouble of a young Hispanic man with Asperger's trying to cope with his disabilities and learning to live on his own. I have worked side by side with a young woman who is intelligent yet has cerebral palsy. She is often judged by her looks. Her disability causes her to look and act differently than her peers, although her skin tone is no different when standing side by side, even though she is Hispanic. As a mother of dark-skinned children, I have witnessed how they are treated wrongly until I step up and claim them as my own. Our children didn't change; the color of their skin is still the same. Their situation is still the same. The other person's perception has changed. They now see them as "White on color." It seems as if by our presence alone we have washed away all the reasons for prejudice until the next time.

I have traveled all over the world and a large part of the United States together with my husband. While we traveled and lived in different places with the military, we developed lifelong friendships and maintained friendships from childhood. These friendships that came from having traveled with the military are diverse in race and culture. Our relationships are diverse geographically as well as diverse in the fact that some of our friends' family members may or may not have disabilities. Their views politically and philosophically may or may not match our own, but that's not the point in our relationship with them. There was something in the relationship that brought us together that was more important, so we all chose to ignore the differences and embrace them for what they brought to our relationships.

As a child development specialist, I am looking at the issue of poverty and how it is affecting our educational system and the students within their learning environments. According to Ruby Payne, children in poverty are already set in their ways, and there isn't really anything we can do about it (Payne, 2013). As I was in the educational field setting, I got to know my student. I witnessed the enriched growth-mindset environment that this school district has set up for these students. There isn't any reason that I can see because of this enriched environment within this school for this student to fail. When it comes to education, it affects all areas, and this child is not playing catch-up. This child has a support system at home and at school. From the moment the student walks in the door of a school building, whether it is a Pre-Preschool Child Development (PPCD) class, Head Start, or kindergarten class, they are running to catch up with their peers from the get-go. If they are malnourished and have not been given the same chances in an enriched home environment, then they will be lagging behind their peers. I know this from the experiences of my own six cases of adoption. In the case of my student in the educational setting in the field, my student's family ensured that they had an enriched environment at home as well as at school.

The student I worked with actually read very well. The parents recently, within the last year or so, had begun to experience the beginnings of poverty. The mother works in the medical field, and the dad recently became disabled. The parents are working diligently to teach their child how to save money and prepare for what they want out of life. The parents take their child to garage sales and cut the child's hair themselves. The child is not unhappy about what they do not have. Instead, they are happy about what they are saving for and looking forward to attaining. The child has books, Legos, and many other building blocks of imagination and fine motor skill developmental toys. The child doesn't realize that the parents are actually giving them the essential building blocks for reading and math that they truly need for problem solving. They just know they are getting to play. When the child tells the dad that they are bored, the dad does not turn on the TV or Xbox. The dad gets down an erector set, and the child then reads the directions and builds a helicopter. The parents are teaching the child problem-solving skills. This family is going through a crisis, yet they are showing their child that they are strong, and they are positively affecting the child's life by being a positive influence in it.

This student had the same type of background that I had growing up and somewhat of what my own children did when they were younger. I was not surprised by the things that the child shared with me—for instance, that their dad cuts their hair. They went on vacations with extended family members and stay in family homes. The family goes garage-sale shopping for the family and for birthday gifts; this was something my family did when I was growing up.

I was able to realize that the mom was trading out two pairs of tennis shoes for the student and matching the shoestrings for each set of clothing. This tells me I am no longer in this low socioeconomic class as I once was. I believe that this family is working hard to improve their socioeconomic situation. They are teaching their child how to plan ahead and at the same time how to think of others. This child talked about their faith in God and how they trusted and prayed to him. This child thinks of others' needs, wants to do good in school, and they love to read more than playing outside with their classmates.

As an educator, I believe that I will be able to learn about others and their cultures, beliefs, and backgrounds. This will help me understand where they are coming from in their responses to issues that arise in the educational settings, specifically where poverty is concerned. When I learn to take the time to invest in the lives of my students instead of just assuming that I know from a preconceived notion, I will be respecting them. I will then be able to help them find ways to meet their family's needs in the community that best supports them. In the educational field, knowing about other people and their cultures shows that I can be trusted enough for them to tell me about themselves. Because of this, I can help their children reach their full potential. Choosing to encourage my students to be themselves and share who they really are shows them that I care about them personally. When I encourage my students (as this educational setting in the field did) to use a mindset of "I can, I will, and this is how it can be done," then I am empowering my students to be more than they are at the moment. I am showing them how to reach out of their comfort zones and dream their dreams and achieve them. At those moments, I will have put aside my own ambitions so that they will be able to achieve theirs. It's not that my dreams for them are not important; it's that they have the right to achieve their dreams and be who they dream they want to be without being overrun by who I perceive them to be. This is what I have taken to be as educationally important.